Land-Use Management - Recent Advances, New Perspectives, and Applications

Edited by Sérgio António Neves Lousada

Published in London, United Kingdom

Land-Use Management - Recent Advances, New Perspectives, and Applications
http://dx.doi.org/10.5772/intechopen.111321
Edited by Sérgio António Neves Lousada

Contributors
Carianne Johnson, Carlos Afonso Nobre, Diego Oliveira Brandão, Elie A. Padonou, Fiacre Ahononga, Gebeyanesh Worku Zerssa, Gianni Lobosco, Huong Le Thi Thu, Indi Braden, Issa Adbou-Kerim Bindaoudou, John Ritter, Julia Arieira, Kirubel Teshome Tadele, Kossi Adjonou, Kouami Kokou, Lam Nguyen Thanh, Linda Johnson-Bhola, Luca Emanueli, Marta Hailemariam, Michael Thomas Aide, Moustapha A. Kolawolé, Raed Najjar, Rodrigue Idohou, Romain Glèlè Kakaï, Salako Valère, Son Cao Truong, Theonestina Kaiza-Boshe, Thorkil Casse, Van Dinh Thi Hai, Vien Tran Duc, Vittoria Mencarini,

First published in London, United Kingdom, 2024 by IntechOpen
IntechOpen is the global imprint of INTECHOPEN LIMITED, registered in England and Wales, registration number: 11086078, 5 Princes Gate Court, London, SW7 2QJ, United Kingdom
Printed in Croatia

British Library Cataloguing-in-Publication Data
A catalogue record for this book is available from the British Library

Additional hard and PDF copies can be obtained from orders@intechopen.com

Land-Use Management - Recent Advances, New Perspectives, and Applications
Edited by Sérgio António Neves Lousada
p. cm.

This title is part of the Sustainable Development Book Series, Volume 13
Topic: Urban Planning and Environmental Management
Series Editor: Usha Iyer-Raniga
Topic Editors: Christoph Lüthi and Rui Alexandre Castanho

Print ISBN 978-0-85014-132-0
Online ISBN 978-0-85014-133-7
eBook (PDF) ISBN 978-0-85014-134-4
ISSN 2753-6580

For EU product safety concerns:
IN TECH d.o.o., Prolaz Marije Krucifikse Kozulić 3, 51000 Rijeka, Croatia,
info@intechopen.com or visit our website at intechopen.com.

IntechOpen Book Series

Sustainable Development

Volume 13

Aims and Scope of the Series

Transforming our World: the 2030 Agenda for Sustainable Development endorsed by United Nations and 193 Member States, came into effect on Jan 1, 2016, to guide decision making and actions to the year 2030 and beyond. Central to this Agenda are 17 Goals, 169 associated targets and over 230 indicators that are reviewed annually. The vision envisaged in the implementation of the SDGs is centered on the five Ps: People, Planet, Prosperity, Peace and Partnership. This call for renewed focused efforts ensure we have a safe and healthy planet for current and future generations.

This Series focuses on covering research and applied research involving the five Ps through the following topics:

1. Sustainable Economy and Fair Society that relates to SDG 1 on No Poverty, SDG 2 on Zero Hunger, SDG 8 on Decent Work and Economic Growth, SDG 10 on Reduced Inequalities, SDG 12 on Responsible Consumption and Production, and SDG 17 Partnership for the Goals

2. Health and Wellbeing focusing on SDG 3 on Good Health and Wellbeing and SDG 6 on Clean Water and Sanitation

3. Inclusivity and Social Equality involving SDG 4 on Quality Education, SDG 5 on Gender Equality, and SDG 16 on Peace, Justice and Strong Institutions

4. Climate Change and Environmental Sustainability comprising SDG 13 on Climate Action, SDG 14 on Life Below Water, and SDG 15 on Life on Land

5. Urban Planning and Environmental Management embracing SDG 7 on Affordable Clean Energy, SDG 9 on Industry, Innovation and Infrastructure, and SDG 11 on Sustainable Cities and Communities.

The series also seeks to support the use of cross cutting SDGs, as many of the goals listed above, targets and indicators are all interconnected to impact our lives and the decisions we make on a daily basis, making them impossible to tie to a single topic.

Meet the Series Editor

Usha Iyer-Raniga is a professor in the School of Property and Construction Management at RMIT University. Usha co-leads the One Planet Network's Sustainable Buildings and Construction Programme (SBC), a United Nations 10 Year Framework of Programmes on Sustainable Consumption and Production (UN 10FYP SCP) aligned with Sustainable Development Goal 12. The work also directly impacts SDG 11 on Sustainable Cities and Communities. She completed her undergraduate degree as an architect before obtaining her Masters degree from Canada and her Doctorate in Australia. Usha has been a keynote speaker as well as an invited speaker at national and international conferences, seminars and workshops. Her teaching experience includes teaching in Asian countries. She has advised Austrade, APEC, national, state and local governments. She serves as a reviewer and a member of the scientific committee for national and international refereed journals and refereed conferences. She is on the editorial board for refereed journals and has worked on Special Issues. Usha has served and continues to serve on the Boards of several not-for-profit organisations and she has also served as panel judge for a number of awards including the Premiers Sustainability Award in Victoria and the International Green Gown Awards. Usha has published over 100 publications, including research and consulting reports. Her publications cover a wide range of scientific and technical research publications that include edited books, book chapters, refereed journals, refereed conference papers and reports for local, state and federal government clients. She has also produced podcasts for various organisations and participated in media interviews. She has received state, national and international funding worth over USD $25 million. Usha has been awarded the Quarterly Franklin Membership by London Journals Press (UK). Her biography has been included in the Marquis Who's Who in the World® 2018, 2016 (33rd Edition), along with approximately 55,000 of the most accomplished men and women from around the world, including luminaries as U.N. Secretary-General Ban Ki-moon. In 2017, Usha was awarded the Marquis Who's Who Lifetime Achiever Award.

Meet the Volume Editor

Sérgio António Neves Lousada holds an International Ph.D. in Civil Engineering - Hydraulics. He teaches courses on hydraulics, environment and water resources, and construction at the University of Madeira, Portugal. He has published articles and books and participated in events focused on hydraulics, urban planning, and land management. Furthermore, he collaborates with the Research Group on Environment and Spatial Planning (MAOT), University of Extremadura (UEx), Spain; Research Center for the Enhancement of Endogenous Resources (VALORIZA), Polytechnic Institute of Portalegre (IPP), Portugal; The Centre for Research, Development and Innovation in Tourism (CiTUR), Portugal; and the Research Centre for Risks and Sustainability in Construction (RISCO), University of Aveiro, Portugal. Moreover, he holds an International master's degree in Ports and Coasts Engineering.

Contents

Preface

Land-use management stands at the crossroads of human development and environmental stewardship, shaping the landscapes that define our communities and the intricate ecosystems that sustain life. As we navigate an era marked by unprecedented global challenges, the importance of thoughtful and sustainable land-use practices has never been more evident.

This book, *Land-Use Management – Recent Advances, New Perspectives, and Applications*, is the result of collaborative efforts from a diverse array of experts who share a common passion for understanding, improving, and responsibly guiding the use of our terrestrial resources. In these pages, we aim to provide a comprehensive exploration of the latest advancements in land-use management, offering fresh perspectives and practical applications that reflect the evolving needs of our societies.

The journey begins with an acknowledgment of the complex interplay between human activities and the environment. We recognize the urgency to adopt innovative approaches that balance development with conservation, harness technology for sustainable outcomes, and embrace the principles of inclusivity and community engagement.

Each chapter within this book is a testament to the dynamism and interconnectedness inherent in effective land-use management. From the intricacies of urban planning to the sustainable practices transforming agriculture, and the integration of cutting-edge technologies, our contributors provide valuable insights into the multifaceted world of land use.

We invite readers to delve into these pages with an open mind and a curiosity for the possibilities that lie ahead. Whether you are a seasoned professional, a policymaker, an academic, or a concerned citizen, we hope this book serves as a valuable resource for understanding the complexities of contemporary land-use challenges and inspires collective action towards a more sustainable and resilient future.

May this exploration into recent advances, new perspectives, and practical applications in land-use management contribute to a broader conversation and drive positive change on a global scale.

This edited book consists of eleven chapters focusing on land-use management.

Chapter 1, "Assessing the Potential Flood Mitigation Services of a Former Golf Course with a Focus on Flood Storage", focuses on golf course closures in the United States since 2006, which present an opportunity for maximizing ecosystem services. A former course in Ohio was assessed for flood storage potential as part of future planning. Reversing culvert flow reconnected the stream to its floodplain. Monitoring, mapping, and two models estimated flood storage, revealing up to 103 K cubic meters and 2.1% of stormflow stored on the surface, with additional subsurface storage. The site also provides ecosystem services such as water purification, soil formation, and nutrient cycling.

Chapter 2, "Carbon Sequestration as a Land Management Strategy", examines the carbon sequestration in the AFOLU sector, which employs land management strategies (afforestation, restoration, soil carbon sequestration, and bioenergy) traded for payments in compliance and voluntary carbon markets. Compliance markets target national emissions reduction per international agreements, while voluntary markets involve governments and private sector engagement for global emission goals. Both face a common challenge: insufficient funding access for forest-dependent communities, impacting land management effectiveness.

Chapter 3, "How Far the Mono Transboundary Biosphere Reserve Protects Biodiversity in the Dahomey-Gap Corridor, West Africa?", describes how the Mono Transboundary Biosphere Reserve (MTBR), spanning Benin and Togo, faces anthropogenic pressures, necessitating prospective analysis for balanced biodiversity. Using land use and land cover (LULC) changes from 1986 to 2015, with Markovian chain analysis, this study predicts future LULC up to 2070. Urban/bare soil increased (8.79 ha/year) from 1986 to 2000, while mangroves expanded (9.81 ha/year) from 2000 to 2015. Projecting this dynamic, mangroves are expected to increase by 6% by 2070, but farmland may increase significantly (13%). Strengthening management strategies within MTBR is crucial for sustainable biological resource management.

Chapter 4, "Improving the Sustainability of Agriculture: Challenges and Opportunities", discusses how agricultural practices underpin global development and how unsustainable production may jeopardize future land capacity. Sustainable agriculture, hindered by issues like reliance on external inputs and climate change, offers a solution. Challenges include technology gaps and climate impacts. Proposed strategies involve reducing artificial fertilizer use, promoting local organic sources, and improving small-scale irrigation with environmental considerations. This chapter provides a brief overview of sustainable agriculture, its components, and challenges in achieving overall sustainability worldwide.

Chapter 5, "Integrated Effect of the Payment for Forest Environmental Services (PFES) in Vietnam", describes how the Payment for Forest Environmental Services (PFES) is a vital tool in global forest resource management, notably in countries like Vietnam. Instituted in 2010, the Vietnamese PFES policy enhances forest protection and livelihoods of forest-dependent communities. This chapter analyzes the PFES policy and evaluates its effectiveness in Ba Be district, Bac Kan province, focusing on environmental, economic, and social aspects. The synthesis highlights the overall positive impact of the PFES program in Vietnam and suggests solutions for its improvement and promotion in Vietnam and other developing nations globally.

Chapter 6, "Moving Horizon, Design Praxis through Soil Transformation: A Landscape Manifesto", describes how the moving horizon originates from a doctoral investigation, exploring the intricate relationship between landscape design and soil transformation. Emphasizing the dynamic nature of soil, the study asserts its pivotal role in landscape evolution. The soil, considered a live and dynamic material, shifts from the background to the foreground in both design practice and theoretical implications. The assessment results in ten propositions forming a landscape manifesto. The approach is applied in the Ravenna Climate Change Adaptation Plan, integrating soil understanding and transformation into territorial adaptation measures for climate change.

Chapter 7, "Perspectives and Application of Land Use Management Strategies to Address Mangrove Ecosystem Degradation in Guyana: A Case Study of Mon Repos", focuses on the coastal mangrove ecosystems in Guyana, which face persistent threats due to erosion, infrastructure development, and environmental degradation. Despite efforts, the National Mangrove Project Office's strategies, including public awareness, have not fully resolved the issues. This chapter advocates for zoning and regionalization effectiveness in combating mangrove degradation at Mon Repos, East Coast Demerara. Literature survey, document analysis, and ArcGIS Pro with remote sensing reveals potential positive impacts on ecosystem services, livelihoods, and waste management. However, a lack of real-time data hinders effectiveness, prompting recommendations for implementing strategies like geographic information systems, remote sensing, and a multiple-use conservation zoning plan.

Chapter 8, "Soil Evolution after Riparian Buffer Installation", describes how the Riparian buffers, engineered for water resource protection, aesthetics, and economic benefits, now showcase a novel role in preserving soil organic carbon. This review explores their support for ecosystem services and carbon sequestration potential and presents a case study from east-central Missouri. After 18 years, the riparian buffer exhibited 3.4% soil organic matter compared to 1.7% in the adjacent field, indicating significant carbon capture and preservation. Ammonium and sulfate concentrations were notably higher in the buffer, emphasizing its positive impact on habitat and soil water quality.

Chapter 9, "Threats and Sustainability of Brazil Nut (*Bertholletia excelsa* Bonpl.) Pre-Industrialization in the Amazon Region", describes how the Brazil nut (*Bertholletia excelsa*) is vital in the Amazon, but its seed production's climate change dynamics are poorly understood. Seed data spanning 1990–2021 in Baixo Amazonas revealed variable annual production (2156–10,235 tons), averaging 5192 tons. Linear regression showed no direct links between seed production and current-year climate variables ($p > 0.05$). However, significant associations emerged with prior-year climatic factors ($p < 0.05$), notably temperature, indicating a 1°C rise correlates with a 2595-to-2673-ton seed volume decrease. Temperature explains 38%–42% of seed volume variability, emphasizing the need to address global warming, enhance seed value processes, and cultivate climate-adapted *B. excelsa* varieties.

Chapter 10, "Towards Overcoming the Challenges to Adopting Ecosystem-Based Management Approach for Protected Areas: The Case of Serengeti Ecosystem", highlights how ecosystem-based planning is crucial for wildlife-protected areas, ensuring ecological integrity and wildlife survival. Most African protected areas were established before this approach, necessitating the adoption of ecosystem-based management (EBM) for ecological integrity and wildlife survival. The vast and complex Serengeti Ecosystem faces challenges, notably human–wildlife conflicts (HWCs). Despite various initiatives, the Greater Serengeti Conservation Society appears promising for successfully implementing EBM, addressing challenges for the Serengeti Ecosystem's sustainability.

Chapter 11, "Urban Planning and Land-Use Management in Jerusalem – Chronological Analysis: Urban Perspectives in Contested Cities", focuses on how Jerusalem's urban policies, shaped by four regimes (Ottoman rule, British mandate, Jordanian control, and Israeli occupation), reveal a complex spatial history. In less than 50 years (1917–1967), the city underwent transformative planning paradigms, impacting population and growth. These changes led to socio-spatial challenges, altering population composition and creating a paradoxical urban fabric. The successive authorities, culminating in the Israeli occupation, established intricate rules, resulting in a complex and spatially unsustainable planning system, exacerbating urban conflicts.

We hope this book will help readers navigate the intricate field of land-use management. This book aspires to be a guiding thread, weaving together the latest insights, diverse perspectives, and innovative applications. As we embark on this collective journey, may the pages that follow inspire a shared commitment to responsible stewardship, sustainable practices, and the harmonious coexistence of humanity and the environment.

Sérgio António Neves Lousada
UMa - Faculdade de Ciências Exatas e da Engenharia,
Campus Universitário da Penteada,
Funchal, Portugal

Chapter 1

Assessing the Potential Flood Mitigation Services of a Former Golf Course with a Focus on Flood Storage

John Ritter

Abstract

Golf course closures in the U.S. have exceeded openings since 2006, creating an opportunity for reuse that maximizes ecosystem service. Flood storage potential on a former course in Ohio was evaluated as part of a planning process for its future use. Flow through culverts that historically provided an outlet for excess surface water to drain to an adjacent stream was reversed, reconnecting the stream to its floodplain. Installation of shallow monitoring wells, surface water and groundwater level monitoring, and mapping of flood events provided the data necessary to assess flooding and flood storage potential. This study illustrates two methods for estimating flood storage, a culvert flow model based on head differences between the stream and ponding on the former course, and a GIS flood volume model based on high watermarks. As much as 103 K cubic meters and as high as 2.1 percent of stormflow was stored on the former course on the surface for a given flood event, with additional storage in the subsurface. Ecosystem services associated with stormflow are also provided, including water purification, soil formation, and nutrient cycling.

Keywords: ecosystem services, flood storage, flood mitigation, surface water-groundwater interaction, golf course

1. Introduction

Annual course closures in the U.S. have exceeded new course openings since 2006. On average, 0.8 percent of the total supply in 18-hole equivalents has closed over the last 30 years, increasing to as high as 2.1 percent immediately prior to COVID-19 [1]. Closed golf courses are mostly repurposed for residential and commercial real estate but some are converted for agricultural or recreational uses. Because of the large areas of open space they comprise, closed golf courses provide an unmatched opportunity to maximize the ecosystem services they provide [2]. In a national study of golf course closures across the United States, Cederberg [2] found that 42 percent of the closed courses examined had no clear plans for future use. Of the courses that had been converted to parks and open spaces, the results indicated that large areas of former courses were converted to open spaces or natural areas with services limited to trail walking, nature viewing, and outdoor education [2].

Since Petrosillo et al. [3]. make the case that urban planners consider early in the planning phase the ecosystem services that new golf courses may provide, it is equally, if not more, important in planning for course closures. Particularly with respect to publicly owned courses facing closure, leaders need to consider whether a closed golf course can support critical ecosystem services beyond cultural services associated with health, well-being, and education. Golf courses account for as much as 29 percent of all urban greenspace and are the most accessible form of greenspace for approximately 3.4 percent of the U.S. urban population [4]. Course closures, by virtue of their extent alone, provide a unique opportunity to integrate those services with others that more directly address current and future challenges that face a community (e.g., water regulation in the case of communities with combined sewer overflows or climate amelioration in urban heat islands).

In the upper Great and Little Miami River watersheds, comprising an area of approximately 8000 km^2, of the 53 golf courses identified, nine have closed since 2012. One of these courses was converted for residential use and another for agricultural use, but the remaining seven are green spaces, mostly fallow since the time of closure. Only one of them (the former Larch Tree Golf Course west of Dayton, Ohio) was assessed for its conservation value and converted into a wetland mitigation bank. In addition to trails, wildlife, and educational opportunities, the former course provides wetland habitat and improves water quality, regulates runoff, and reduces erosion in addition to the host of other regulating and supporting services. Another one of the closed courses, the former Snyder Park Golf Course (SPGS), an 18-hole municipal course in Springfield, OH, is the subject of this study. It was closed in 2014 without a post-closure plan.

The goal of this chapter is to provide an example of how a select ecosystem service can be assessed to maximize the sustainable reuse of a golf course. The former golf course could provide a number of ecosystem services, including provisioning services (food, fresh water, fiber, and fuel), regulating services (climate regulation, water regulation, erosion control, water purification, and pollination), cultural services (education, recreation, and tourism), and supporting services (soil formation, nutrient cycling, and primary production) [5]. The focus of this study is on the role the former golf course plays in water regulation. Two different processes are associated with water regulation, flood prevention, associated with runoff generation occurring at the watershed scale, and flood mitigation, associated with storage of water once it has accumulated in the stream [6]. In cases of prevention, the need for vegetation biomass and forest to prevent runoff is critical, whereas available storage space for stormflow along the stream corridor is critical for mitigation [6]. In this study, I examine the stormflow conditions under which the former course floods, the surface water-groundwater interaction during flooding, and the volume of flood storage it provides.

2. Study area

Snyder Park Golf Course opened in 1920 as an 18-hole public golf course operated by the City of Springfield and National Trail Parks and Recreation District. The original course was constructed on the floodplain at the confluence of Mad River and

Buck Creek, utilizing in its design extant floodplain and channel features that were preserved following channelization and levee construction on Buck Creek. **Figure 1** illustrates the topography of the former course. It is higher to the north and generally slopes downward toward the confluence at a gradient similar to the current streams, 0.175 percent or 1.75 m/km. Former channels of Buck Creek are especially evident in **Figure 1**, recognized by their narrow sinuous features. Following closure in 2014, the higher elevations were developed into community gardens, but the lower elevations, which experienced periodic flooding (**Figure 2**), were left fallow. Currently, approximately 40 acres to the north and northeast are mowed to maintain a park-like setting, with a portion of it developed into test gardens for landscape plants and an

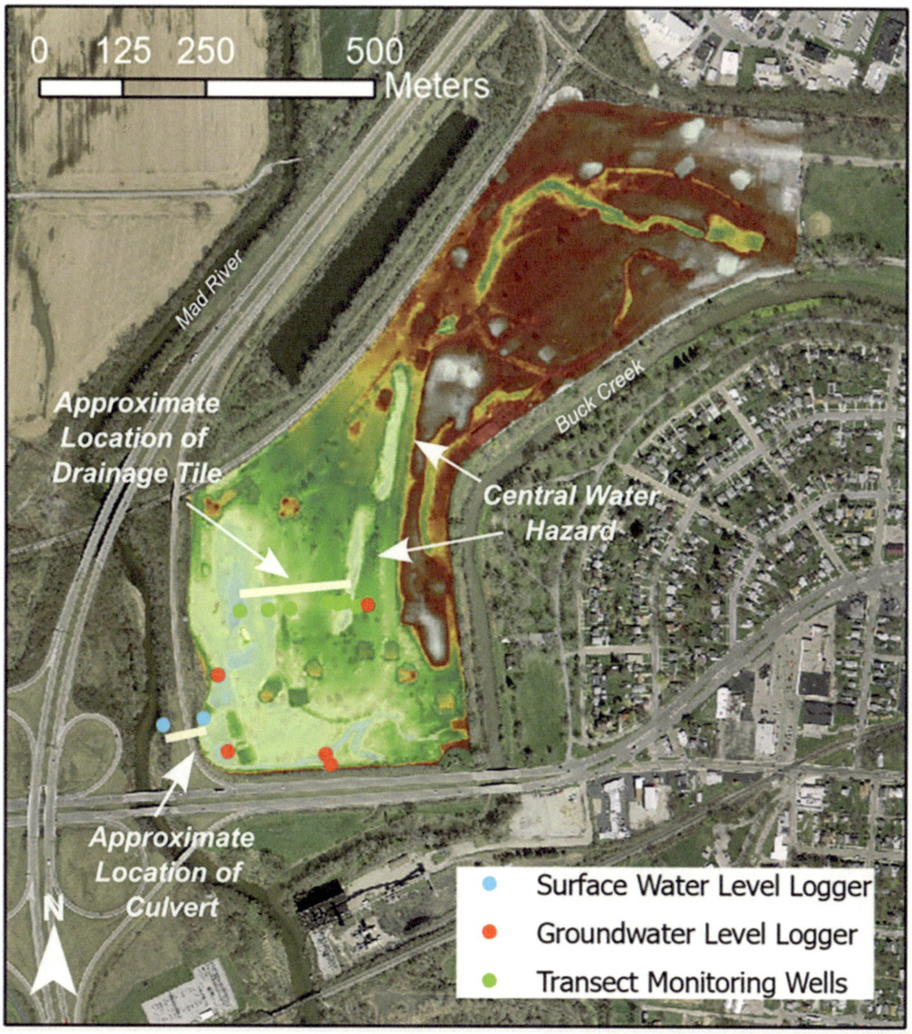

Figure 1.
DEM of the former Snyder Park golf course in Springfield, Ohio illustrating the floodplain and channel topography on which it was built. The location of monitoring wells and water level loggers used in this study are shown in relation to key features. Following closure in 2014, the higher elevations (brown area to the northeast) were developed into community gardens, but the lower elevations (green and light blue area to the southwest), with periodic flooding, were left fallow. The relatively low, narrow sinuous features are former channel positions of Buck Creek.

Figure 2.
Flooding in March 2020 covered approximately 18 acres of the former course. Buck Creek is separated from the course by a levee.

arboretum. Walking trails are maintained at lower elevations, but because of the flooding, it is otherwise rewilding with a mix of native and invasive vegetation and noxious weeds.

The former course is underlain primarily by glacial sand and gravel outwash and more recent stream alluvium. Although mapped as Westland silty clay loam [7], its field soil description suggests it is more likely a Tremont silt loam (**Figure 3**). The Tremont silt loam exhibits gleyed colors with reddening around concentrations of organic matter indicative of occasional flooding with a seasonally high-water table. It is rated as a hydric soil. A narrow ridge that runs the length of the southeastern border of the course (**Figure 1**) is underlain by glacial sand and gravel and soil profile development is indicative of an Eldean silt loam. It offers a striking contrast in soil profile development to that of the Tremont silt loam (**Figure 3**).

The decision to focus on water regulation and, specifically, flooding was based on the topographic setting, the extent of hydric soils, and early observations of flooding. When the golf course was in operation, excess water was drained to Mad River through a network of ponds connected by a tile network and two side-by-side, culverts that were installed to drain the golf course to Mad River (**Figure 4**). The culverts are 82.6 cm (30 in) in diameter, approximately 57.0 m (187.0 ft) in length, with a fall of 0.35 m (13.8 in) sloping toward Mad River (**Figure 4**) with a fall of 0.35 m (13.8 in) over that length. Closed flap gates on the Mad River side of the culverts prohibited back-flooding from the Mad River. Following closure, the flap gates were inactivated, in effect hydrologically reconnecting the river to its floodplain under

DOI: http://dx.doi.org/10.5772/intechopen.113107

Figure 3.
Two soils are present on the former SPGC, Eldean (left) and Tremont (right) soil series. The Tremont soil series is rated as a hydric soil in Ohio and comprises more than 98 percent of the former course. The sand and gravel that form the parent material for the Eldean underlie the entire area.

Figure 4.
Illustration of the relation of the culvert between Mad River and the former course showing a stormflow event on Mad River at a higher stage than surface water on the course. The elevations shown are surface water elevation on the former course at peak stormflow elevation on Mad River according to the hydrographs in **Figure 5**.

stormflow conditions. The ponds and tile network have not been modified so flow is currently governed by relative elevation of water on Mad River and the former course. The Mad River watershed at this point is 337 sq. km. When Mad River exceeds 50 cm (1780 cfs) at the St. Paris Pike at Eagle City, OH stream gage (USGS gage 03267900) just upstream from the culverts, the stage is sufficient for flow onto the course. Once water floods the course, it is distributed through a series of ponds and water hazards that are connected by a network of culverts at cart crossings and tiles, particularly one connecting pond with a central water hazard (**Figure 1**).

3. Methodology

From 2014 to the present, surface water and groundwater elevations in various areas of the course have been surveyed or measured during and after floods (**Figure 1**). Water-level loggers were installed in various configurations to examine (1) groundwater elevations on the former course and its fluctuation in response to streamflow and flooding, and (2) surface water elevations and head differences between Mad River and the former course during flood events (**Figure 1**). At any given time, between two and four Solinst Leveloggers were deployed during the course of the study at various locations to measure surface water and groundwater water depths at 15- to 60-min intervals. Depths were compensated for barometric pressure and converted to water-level elevations using surveyed water levels during the period of measurement. Shallow monitoring wells were hand-augured to depths of approximately 2 m. While some were equipped with water-level loggers, depth to water was periodically measured in others using a steel-measuring tape and converted to water-level elevations. Open bodies of water (i.e., water hazards on the former course) were considered to represent groundwater level because all were excavated in sand and gravel outwash.

During the initial stages of this study, I realized flooding from stormflow events on Mad River was more frequent than anticipated, presenting an opportunity to study flood storage potential. Immediately following many of these flood events, the elevations of high-water marks, indicated by the highest accumulations of organic debris or surface ice, were surveyed. Flood storage potential was estimated by two means, modeling culvert flow based on the head difference between the Mad River

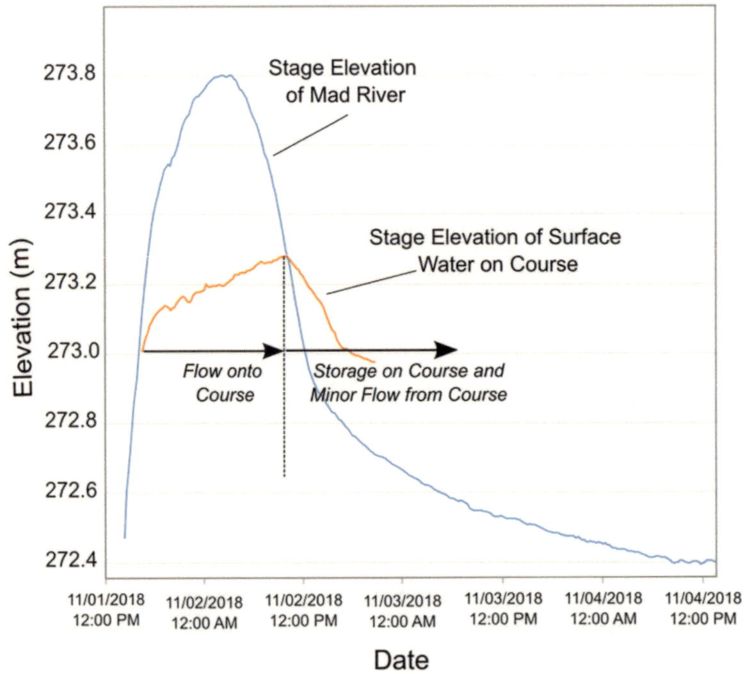

Figure 5.
To examine flood storage potential, water level was logged at 15-min intervals on either end of the culvert and converted to elevation. The difference in elevation, or head, was used in calculating culvert flow.

and surface water elevation on the course and calculating the volume difference between the golf course surface and high-water elevation of a given flood.

Under flood conditions on Mad River, the culverts connecting Mad River with the former Snyder Park Golf Course exhibit full barrel flow [8]. In this case, the culverts are in pressure flow throughout their length, driven by the positive head between the river and the golf course. For the floods modeled in this study, datalogger data confirm that the inlet and outlet are fully submerged. This condition is often assumed in calculations [8] and is the basis for the nomograph estimations of discharge presented here. They also note that the equations and nomographs for submerged, full flow can be reasonably applied to culverts with no slope or an adverse slope. The culvert in this study has an adverse slope (**Figure 4**). Culvert discharge was calculated at a 15-min interval using a spreadsheet solution to the flow equation in [8] based on the head difference (**Figure 5**), an entrance loss coefficient (Ke), and culvert length and diameter. A value of 0.9 for Ke, representing a corrugated metal pipe projecting on either side, was used.

Flood storage was also estimated using the Cut Fill tool in ArcGIS ArcMap 10.8.2. The Cut Fill tool is used to calculate a volume difference between two input raster surfaces at two different time periods, prior to flooding and at peak flood. The surface prior to flooding is the bare earth digital elevation model (DEM) based on LiDAR. The surface at peak flood is created for each flood based on high-water marks or peak surface water elevation. Flood surfaces for two events are shown in **Figure 6**. Peak flood elevation is assumed flat for calculation purposes, but there is a negligible slope from the culverts to distant points of flooding.

Figure 6.
The lower elevations of the former course frequently flood. Two floods are depicted here from the sequence of floods used in the study to estimate flood storage. The November 2, 2018 and may 17, 2019 floods inundated 13 and 17 acres, respectively.

4. Results

4.1 Groundwater fluctuations

Depth to groundwater varied seasonally and as a result of floods, from 0 m during floods to greater than 2 m during extended dry periods in late summer and fall. **Figure 7** shows variation in water level along a central transect of monitoring wells (**Figure 1**) at representative times during the study. Three surveys are illustrated. The May 27, 2022 survey occurred during a wet period, concurrent with a minor stormflow event (peak discharge 29 m^3s^{-1}) on Mad River. The water table is fairly flat at an elevation of 272.3 m (**Figure 7**). The Jun 28, 2022 survey occurred 15 days after a significant flood event but with trace rainfall since then. Groundwater lies below the central water hazard (**Figure 7**) and is falling. The Jul 13, 2022 survey occurred 7 days after a stormflow event (peak discharge 131 m^3s^{-1}) on Mad River sufficient to flood lower elevations of the former course. Surface water in the central water hazard is still elevated as it is the pond along the west side of the course (at 0 m on the transect) with standing water along the western side of the transect. Groundwater elevations on either side of the central hazard are lower (**Figure 7**).

The groundwater response to two flood events, shown as a range of elevations, is also shown in the cross section in **Figure 7** for the monitoring well along the eastern edge of the transect. The respective groundwater hydrographs for stormflow events

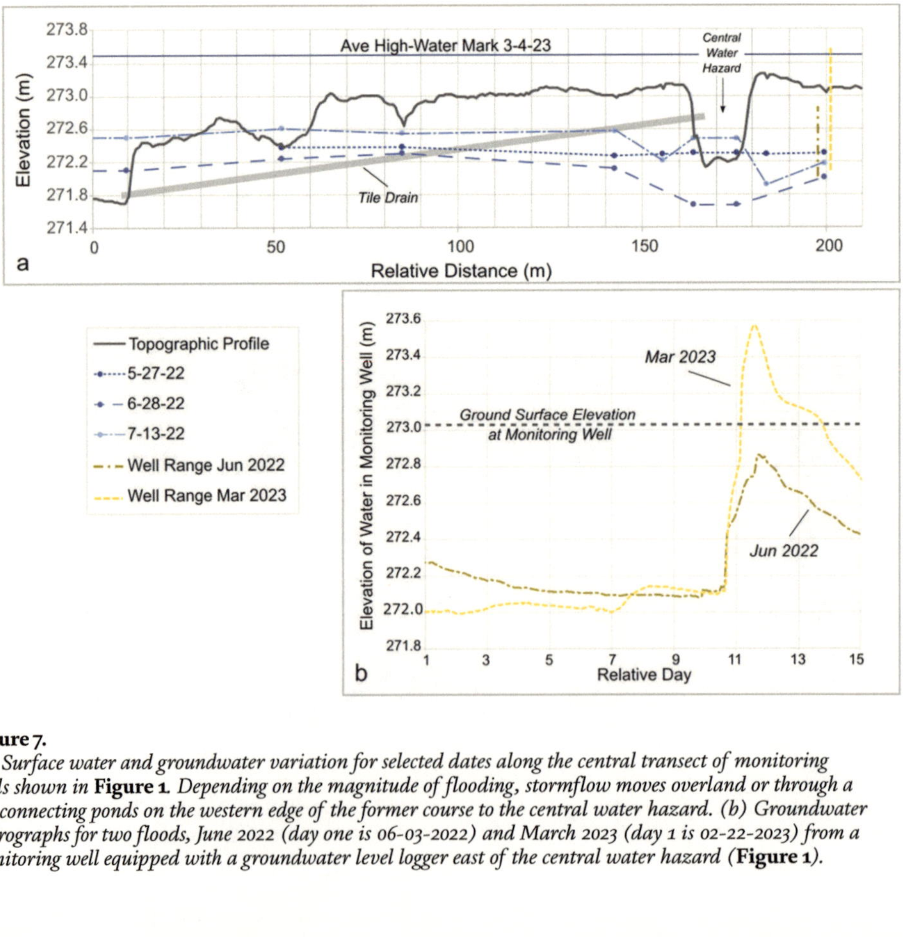

Figure 7.
(a) Surface water and groundwater variation for selected dates along the central transect of monitoring wells shown in **Figure 1**. *Depending on the magnitude of flooding, stormflow moves overland or through a tile connecting ponds on the western edge of the former course to the central water hazard. (b) Groundwater hydrographs for two floods, June 2022 (day one is 06-03-2022) and March 2023 (day 1 is 02-22-2023) from a monitoring well equipped with a groundwater level logger east of the central water hazard* (**Figure 1**).

on Mad River are also shown (**Figure 7**). The base groundwater elevations prior to the flood events were similar (272. 1 m). The Jun 13, 2022, stormflow event, which peaked on Mad River at 118 m^3s^{-1}, is associated with a peak groundwater elevation of 272.9 m (**Figure 7**). The Mar 3, 2023, stormflow event, which peaked on Mad River at 173 m^3s^{-1}, is associated with a peak groundwater elevation of 273.6 m. High-water marks for this event surveyed on the course ranged from 273.33 m to 273.49 m; the average high-water mark, 273.42 m, is shown on the transect (**Figure 7**). The entire transect was flooded during this event. It is important to note that the average high-water mark is approximately 15 cm below the maximum peak recorded by the water level logger (**Figure 7**).

4.2 Flood storage on the former course

From November 2018 to June 2019, 20 streamflow events occurred on Mad River upstream of the former course with peak discharges in excess of 50 m^3s^{-1}, the approximate flow magnitude necessary for Mad River to backflow through the culverts connecting Mad River to the former course. Seven events, two of which exceeded floods with a return period of more than 5 years, were selected for the study of flood storage potential. Seven stormflow events on Mad River (circled, **Figure 8**) were selected for the study of flood storage potential on the former course. Peak discharge and total stormflow discharge for these events are summarized in **Table 1**. The total stormflow of these events accounts for 1845–13,219 K m^3 (**Table 1**). Of that, it is estimated that 37–103 K m^3, or 0.4–2.1 percent of total stormflow, was stored on the former course

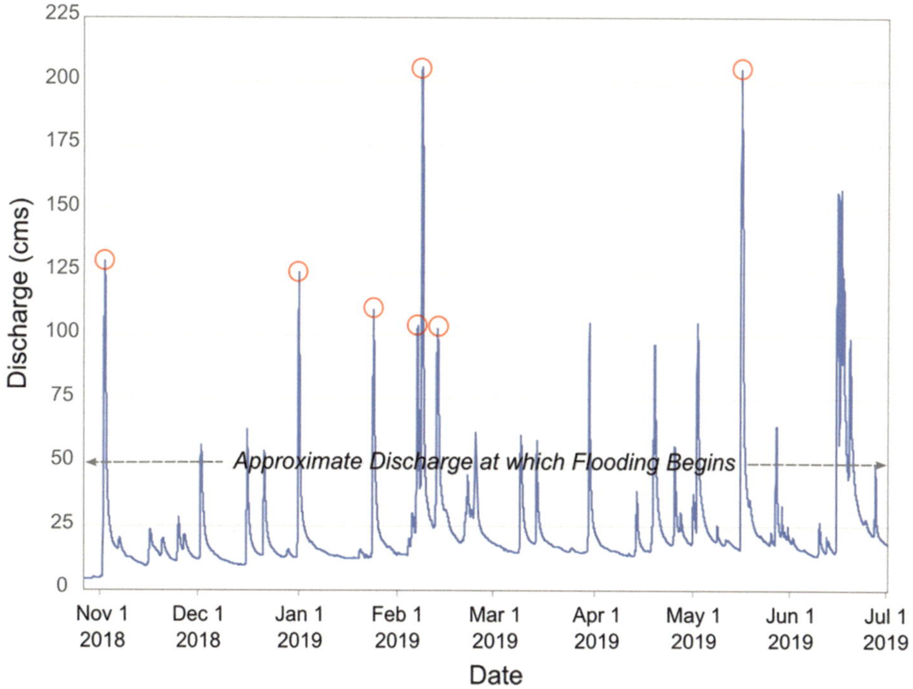

Figure 8.
From November 2018 to June 2019, 20 stormflow events occurred on Mad River at St. Paris pike at Eagle City, OH stream gage (USGS gage 03267900) with peak discharges in excess of 50 m^3s^{-1}, the approximate flow magnitude necessary for the Mad River to flood onto the former course. Flood storage was estimated for the seven events circled events.

			Culvert-based Volume		GIS-based Volume	
Date(s) of Stormflow Event	Peak Discharge[1] (m^3/s)	Total Stormflow Discharge[2] (m^3)	Stormflow Volume[3] (m^3)	% Stormflow Stored	Stormflow Volume[4] (m^3)	% Stormflow Stored
Nov 1–2, 2018	130.5	9,782,216	59,303	0.6	48,675 (49,843)	0.5
Dec 31, 2018 -Jan 1, 2019	126.0	10,272,094	37,993	0.4	34,245	0.3
Jan 23–24, 2019	111.3	1845,330	38,399	2.1	29,406	1.6
Feb 6–7, 2018	104.8	4,304,795	37,110	0.9	31,651	0.7
Feb 7–8, 2019	206.7	13,219,644	93,245	0.7	103,442 (103,537)	0.8
Feb 12–13, 2019	103.6	8,709,809	42,191	0.5	43,776	0.5
May 17, 2019	205.0	13,057,374	103,445	0.8	103,443 (103,623)	0.8

Table 1.
Flood storage on the former Snyder Park golf course for seven flood events between November 2018 and July 2019.

based on modeling of culvert flow (**Table 1**). The volume of storage tends to increase with the peak discharge. GIS estimates based on the difference between the elevation of the course and a flood surface representing the elevation of the flood are similar: 29–103 K m^3, or 0.3–1.6 percent of total stormflow (**Table 1**). To put this in a different perspective, the stormflow volumes reported would amount to the equivalent of storing between 5 and 8 minutes of peak streamflow discharge for the events studied.

5. Discussion

With golf course closures exceeding openings in the recent past and their location and extent in predominantly urban and peripheral-urban areas, evaluating the potential reuse of golf courses for water regulation or other ecosystem services is critical. Water regulation services are considered from two perspectives, flood prevention and flood mitigation [6]. The factors most often associated with flood prevention, increased biomass, proportion of permeable surface area, infiltration capacity, and soil quality [6], also characterize golf courses. Former courses in upland urban areas are particularly well-suited to serve this function. However, it is not unusual for golf courses to be developed on "unbuildable" land, even land that is or was formerly floodplain (e.g., see the discussion thread in [9], a site dedicated to golf course architecture). Reconnecting streams to former floodplains are widely recognized as a sustainable means of flood mitigation with the added benefits of increasing floodplain goods and services and resiliency to climate change impacts [10]. The former Snyder Park Golf Course, situated on a former floodplain at the confluence of two streams, was reconnected to Mad River utilizing the existing side-by-side culverts that had historically drained excessive standing water from the operating golf course.

Flood storage was estimated by two different methods with remarkably similar results (**Table 1**). During stormflow events of sufficient stage-discharge, stormflow stored on the course amounts to as much as 2.1 percent of the total stormflow volume on Mad River (**Table 1**). Results from either method of estimation are conservative as both methods rely on the stage elevation of water on the former course and do not account for infiltration as the flood wave inundates the course (i.e., the stage elevation of water does not include these concurrent losses) as it will be discussed later. There is also loss through the culverts as the flood elevation exceeds the stage elevation of Mad River as the flooding wanes. The largest stormflow event for which flood storage was estimated occurred on May 2019, amounting to 103, 455 cu m of flood storage (**Table 1**). With a high-water mark of 273.7 m, the May 2019 flood inundated more than 39.6 acres of the former course, about 91 percent of that part of the course that is not mowed or in gardens. The maximum flood storage, without impacting current maintained areas, with a high-water mark of 274.0 m, would amount to 162, 437 cu m of stormwater. The former course could receive additional stormflow, but it is ultimately limited by the volume of water able to move through the culverts.

Flood storage is likely underestimated as noted previously. Water-level data from the monitoring wells indicate that groundwater and surface water are hydraulically connected during flooding events, with surface flooding causing rapid changes in groundwater levels. By implication, the former course offers both surface and subsurface flood storage, the latter not included in the flood storage estimations. Groundwater levels rise in wells nearest Buck Creek and Mad River even during stormflow events that do not exceed the threshold necessary for surface flooding of the course, similar to bank storage [11] with some of the same benefits for flood mitigation. The two groundwater hydrographs in **Figure 7** illustrate this for events that flooded the former course. Elevation of the flood surface during June 2022 was sufficient to push water, through the tile drain, to the central water hazard. Seepage into the banks of the water hazard produced a 0.78-m rise in groundwater elevation in a monitoring well approximately 16 m further east of the central water hazard. For the May 2023 flood event, the central water hazard and well location were both inundated (**Figure 7**). The monitoring well was submerged by approximately 0.5 m of water. Though it is not possible to know whether the subsurface at the location of the monitoring well was recharged by lateral flow from the central water hazard or vertically from rapid surface flooding, it is clear that flood storage at this point on the course included approximately 1.1 m of groundwater storage and 0.5 m of surface water storage (**Figure 7**). The hydraulic connection between surface water and groundwater on the former course is facilitated by the sand and gravel outwash deposit which underlies the entire course. Diminishing groundwater levels in the days and weeks following stormflow events and flooding suggest that groundwater beneath the former course is gradually supplying baseflow on Buck Creek and Mad River.

Flood storage on the former course is fairly frequent. Streamflow discharge in excess of the 50 m^3s^{-1} needed to overflow onto the course occurs with an annual exceedance probability of less than 50 percent and an average recurrence interval of less than 2 years [12]. Ecosystem services directly or indirectly related to flooding and flood storage are also potentially (and frequently) provided by the former golf course. Several ecosystem services were observed or inferred, but not measured, here. Given the nature of stormflow in Midwestern U.S. watersheds dominated by agricultural uses (e.g., excessive sediment and nutrient loads), the former course provides supporting services like soil formation and nutrient cycling. Sandy deposits nearest the culverts and cores from ponds nearer the culverts showing fine sand, silt, and clay, and fine silt recently deposited on reduced muck and sand and gravel, and a thin layer of clay coating vegetation on flooded surfaces all indicate sediment accumulation. Carbon storage on the reconnected floodplain provides climate regulation, especially as the formerly hydric soils are more routinely saturated due to flooding. The increased residence time associated with flooding and the infiltration of stormflow would result in increased water quality, which is returned to Buck Creek and Mad River as baseflow. A conceptual plan for the park district managing restoration of the former course is based on these services in its early stages. It includes excavating a waterway near the culverts to promote flow onto the course, removing barriers between, and enlarging, ponds on the western edge to increase storage, and lowering the topography in and adjacent to the central water hazard to restore it as a wetland. In addition to walking trails and wildlife observation decks, different land covers include woodland, prairie, wet meadow, and pond.

6. Conclusions

Golf course closures exceed new course openings in the U.S. and many comprise large tracts of green space in urban areas without clear plans for future use. Course closures in urban areas and the periphery provide an opportunity for maximizing ecosystem services beyond typical cultural services (i.e., trail walking, nature viewing, and outdoor education), increasing community resilience. The focus of this study is a closed golf course on a former floodplain at the confluence of two streams, Buck Creek and Mad River, the latter of which is connected to the course through two culverts that historically drained excess water from the course. This study reports the results of two methods for estimating flood storage, a culvert flow model based on head differences between the stream and ponding on the former course and a GIS flood volume model based on high watermarks. Streamflow on Mad River in excess of 50 m^3s^{-1}, a relatively minor flood with an exceedance probability of greater than 50 percent, is sufficient to flow onto the former course. For the stormflow events modeled, the former course stores 0.3–2.1 percent of total stormflow with good agreement between the two methods, but they likely underestimate actual storage. Concurrent with surface flooding, stormflow is being infiltrated causing groundwater levels to rise in flooded areas as well as in areas without surface flooding.

Acknowledgements

Students in my watershed hydrology course helped to install monitoring wells during preliminary investigations. Andrew Francis and Christian Smith maintained, collected, and analyzed water-level data from them as well as helped with water level surveys.

Author details

John Ritter
Wittenberg University, Springfield, USA

*Address all correspondence to: jritter@wittenberg.edu

References

[1] National Golf Foundation. Big Shift for Course Closures in 2021 [Internet]. 2022. Available from: https://www.ngf.org/course-closures-continued-to-decline-in-2021/ [Accessed: 2023-08-08]

[2] Cederberg K. Taking golf out of golf course: Trajectories to convert facilities to parks and open space preserves. Landscape Research Record. 2018;**7**:158-171. Available from: https://thecela.org/wp-content/uploads/214F.pdf [Accessed 2023-08-08]

[3] Petrosillo I, Valente D, Pasimeni MR, Aretano R, Semeraro T, Zurlini G. Can a golf course support biodiversity and ecosystem services? The landscape context matter. Landscape Ecology. 2019;**34**:2213-2228. DOI: 10.1007/s10980-019-00885-w

[4] Ryan JC. Do urban golf courses provide barriers to equitable greenspace access in the United States? Annals of the American Association of Geographers. 2023;**113**:1057-1070. DOI: 10.1080/24694452.2023.2166011

[5] Millennium Ecosystem Assessment. Ecosystems and Human Well-Being: Wetlands and Water Synthesis: World Resources Institute [Internet]. 2005. Available from: https://www.millenniumassessment.org/documents/document.358.aspx.pdf [Accessed: 2023-08-08]

[6] Vári Á, Kozma Z, Pataki B, Jolánkai Z, Kardos M, Decsi B, et al. Disentangling the ecosystem service 'flood regulation': Mechanisms and relevant ecosystem condition characteristics. Ambio. 2022;**51**:1855-1870. DOI: 10.1007/s13280-022-01708-0

[7] Soil Survey Staff, Natural Resources Conservation Service, United States Department of Agriculture. Soil Survey Geographic (SSURGO) Database for Clark County, Ohio [Internet]. 2023. Available from: https://websoilsurvey.nrcs.usda.gov/. [Accessed: 2023-08-08]

[8] Schall JD, Thompson PL, Zerges SM, Kilgore RT, Morris JL. Hydraulic Design of Highway Culverts. In: Hydraulic Design Series No. 5. 3rd ed. Washington: D.C. Publication No. FHWA-HIF -12-026: Federal Highway Administration; 2012. p. 323 [Accessed: 2023-08-08]. Available from: https://www.fhwa.dot.gov/engineering/hydraulics/pubs/12026/hif12026.pdf

[9] Golf Club Atlas. Golf Courses in Floodplain? [Internet]. 2018. Available from: https://www.golfclubatlas.com/forum/index.php/topic,65537.msg1563694.html#msg1563694 [Accessed: 2023-08-27]

[10] Opperman JJ, Galloway GE, Fargione J, Mount JF, Richter BD, Secchi S. Sustainable floodplains through large-scale reconnection to rivers. Science. 2009;**326**:1487-1488. DOI: 10.1126/science.1178256

[11] Ferraz G, Tamás K. Surface water–groundwater interactions and bank storage during flooding: A review: Periodica Polytechnica. Civil Engineering. 2022;**66**:149-163. DOI: 10.3311/PPci.18594

[12] U.S. Geological Survey. Streamflow statistics for Mad River at St. Paris Pike at Eagle City OH: USGS Station Number 03267900. Available from: https://streamstats.usgs.gov/ss/ [Accessed: 2023-08-27]

Chapter 2

Carbon Sequestration as a Land Management Strategy

Carianne Johnson

Abstract

Carbon sequestration mechanisms were developed as a land management strategy in the AFOLU sector. The principal land management strategies to obtain payment for ecosystem services include afforestation and restoration, soil carbon sequestration and bioenergy. Improvements in land management can then be traded for payments in two mechanisms—the compliance carbon market and voluntary carbon market. While the compliance market focuses on reducing carbon emissions at the national level in accordance with international agreements the voluntary markets have a multi-level focus working not only with governments but also emphasizes direct engagement with private sector to achieve global emission reduction goals. Each mechanism's structure has benefits and drawbacks with one key shortcoming in both—the access to funding for communities reliant on forest ecosystems which directly impacts the effectiveness of the mechanism to improve land management.

Keywords: AFOLU, carbon markets, land management, rural development, carbon rights

1. Introduction

Carbon sequestration is the process of storing carbon. Forests sequester carbon by retaining carbon through the soils, woody debris, litter and biomass [1]. Initially research that determined the carbon sequestration potential of soil, woody debris, litter and biomass was very intensive and time consuming, namely laboratory examinations of soil samples [2–4]. To address this, allometric equations were developed to be less time consuming and included calculations based on the diameter at breast height, crown diameter, tree height, tree species [5]. Obtaining forest inventory data of different tree species became the primary method to determine carbon stocks and once inventory data was collected consistently changes in the carbon stock of the forest were quickly determined [6, 7].

In an effort to reduce the greenhouse gases (GHGs) in the atmosphere several global mechanisms were developed to 'offset' the GHGs emissions by preserving forests [8]. A carbon offset is measured in tons of carbon dioxide (tCO2e) and is defined by [9, 10] as the amount of carbon sequestration or emission reduction of carbon dioxide. Carbon offsets are quantifiable units of GHG reductions [11] 'traded' through a cap-and-trade program where carbon emissions in the developed countries are offset by carbon sequestration efforts in the developing countries. Each cap-and-trade program determines a set amount of emissions allowed which is known as the cap and in order to prevent the emissions from exceeding the prescribed cap, companies offset their emissions by investing in programs that sequester carbon through carbon market trading.

There are two types of carbon markets to date compliance and the voluntary market. These mechanisms were originally envisioned under the Kyoto Protocol which allowed for countries to develop cap-and-trade programs and offset their emissions. Developing countries committed to preserving their ecosystems with carbon sequestration potential while developed countries committed to developing cap-and-trade programs to offset their emissions [12]. Cap-and-trade programs were not developed by all countries, so the Paris agreement extended the requirements of reducing global emissions and requested for all signing parties to outline their emission reduction goals in the National Determined Contributions (NDC). The compliance mechanisms developed were not easily accepted and did not provide the expected impetus for global emission reductions. The effectiveness of the carbon markets continues to be the focus of debate as the cap-and-trade structure allows for buyers to obtain carbon offsets to keep their emissions within allowable limits [12]. The carbon offsets are then seen as licenses to continue business as usual. While some developed countries have national cap-and-trade programs, others only have regional/state-based programs. Existing programs have stark differences allowing for discrepancies in emissions CAPs and acceptable methods for trading on carbon offsets [12, 13]. Additionally, structures for engaging in carbon trading are very cumbersome and require extensive time and technical acumen to receive verifiable credits that would be utilized in trading.

Concurrently, the voluntary mechanisms focused on engaging the private sector to develop emissions reductions commitments and offset their emissions through directly investing in carbon sequestration projects and programs [12]. The voluntary market is seen as the commodification of emissions that favor the companies with the resources to purchase the trades and therefore determine the demand of the credits [14, 15]. Market driven incentives are then unable to produce equitable and ecological results for communities reliant on forest resources [16–20]. However stronger regulation in the voluntary market could alienate small business and forest dependent communities that lack the resources to monitor and report their emission reductions using time consuming methodologies with extensive technical requirements [21–26].

2. Carbon sequestration strategies in AFOLU sector

In the AFOLU sector there are a few principal strategies for reducing emissions and removing emissions. These strategies rely heavily on the science of carbon sequestration. The following is by no means a comprehensive list but provides an overview of the widely recognized strategies that are utilized to improve land management.

2.1 Afforestation or restoration

Afforestation and restoration (AR) is most widely utilized strategy of the list and is defined as conversion of non-forest land to forest through planting and seeding [27]. According to the Clean Development Mechanism (CDM) afforestation applies when the land was not forested for 50 years whereas reforestation applies to land that did not contain forest before 1990 [27, 28]. Assisted Natural Regeneration (ANR) also applies to this category. It is important to note that afforestation and restoration does not stipulate a time frame for the forest cover to be maintained only that a forest must have a crown cover greater than 105 [27, 28].

However, planting and seeding for mono or multi-species plantations also apply to this category. Plantations that are planted after cutting forests would not be considered in this category unless the plantation was established on grasslands, agricultural croplands or degraded forests with less than 10% crown/canopy cover [27, 29, 30].

Wetland restoration is the most significant aspect of AR due to the enhanced carbon sequestration of mangroves through their extensive root structures and soil composition [8]. This strategy is very variable due to the climate, geomorphology, relative sea level rise, wave energy and anthropogenic factors impacting a wetland system [8]. Wetland restoration requires more extensive assessments of conditions and tends to benefit from ANR activities versus human induced planting and seeding [8, 27]. Primary forests are more effective at sequestering carbon due to the age of the trees and their uninterrupted growth while afforestation and restoration activities require time to allow the forest to regenerate. This strategy is effective at reducing carbon emissions for extended periods and has even prompted countries to grow secondary forests in areas cleared for agricultural production. Agroforestry is also a practice that applies to this category allowing for agricultural production under the forest canopy. As a land management strategy carbon trading for AR projects and programs continues to be a substantial contributor to both the compliance and voluntary markets.

2.2 Soil carbon sequestration

Given the carbon sequestration potential of soil, cultivation practices can contribute to the release of carbon into the atmosphere and the loss of soil organic carbon [31]. Soil organic carbon is beneficial to promote stability in the soil and suppress the proliferation of diseases [32]. Soil carbon sequestration activities include the reducing tillage, green manuring through the use of tree litter, organic fertilizers as noted in [33–35]. While the strategy is effective at community and regional levels the global potential for sequestration has been subject to scrutiny particularly in agricultural settings [36, 37]. Soil organic carbon stocks are not only vulnerable to agricultural activities, it is also vulnerable to climate change through heterotrophic respiration [38–44] and are dependent on time and scale [38, 45–47].

However, carbon trading for soil carbon sequestration activities is widely utilized by the agricultural sector and benefits individual farm holders with additional financing to support their sustainable agriculture practices.

2.3 Bioenergy and biochar

Biochar is the conversion of biomass or plant material into charcoal through pyrolysis—the heating of the biomass material until the charcoal is formed [48]. During the process of developing biochar the gases are captured and condensed into liquid fuels namely bio-diesel and ethanol [48]. This process reduces emissions by using agricultural waste to create clean energy resulting in a carbon dense product that can be used with compost as fertilizer [48]. With an increase in demand for biofuels as a form of clean energy, the process of using plant material for energy has increased the use of land for crop plantations namely soy for bio-diesel and corn for ethanol [48–50]. Carbon offsets are traded for the creation of bio-energy and bio-char and the bio-energy created from agricultural waste provides greater opportunities for emission reduction [48, 50, 51].

Utilizing agricultural waste allows for combination of the three aforementioned strategies for overall ecosystem protection. Commercial production of bio-energy is also possible in agroforestry systems. However, land management practices that combine afforestation and reforestation, soil carbon sequestration and bioenergy production are only viable at limited landscape scales. On a commercial scale, there is the challenge of maintaining soil quality versus utilizing agricultural wastes for bio-energy [50, 51]. Emission reduction, land management strategies are feasible for rural, forest dependent communities to develop and maintain. This drives the popularity of these strategies in AFOLU sector for carbon trading and they can be traded in the compliance and voluntary market through different mechanisms.

3. Compliance carbon market mechanisms

Under the compliance market there are multiple mechanisms, however two of them are noteworthy. The Clean Development Mechanism (CDM) whose purpose is to support countries in meeting their sustainable development goals and achieve their reduction commitments [52]. There is continued optimism that the potential investment created from the CDM projects can directly support rural, forest dependent communities once the right structures and incentives are created [52–54]. For example, under the CDM-AR projects support the adoption of agroforestry in small holder farms as a way of engaging small holder farmers [54]. However, in forest dependent communities with unequal or unresolved tenure rights and direct access to the benefits of the projects remains a key concern [52–54]. Additionally, CDM structure and process for project development is managed by a board. The board are elected by parties to the Kyoto Protocol and they oversee the CDM process [55]. The process includes assessing projects, registering projects, issuing credits to registered projects, Additionally the board approves new methodologies, adopt new CDM rules and supervise the accreditation of independent auditing firms. Developing a project under the CDM must provide detailed information on the technologies employed, the expected impacts and calculation of the projected emission reductions using one the 140 methodologies in the CDM library [55]. While new methodologies can be proposed their approval relies on a review process though different groups—the UNFCCC secretariat, independent experts, and CDM methodology panel and the board which extends the process taken to get the project approved [55]. Once a project proposal has been reviewed it then needs to be validated by an independent auditor who then determines if the project follows all the CDM requirements [55]. Once the project is cleared by the auditor it goes into a 30-day public comment period where stakeholders can provide comments on the project. After the public comment period the auditor completes a report with recommendations on how to proceed with the project [55]. In addition to the auditor the CDM Board registration and issuance team reviews the project and provides recommendations. In the event that the two assessment differ the final decision to approve and register or reject the project is in the hands of the full board of the CDM [55]. If the project is approved, they can move forward with implementation.

However, the creation of tradable units or credits for the emissions reductions do not happen right away [55]. A second auditor, different from the one hired previously is required to verify the number of emission reductions which typically happens after 1 year of the project being in operation. The reports from the project activity are known as monitoring reports and they are then used to verify the emission reductions [55]. The auditor must verify that the project contributes to emissions reductions. Another board approval is needed to allow for CERs (CDM credits) to be issued to the project. When the CERs are issued then they can be traded. Credits are issued every monitoring period under the CDM system every 7 years [55]. There is the opportunity to apply for two 7-year renewals for credits to be issued or a 10-year non-renewable [55].

The process for CDM credits is long and rigorous requiring multiple approvals from the CDM board committees, auditors and engagement with national agencies and local stakeholders. Projects rejected by CDM struggled to provide a strong case for additionality—the case that the reduction of emissions would not have occurred with the sale of the credits of the proposed carbon project and incorrect use of the methodologies to determine the accurate emissions [56]. CDM has diverse interpretations of sustainable development that results in low standard assessment criteria for monitoring [56, 57]. In this case countries have not comprehensively developed monitoring systems to ensure that projects are achieving sustainable benefits. This impacts the quantity and quality of project benefits to forest dependent communities leaving developers to focus solely on the emission reductions aspects of the projects over the sustainable development benefits to these communities [58]. CDM also does not monetary incentives to benefit these communities and depends on the gaps to be filled by voluntary action on the part of the project developers or national agencies involved in the project [56, 59]. Under CDM projects that generate large volumes of CERs with low implementation costs are favored even as their projects generate no to very low benefits to communities reliant on forest resources [59].

The reducing emissions from deforestation and forest degradation in developing countries (REDD) mechanism sought to improve upon the shortcomings of CDM by emphasizing sustainable forest management of forests as a plus to mechanism [60]. REDD+ outlines how countries must use payments to reduce emissions through sustainable forest management and improved forest protection [60, 61]. A key component of REDD+ projects is the requirement of strategies that support national land-use and forest sector planning, stakeholder negotiations to determine provision of funds and services to local actors, carbon brokering and national level carbon accounting [61–63]. An integrated national approach is a key indication of the success of a REDD+ project giving principal responsibility for forest management to national governments [61–63]. Unlike CDM, not all REDD+ facilities require the generation of tradable units and the corresponding creation of registries, verification requirements and stringent rules for accounting [14, 64–70]. These transactions that do not meet carbon-market standards and would require additional structure to develop tradable offsets. Action for ERR issued under REDD+ to become legally defined certificates will allow for an established registry to track transfers of the offset [71]. The one facility under REDD+ mechanism that requires tradable units is the World Bank's Forest Carbon Partnership Facility (FCPF). This facility precisely outlines the activities that contribute to sustainable forest management namely improving forest law management, strengthening protected areas network, direct payments for environmental services, reduced impact logging, removing subsidies leading to deforestation and degradation [71]. The facility provided funds for countries to set up structures for assessments and monitoring of carbon stocks through a readiness mechanism and then created a verifiable, tracking system for the compensation of reductions [71]. Until the growth of voluntary market REDD+ plus credits under the mechanism are largely sold to offset emission in aviation through the Carbon Offsetting and

Reduction Scheme for International Aviation (CORSIA) [72, 73]. Under its current system the REDD+ experiences the challenges of double counting—which is the country of buyer and the country of the seller claiming the credits as part of their nationally determined contributions [14]. Additionally, double selling which are selling the offsets of the same land area to multiple buyers [14, 74–76].

On the whole the compliance market has drawn strong criticism in several ways. Under the CDM a disproportionately high number of projects are implemented in emerging economies with limited attention to low-income countries [77–81]. With the sole emphasis on forest management, the REDD+ mechanism does not create substantial results for SIDS with limited forested land. This droves the growth of the voluntary carbon market (VCM). As the programs normally referred to as standards under the VCM developed they utilized methodologies developed under the CDM and REDD+ and created premium prices on projects that supported sustainable development goals [81–84].

4. Voluntary carbon market

The voluntary carbon market is structured in a similar way to both the CDM and the REDD+ and differs in that it allows for companies seeking to voluntarily offset their emissions to invest in projects that are reducing emissions at varying scales [85, 86]. VCM was developed in tandem with CDM and REDD+ to provide alternatives to the slow and inconsistent regulatory action [86]. It also sought to address the concerns of developing countries that offsets were utilized to outsource reduction commitments and exploit low-cost mitigation projects and provide limited benefit to communities reliant on forest resources [76, 87, 88]. As a result, VCM standards define requirements to measure reductions, accounting and sustainability. Under the VCM carbon credits can direct private financing to sustainable development activities at the local level [88–92] and require projects to have additional benefits such as job creation, biodiversity protection, public health improvements and scaled up these projects could supply much needed financing to the forest dependent communities of the Global South [92].

The process to develop a project under the VCM differs by the standard utilized but follows the similar process to CDM including developing a proposal, accommodating for a period of public comment, having the proposal audited for accuracy of methodology and technical soundness, approval of the project, preparation of a monitoring report to ensure that the project activities are contributing to a reduction on emissions, having the findings of monitoring report audited, approval and determination of the credits. While the structure of the VCM is similar there is more flexibility in the lengths of the monitoring periods and the frequency of issuing credits over a period of time determined by an individual project or program. As an example, a project under the VCM can have multiple monitoring periods within the 7-year time frame stipulated by the CDM, leading to a higher frequency of trades and corresponding payments. Each monitoring period does require the completion of a monitoring report that is audited and approved before the credits can be traded.

After an initial growth the voluntary carbon market was subject to slow market volumes and market value. Even after the adoption of the Paris Agreement the growth was stymied due to the uncertainty of legitimacy of voluntarily offsetting [93–95]. This lack of growth was due to the demand in the initial stages driven by public institutions while the recent demand is being driven by private institutions [96, 97]. An increased number of private companies have committed to reducing emissions through innovation and investments in the VCM. This drastic increase in interest now drives the demand for the VCM and projects that are developed with sustainable development activities receive a premium due to the emphasis on providing financing directly to forest dependent communities [93, 98]. Companies engaged in the carbon markets cover a wide range of sectors for some phasing out carbon emissions are quickly attainable particularly through utilizing renewable energy sources for electricity and transportation [93, 99]. In this case utilizing offsets are a part of the overall emissions reduction strategies. The VCM also includes companies whose business models feature very high emissions and their path towards full decarbonization is not commercially available or feasible. For companies VCM is the only viable option to achieve carbon neutrality. In a survey conducted with oil and gas companies it was determined that as companies fall short of adjusting their business-as-usual practices of exploration, offsetting would be the only option for them to meet their commitments and will continue to drive the demand for credits on the voluntary carbon market [100, 101].

The major challenge for the VCM is the occurrence of double claiming and double counting particularly in areas where payments are already being received under a compliance market mechanism [102, 103]. Double claiming and double counting will continue to be a challenge as registries under the compliance and voluntary market remain segregated. Article 6 of the Paris Agreement addresses this through corresponding adjustments ensuring that once a mitigation outcome is counted towards one party's mitigation pledge it must be 'un-counted' from the other country's pledge. While guidelines are available to avoid double counting, penalties are not forthcoming [93]. The Taskforce for Scaling the Voluntary Carbon Markets (TSVCM) published report based on consultations which noted that while private and national emissions accounting can exist separately, there may be opportunities for climate neutrality claims under the VCM to 'be made on the back of mitigation outcomes' outlined in the NDCs [104]. The document also notes that double counting at the national level must be avoided. Notwithstanding the strong rhetoric against double counting developing countries continue to face the multi-faceted issues associated with climate change and with limited financial resources to fund mitigation and adaptation measures the potential for funding for project to the most vulnerable and the frequency of payments continue to support a growing interest in the market.

Another key challenge of the VCM is the viability of proposed sustainable development benefits that can also reduce emissions. As case study [105] on the use of cookstoves in rural Kenya illustrates this point. Cookstoves are seen to contribute to improved air quality, fuel reduction, forest conservation and reduction of emissions but there are several issues that can affect the effectiveness of cookstoves including poor design, defects in construction maintenance and the limited firewood requirements [105]. Due to the traditional food preferences and labor requirements for construction and maintenance cookstove use is typically lower than proposed under the project [105]. However, the structure of projects emphasize incentivizes to adopt best practices in place of traditional preferences and tend to alienate beneficiaries leading inconsistent cookstove adoption by forest dependent communities from general abandonment, infrequent and unpredictable use [105]. There are also concerns over commodification of these sustainable benefits especially the 'property' rights over the emission reductions [105]. While these rights are key commodities in the projects there are instances when the rights associated with the activity are not directly owned by the forest dependent communities preventing them from directly benefiting from adoption of new practices [105]. It was discovered that women were required to pay a portion of the initial costs for the cookstoves whether directly out of pocket or a group lending schemes, repayment occurred over a period of time resulting in the women 'paying' for a cookstove that was not being utilized [105]. Additionally, the rights to the carbon offsets did not belong directly to the women and even as some of the cookstove remain idle the carbon traders continue to reap the benefits of carbon rights for an entire community [105]. As pointed out earlier in the chapter, the key challenge of carbon offsets is the emphasis on an adjustment of the behavior of the most marginalized communities in the developing countries in an effort to offset the continued practices of pollution in the developed countries [105].

The effectiveness of sustainable development projects to alter the behavior of communities reliant on forest resources contributes to the concerns on the integrity of the VCM [105] and the multifaceted nature of credits that provide sustainable development credits leads to errors and fraud [92]. High quality carbon credits—projects with sustainable development benefits are seldom well defined leading to discrepancies in accounting and verification [92]. While the market demand increases exponentially the extended time frame between the development of the project proposal and the completed sale of credits detracts buyers from making investments [92]. The varying potential of carbon offsets in the projects drive the market and projects with lower carbon potential are often overlooked based on profitability [92]. While sustainable development benefits and climate neutrality are the ultimate rewards of the projects in the VCM, their development and implementation are driven by market conditions and therefore contingent on profitability [92].

Proponents of reform in the VCM have supported the use of digital tools to provide the much-needed transparency [92]. These digital tools can be utilized for registries providing detailed information on when credits are verified and issued. More importantly they can be utilized to track the impact of projects at regular intervals and not just the end of monitoring periods when payments for credits are issued [92]. This will allow for the traceability of credits and provide greater accuracy in the offset claims used by buyers. Digital tools can also increase the involvement of individuals in the goal towards climate neutrality providing opportunities for customers to better understand the carbon footprint and provide them with opportunities to offset their emissions by contributing to projects [92].

With a growing global climate consciousness many customers are concerned with environmental issues and have expressed willingness to pay for low-carbon products which are seen as having a lower environmental impact [106–109]. This incentivizes companies to provide low-carbon products and services and offset their practices that are not aligned with low carbon strategies [109–113]. Companies are moving towards providing information on the carbon footprint of the products and services as well providing information on the potential carbon footprint of customers utilizing the services [114]. Engaging directly with customers in the carbon markets is growing but managing the scale of investments from individuals versus the scale of investments continues to be a challenge [115]. As outlined in a study conducted by [116] utilizing blockchain technology can support data sharing which supports more efficient carbon trading and transparency in the carbon prices.

5. Conclusion

Carbon offsets provide very distinct opportunities for land management however how a country determines and assign carbon rights to their forest resources will impact the extent that payment in carbon offsets benefit the most marginalized communities [14, 93]. The success of the improved land management and the viability of the carbon offsets for forested areas contingent on the adoption of new practices by these communities. Countries however tend to retain latitude to assign rights to communities as the forest resources are the de facto property of the state [14, 93]. While countries enact certain legislation to afford communities reliant on forest resources land rights over forests most of fall short of explicitly assigning rights to payments from carbon offsets to these communities [14, 93]. As national governments seek to benefit from carbon rights, they are met with legal challenges due to the commodification of environmental services on a given land and the true 'ownership' of those services [14, 93]. While private land ownership as an indication of ownership of carbon rights is more acceptable in certain countries, the determination of rights for forest dependent communities are in flux as they are seen as stewards of the forest resources and not official owners. Countries are now faced with the challenge of differentiating between rights of communities reliant on forest resources to own land therefore benefit from the sale of offsets [14, 93].

Some countries have struck a balance by allowing communities and landowners to benefit from carbon rights subject to taxes or allowing for landowners to claim benefits that are then counted towards the country's contribution to their NDCs [14, 93]. The corresponding adjustments are made to avoid double counting and provide progress for the country meeting their global commitments. Ultimately until there are national laws that connect compliance market or domestic schemes and the voluntary carbon markets, the credits issued under private standards remain independent from result-based payments [14, 93]. The communities' dependency on forest resources requires keen attention to better improve the socio-economic conditions and equitable land management [117, 118]. While the importance of receiving payments for the improvement of land management is a tool to achieving global climate neutrality goals without due attention to the needs of the communities the incentives for these key actors remain woefully insufficient.

Conflict of interest

The authors declare no conflict of interest.

Author details

Carianne Johnson
University of Salford, Salford, UK

*Address all correspondence to: carianne@buffalo.edu

References

[1] Farooqi T, Li X, Yu Z, Liu S, Sun O. Reconcilation of research on forest carbon sequestration and water conservation. Journal of Forestry Research. 2021;**32**(1):7-14. DOI: 10.1007/s11676-020-01138-2

[2] Zhou XL, Lei XD, Liu CX, Huang HB, Zhou C, Peng CH. Reestimating the changes and ranges of forest biomass carbon in China during the past 40 years. Forest Ecosystems. 2019;**6**:51

[3] Sun WL, Liu XH. Review on carbon storage estimation of forest ecosystem and applications in China. Forest Ecosystems. 2020;**7**:4

[4] Tang X, Zhao X, Bai Y, Tang Z, Wang W, Zhao Y, et al. Carbon pools in China's terrestrial ecosystems: New estimates based on an intensive field survey. Proceedings of the National Academy of Sciences. 2018;**115**:4021-4026

[5] Vashum KT, Jayakumar S. Methods to estimate above-ground biomass and carbon stock in natural forests-a review. Journal of Ecosystem and Ecography. 2012;**2**:1-7

[6] Law BE, Turner D, Campbell J, Sun OJ, Lefsky M, Guzy M, et al. Disturbance and climate effects on carbon stocks and fluxes across the forested region of Oregon USA. Global Change Biology. 2004;**10**:1429-1444

[7] Fang J, Chen A, Peng C, Zhao S, Ci L. Changes in forest biomass carbon storage in China between 1949 and 1998. Science. 2001;**292**:2320-2322

[8] Sapkota Y, White J. Carbon offset market methodologies applicable for coastal wetland restoration and conservation in the United States: A review. Science of the Total Environment. 2020;**701**:134497. DOI: 10.1016/j.scitotenv.2019.134497

[9] Lane RR, Mack SK, Day JW, et al. Fate of soil organic carbon during wetland loss. Wetlands. 2016;**36**:1167-1181. DOI: 10.1007/s13157-016-0834-8

[10] Murray BC, Pendleton L, Jenkins WA, Sifleet S. Green Payments for Blue Carbon: Economic Incentives for Protecting Threatened Coastal Habitats. Durham, NC: Nicholas Institute for Environmental Policy Solutions, Duke University; 2011. p. 52

[11] Hamrick K, Gallant M. Voluntary Carbon Markets Insights: 2018 Outlook and First-Quarter Trends. Washington, DC: Forest Trends' Ecosystem Marketplace; 2018

[12] Mack SK, Lane RR, Day JW, Kempka R, Mack J, Hardee E, et al. Carbon market opportunities of Louisiana's coastal wetlands. In: Report by Tierra Resources LLC and the Climate Trust. 2015. Available from: http://tierraresourcesllc.com/coastal-protection-projects/louisianablue-carbon-study/ [Accessed: July 3, 2023]

[13] Ecosystem Marketplace. Market Watch: Compliance Market. Washington, DC: Ecosystem Marketplace, Forest Trends; 2019. Available from: http://www.ecosystemmarketplace.com/marketwatch/carbon/north-america/#compliance-markets [Accessed: July 3, 2023]

[14] Streck C. Who owns REDD+? Carbon markets, carbon rights and entitlements to REDD+ finance. Forests. 2020;**11**:959. DOI: 10.3390/f11090959

[15] Torres G. Who owns the sky past garrison lecture reprints & addenda—Seventh annual Lloyd, K. Garrison lecture on environmental law. Pace Environmental Law Review. 2001;**19**:515-574

[16] Blumm MC. Fallacies of free market environmentalism. The free market environmentalism: The role of the market in environmental protection northwest school of law at Lewis and Clark College-1991. Harvard Journal of Law and Public Policy. 1992;**15**:371-390

[17] Menell PS. Institutional fantasylands: From scientific management to free market environmentalism free market environmentalism: The role of the market in environmental protection northwest School of Law at Lewis and Clark College-1991. Harvard Journal of Law and Public Policy. 1992;**15**:489-510

[18] Newell P, Paterson M. A climate for business: Global warming, the state and capital. Review of International Political Economy. 1998;**5**:679-703

[19] Newell P, Roberts JT. The Globalization and Environment Reader. Hoboken, NJ, USA: John Wiley & Sons; 2016

[20] Ciplet D, Roberts JT. Climate change and the transition to neoliberal environmental governance. Global Environmental Change. 2017;**46**:148-156

[21] MacKenzie D. Making things the same: Gases, emission rights and the politics of carbon markets. Accounting, Organizations and Society. 2009;**34**:440-455

[22] Government of New Zealand. Climate Change Response (Emissions Trading) Amendment Act 2008. New Zealand Legislation: Wellington, New Zealand; 2008

[23] Leining C, Kerr S, Bruce-Brand B. The New Zealand emissions trading scheme: Critical review and future outlook for three design innovations. Climate Policy. 2020;**20**:246-264

[24] Government of New Zealand. Deforesting Forest Land, Te Uru Rakau, Forestry New Zealand. Available from: https://www.mpi.govt.nz/growing-and-harvesting/forestry/forestry-in-the-emissionstrading-scheme/deforesting-forest-land/ [Accessed: July 3, 2023]

[25] Savaresi A, Perugini L. The land sector in the 2030 EU climate change policy framework: A look at the future. Journal for European Environmental and Planning Law. 2019;**16**:148-164

[26] European Commission. Commission Staff Working Document, Impact Assessment on the Role of Land Use, Land Use Change and Forestry (LULUCF) in the EU's Climate Change Commitments. Brussels, Belgium: European Commission; 2012

[27] Smith J. Afforestation and reforestation in the clean development mechanism of the Kyoto protocol: Implications for forests and forest people. International Journal of Global Environmental Issues. 2002;**2**(3/4):322-343

[28] UNFCCC (United Nations Framework Convention on Climate Change). The Marrakesh Accords & The Marrakesh Declaration. 2001. Available from: http://www.unfccc.int./

[29] IISD. Summary of the sixth conference of the parties to the framework convention on climate change. Earth Negotiations Bulletin. 2000;**12**(163):11

[30] IPCC. Land Use, Land-use Change and Forestry. Cambridge: Cambridge University Press; 2000

[31] Lessmann M, Ros G, Young M, Vries W. Global variation in soil carbon sequestration potential through improved cropland management. Global Change Biology. 2021;**28**(3):1162-1177

[32] Bünemann EK, Bongiorno G, Bai Z, Creamer RE, De Deyn G, de Goede R, et al. Soil quality – A critical review. Soil Biology and Biochemistry. 2018;**120**:105-125. DOI: 10.1016/j.soilbio.2018.01.030

[33] Bolinder MA, Crotty F, Elsen A, Frac M, Kismányoky T, Lipiec J, et al. The effect of crop residues, cover crops, manures and nitrogen fertilization on soil organic carbon changes in agroecosystems: A synthesis of reviews. Mitigation and Adaptation Strategies for Global Change. 2020;**25**(6):929-952. DOI: 10.1007/s11027-020-09916-3

[34] Singh BP, Setia R, Wiesmeier M, Kunhikrishnan A. Agricultural management practices and soil organic carbon storage. In: Singh B, editor. Soil Carbon Storage: Modulators, Mechanisms and Modeling. London: Academic Press-Elsevier; 2018. pp. 1-28. DOI: 10.1016/B978-0-12-812766-7.00007-X

[35] Spiegel H, Schlatter N, Haslmayr H-P, Lehtinen T, Baumgarten A. Compatibility of agricultural management practices and types of farming in the EU to enhance climate change mitigation and soil health policy bundles framing agricultural soil protection in EU and selected member states. Netherlands: Wageningen Research, Wageningen University; 2014. Available from: https://research.wur.nl/en/projects/compatibility-of-agricultural-management-practices-and-types-of-f-2

[36] Van Groenigen KJ, Qi X, Osenberg CW, Luo Y, Hungate BA. Faster decomposition under increased atmospheric CO_2 limits soil carbon storage. Science (New York, N.Y.). 2014;**344**(6183):508-509. DOI: 10.1126/science.1249534

[37] De Vries W. Soil carbon 4 per mille: A good initiative but let's manage not only the soil but also the expectations. Geoderma. 2018;**292**:111-112. DOI: 10.1016/j.geoderma.2017.05.023

[38] Beillouin D et al. A Global Overview of Studies about the Land Management, Land-use Change, and Climate Change Effects on Soil Carbon. New Jersey, United States: Wiley; 2021. DOI: 10.1111/gcb.15998

[39] Batjes NH. Total carbon and nitrogen in the soils of the world. European Journal of Soil Science. 1996;**47**(2):151-163. DOI: 10.1111/j.1365-2389.1996.tb01386.x

[40] Goldstein A, Turner WR, Spawn SA, Anderson-Teixeira KJ, CookPatton S, Fargione J, et al. Protecting irrecoverable carbon in Earth's ecosystems. Nature Climate Change. 2020;**10**(4):287-295. DOI: 10.1038/s41558-020-0738-8

[41] Don A, Schumacher J, Freibauer A. Impact of tropical land-use change on soil organic carbon stocks—A metaanalysis. Global Change Biology. 2011;**17**(4):1658-1670. DOI: 10.1111/j.1365-2486.2010.02336

[42] Friedlingstein P, O'Sullivan M, Jones MW, Andrew RM, Hauck J, Olsen A, et al. Global carbon budget 2020. Earth System Science Data. 2020;**12**(4):3269-3340. DOI: 10.5194/essd-12-3269-2020

[43] Crowther TW, Todd-Brown KEO, Rowe CW, Wieder WR, Carey JC, MacHmuller MB, et al. Quantifying global soil carbon losses in response to warming. Nature. 2016;**540**:104-108. DOI: 10.1038/nature20150

[44] Paul EA. The nature and dynamics of soil organic matter: Plant inputs, microbial transformations, and organic matter stabilization. Soil Biology and Biochemistry. 2016;**98**:109-126. DOI: 10.1016/j.soilbio.2016.04.001

[45] Dignac M-F, Derrien D, Barré P, Barot S, Cécillon L, Chenu C, et al. Increasing soil carbon storage: Mechanisms, effects of agricultural practices and proxies. A review. Agronomy for Sustainable Development. 2017;**37**(2):14. DOI: 10.1007/s13593-017-0421-2

[46] Fujisaki K, Chevallier T, Chapuis-Lardy L, Albrecht A, Razafimbelo T, Masse D, et al. Soil carbon stock changes in tropical croplands are mainly driven by carbon inputs: A synthesis. Agriculture, Ecosystems & Environment. 2018;**259**:147-158. DOI: 10.1016/j.agee.2017.12.008

[47] Wiesmeier M, Urbanski L, Hobley E, Lang B, von Lützow M, MarinSpiotta E, et al. Soil organic carbon storage as a key function of soils—A review of drivers and indicators at various scales. Geoderma. 2019;**333**:149-162. DOI: 10.1016/j.geoderma.2018.07.026

[48] Lehmann J et al. Biochar in climate change mitigation. Nature Geoscience. 2021;**14**:883-892. DOI: 10.1038/s41561-021-00852-8

[49] Hansen et al. Agriculural residues bioenergy potential that sustain soil carbon depends on energy conversion pathways. CCB-Bioenergy. 2020;**12**(11):1002-1013. DOI: 10.1111/gcbb.12733

[50] Scarlat N, Martinov M, Dallemand JF. Assessment of the availability of agricultural crop residues in the European Union: Potential and limitations for bioenergy use. Waste Management. 2010;**30**(10):1889-1897. DOI: 10.1016/j.wasman.2010.04.016

[51] United States Department of Agriculture-Natural Resource Conservation Service (USDA-NRCS), 2006. White Paper Crop Residue Removal for Biomass Energy Production: Effects on Soils and Recommendations. Available from: http://soils.usda.gov/sqi/management/files/AgForum_Residue_White_Paper.pdf

[52] Zomer R. Climate change mitigation: A spatial analysis of global land suitability for clean development mechanism afforestation and reforestation. Agriculture, Ecosystems and Environment. 2008;**126**:67-80. DOI: 10.1016/j.agee.2008.01.014

[53] Cosbey A, Parry JE, Browne J, Babu YD, Bandachari P, Drexhage J, et al. Realizing the Development Dividend: Making the CDM Work for Developing Countries. Moanitoba, Canada: International Institute for Sustainable Development; 2005. 72 p

[54] Smith J, Scherr S. Forests, Carbon and Local Livelihoods: An Assessment of Opportunities and Policy Recommendations. Bogor, Indonesia: CIFOR; 2002

[55] Gillenwater M, Seres S. The clean development mechanism: A review of the first international offset programme. Greenhouse Gas Measurement and Management. 2011;**1**(3-4):179-203

[56] Hultman N. A review of community co-benefits of the clean development mechanism. Environmental Research Letters. 2020;**15**:053002. DOI: 10.1088/1748-9326/ab6396

[57] Dirix J, Peeters W, Sterckx S. Is the clean development mechanism delivering benefits to the poorest communities in the

developing world? A critical evaluation and proposals for reform. Environment, Development and Sustainability. 2016;**18**:839-855

[58] Petticrew M, Roberts H. Systematic Reviews in the Social Sciences: A Practical Guide. New York: Wiley; 2008

[59] Pearson B. Market failure: Why the clean development mechanism will not promote clean development. Journal of Cleaner Production. 2007;**15**: 247-252

[60] Phelps J, Webb E, Agrawal A. Does REDD+ threaten to recentralize forest governance. Science. 2010;**328**(5976): 312-313. DOI: 10.1126/science.1187774

[61] Miles L, Kapos V. Reducing greenhouse gas emissions from deforestation and forest degradation: Global land-use implications. Science. 2008;**320**:1454-1455. DOI: 10.1126/science.1155358

[62] Angelsen A, Wertz-Kanounnikoff S. In: Angelsen A, editor. Moving Ahead with REDD: Issues, Options and Implications. Bogor, Indonesia: Center for International Forestry Research; 2008. pp. 11-22

[63] Minang PA, Murphy D. REDD after Copenhagen: The Way Forward. Nairobi: World Agroforestry Center; 2010. Available from: www.asb.cgiar.org/PDFwebdocs/REDD_After_Copenhagen-EN.pdf

[64] United Nations. Framework Convention on Climate Change. 1771 UNTS 107: New York, NY, USA: United Nations Treaty Collection; 1994

[65] UNFCCC. Warsaw Framework for REDD-Plus. Bonn, Germany: UNFCCC; 2013; Decisions 9-15/CP19

[66] UNFCCC. Warsaw Framework for REDD-Plus, Modalities for Measuring, Reporting and Verifying. Bonn, Germany: UNFCCC; 2013; Decision 14/CP.19; Para. 15

[67] NYDF Assessment Partners. Goal 9: Reward Positive Results/New York Declaration on Forests; Goal Assessment Update. Washington, DC, USA: NYDF Assessment Partners; 2019. p. 9

[68] International Bank on Reconstruction and Development. General Conditions Applicable to Emission Reductions Payment Agreements; The Forest Carbon Partnership Facility. Washington, DC, USA: World Bank; 2014. Available from: https://www.forestcarbonpartnership.org/erpa-general-conditions [Accessed: July 1, 2023]

[69] United Nations. The Kyoto Protocol to the United Nations Framework Convention on Climate Change. New York, NY, USA: United Nations Treaty Collection, C.N.101.2004; 1997

[70] Johns T et al. A three-fund approach to incorporating government, public and private forest stewards into a REDD funding mechanism. International Forestry Review. 2008;**10**(3):458-464

[71] Karsenty A. The architecture of proposed REDD schemes after Bali facing critical choices. International Forestry Review. 2008;**10**(3):443-457

[72] Verified Carbon Standard. Data Insights. 2020. Available from: https://verra.org/datainsights/april-2020/ [Accessed: July 1, 2023]

[73] Chagas T, Galt H, Lee D, Neeff T, Streck C. Should Forest Carbon Credits Be Included in Offsetting Schemes Such as CORSIA? Washington, DC, USA: Climate Focus; 2019

[74] Andonova L, Sun Y. Private governance in developing countries: Drivers of voluntary carbon offset programs. Global Environmental Politics. 2019;**19**:1. DOI: 10.1162/glep_a_00496

[75] Green J. Rethinking Private Authority Agents and Entrepreneurs in Global Environmental Governance. Princeton, NJ: Princeton University Press; 2014

[76] Paterson M, Hoffmann M, Betsill M, Bernstein S. The micro foundations of policy diffusion toward complex global governance: An analysis of the transnational carbon emission trading network. Comparative Political Studies. 2014;**47**(3):420-449

[77] Biedenkopf K, Müller P, Slominski P, Wettestad J. A global turn to greenhouse gas emissions trading? Experiments, actors, and diffusion. Global Environmental Politics. 2017;**17**(3):1-11

[78] Hale T, Roger C. Domestic politics and Chinese participation in transnational climate governance. In: Kennedy S, editor. China and Global Governance: The Dragon's Learning Curve. London, England: Routledge; 2017

[79] Schröder M. Local Climate Governance in China: Hybrid Actors and Market Mechanisms. New York, NY: Palgrave Macmillan; 2012

[80] Castro P, Michaelowa A. Would preferential access measures be sufficient to overcome current barriers to CDM projects in least developed countries? Climate and Development. 2011;**3**(2):123-142

[81] Andonova LB. Public–private partnerships for the Earth: Politics and patterns of hybrid authority in the multilateral system. Global Environmental Politics. 2010;**10**(2):25-53

[82] Michaelowa A, Michaelowa K. Climate business for poverty reduction? The role of the World Bank. Review of International Organizations. 2011;**6**(3-4):259-286

[83] Green J. Order out of chaos: Public and private rules for managing carbon. Global Environmental Politics. 2013;**13**(2):1-25

[84] Lovell HC. Governing the carbon offset market. Wiley Interdisciplinary Reviews: Climate Change. 2010;**1**(3): 353-362

[85] Bumpus AG, Liverman DM. Accumulation by decarbonization and the governance of carbon offsets. Economic Geography. 2008;**84**(2):127-155

[86] Abbott KW, Green JF, Keohane RO. Organizational ecology and institutional change in global governance. International Organization. 2016;**70**(2):247-277

[87] Hamilton K, Sjardin M, Shapiro A, Marcello T. Fortifying the Foundation: State of the Voluntary Carbon Markets 2009. New York, NY: New Carbon Finance; 2009

[88] Bernstein S. Liberal environmentalism and global environmental governance. Global Environmental Politics. 2002;**2**(3): 1-16

[89] Newell P, Paterson M. Climate Capitalism: Global Warming and the Transformation of the Global Economy. Cambridge, England: Cambridge University Press; 2010

[90] Roberts JT, Parks B. A Climate of Injustice: Global Inequality, North-South Politics, and Climate Policy. Cambridge, MA: MIT Press; 2006

[91] Wara M, Victor D. A Realistic Policy on International Carbon Offsets. PESD Working Paper 74. CA: Stanford University; 2008

[92] Blaufelder C; Levy C; Mannion P.; Pinner D.A blueprint for scaling voluntary carbon markets to meet the climate challenge. Available from: https://www.mckinsey.com/capabilities/sustainability/our-insights/a-blueprint-for-scaling-voluntary-carbon-markets-to-meet-the-climate-challenge

[93] Kreibich N, Hermwille L. Caught in between: Credibility and feasibility of the voluntary carbon market post-2020. Climate Policy. 2021;**21**(7):939-957. DOI: 10.1080/14693062.2021.1948384

[94] Donofrio S, Maguire P, Zwick S, Merry W. Voluntary carbon and the post-pandemic recovery. In: Forest Trends. Available from: https://www.ecosystemmarketplace.com/carbon-markets/. 2020 [Accessed: July 1, 2023]

[95] Hermwille L. Climate change as a transformation challenge – A new climate policy paradigm? GAIA – Ecological Perspectives for Science and Society. 2016;**25**(1):19-22. DOI: 10.14512/gaia.25.1.6

[96] Donofrio S, Maguire P, Zwick S, Merry W. The only constant is change – State of the voluntary carbon markets 2020, second installment. Forest Trends. 2020:23. Available from: https://share.hsforms.com/1FhYs1TapTE-qBxAxgy-jgg1yp8f [Accessed: July 1, 2023]

[97] Rogelj J, Geden O, Cowie A, Reisinger A. Net-zero emissions targets are vague: Three ways to fix. Nature. 2021;**591**(7850):365-368. DOI: 10.1038/d41586-021-00662-3

[98] UNEP Finance Initiative. The Portfolio Decarbonization Coalition. 2020. Available from: https://unepfi.org/pdc/ [Accessed: July 3, 2023]

[99] Machnik D, Sun P, Tänzler D. Climate neutrality targets of European companies and the role of carbon offsetting. Adelphi. 2020:60

[100] Tong D, Trout K. Big oil reality check – Assessing oil and gas company climate plans. Oil Change International. Available from: http://priceofoil.org/content/uploads/2020/09/OCI-Big-Oil-Reality-Check-vF.pdf. 2020 [Accessed: July 3, 2023]

[101] Kachi A, Mooldijk S, Warnecke C. Climate Neutrality Claims. Cologne, Germany: NewClimate Institute; 2020. p. 23. Available from: https://newclimate.org/wp-content/uploads/2020/09/Climate_neutrality_claims_BUND_September2020.pdf [Accessed: July 3, 2023]

[102] Gold Standard. A New Paradigm for Voluntary Climate Action: 'Reduce Within, Finance Beyond'. 2017. Available from: https://www.goldstandard.org/sites/default/files/documents/a_new_paradigm_for_voluntary_climate_action.pdf [Accessed: July 3, 2023]

[103] Hamrick K, Gallant M. Unlocking Potential – State of the Voluntary Carbon Markets 2017. 2017. Available from: http://www.forest-trends.org/documents/files/doc_5591.pdf

[104] TSVCM. Consultation Document. Taskforce on Scaling Voluntary Carbon Markets. 2020. Available from: https://www.iif.com/Portals/1/Files/TSVCM_Consultation_Document.pdf [Accessed: July 1, 2023]

[105] Wang Y, Corson C. The making of a 'charismatic' carbon credit: Clean cookstoves and 'uncooperative' women

in Western Kenya. Environment and Planning A: Economy and Space. 2015;**47**(10):2064-2079

[106] Tong W et al. The impact of cap-and-trade mechanism and consumers' environmental preferences on a retailer-led supply chain. Resources, Conservation & Recycling. 2019;**142**:88-100. DOI: 10.1016/j.resconrec.2018.11.005

[107] Manohar HL, Kumar RG. Impact of green supply chain management attributes on sustainable supply chains. International Journal of Supply Chain and Operations Resilience. 2016;**2**:291-314. DOI: 10.1504/IJSCOR.2016.084030

[108] Xu L, Wang C. Sustainable manufacturing in a closed-loop supply chain considering emission reduction and remanufacturing. Resources, Conservation and Recycling. 2017;**131**:297-304. DOI: 10.1016/j.resconrec.2017.10.012

[109] Du S, Zhu J, Jiao H, Ye W. Game-theoretical analysis for supply chain with consumer preference to low carbon. International Journal of Production Research. 2015;**53**:3753-3768. DOI: 10.1080/00207543.2014.988888

[110] Janssen M, Jager W. Stimulating diffusion of green products. Journal of Evolutionary Economics. 2002;**12**:283-306. DOI: 10.1007/s00191-002-0120-1

[111] Swami S, Shah J. Channel coordination in green supply chain management. The Journal of the Operational Research Society. 2013;**64**:336-351. DOI: 10.1057/jors.2012.44

[112] Pu X, Shi Q, Ling L. Effect of direct marking on retailing channels where large retailers exist. Journal of Management Sciences in China. 2007;**10**:49-56. DOI: 10.3321/j.issn:1007-9807.2007.06.006

[113] Lai K, Tang AKY. Green retailing: Factors for success. California Management Review. 2010;**52**:6-31. DOI: 10.1525/cmr.2010.52.2.6

[114] Styles D, Schoenberger H, Galvez-Martos JL. Environmental improvement of product supply chains: A review of European retailers' performance. Resources, Conservation & Recycling. 2012;**65**:57-78. DOI: 10.1016/j.resconrec.2012.05.002

[115] Tuten T. Promoting sustainability by marketing green products to non-adopters. Gest. 2013;**2000**(30):93. DOI: 10.3917/g2000.302.0093

[116] He H, Luo Z, Wang Q, Chen M, He H, Gao L, et al. Joint operation mechanism of distributed photovoltaic power generation market and carbon market based on cross-chain trading technology. IEEE Access. 2020;**8**:66116-66130. DOI: 10.1109/ACCESS.2020.2985577

[117] Johnson CAB. Evaluation of Spatial Fragmentation of Protected Areas Using the Spatial Assessment for Coastal Protected Areas in Caribbean Small Island Developing States. ProQuest Dissertations & Theses. 2020

[118] Moreaux C, Zafra-Calvo N, Vansteelant NG, Wicander S, Burgess ND. Can existing assessment tools be used to track equity in protected area management under Aichi Target 11? Biological Conservation. 2018;**224**:242-247

Chapter 3

How Far the Mono Transboundary Biosphere Reserve Protects Biodiversity in the Dahomey-Gap Corridor, West Africa?

Kossi Adjonou, Elie A. Padonou, Rodrigue Idohou, Moustapha A. Kolawolé, Issa Adbou-Kerim Bindaoudou, Salako Valère, Fiacre Ahononga, Romain Glèlè Kakaï and Kouami Kokou

Abstract

Mono Transboundary Biosphere Reserve (MTBR) is rich in biodiversity associated with different multi-functional ecosystems in the Dahomey-Gap corridor in the southern border between Benin and Togo. The reserve has been facing many anthropogenic pressures since few years including the uncontrolled exploitation of forest resources, and fragmentation of habitats and permanent search for arable land. Thus, it becomes important to develop prospective analysis approaches in order to provide specific insights for a balanced biodiversity. This study aims to provide scientific evidence to better understand and project future changes in LULC in the MTBR at different spatial and temporal scales. Changes in LULC were used to map the MTBR in 1986, 2000, and 2015 and to predict the LULC in the future up to 2070 using Markovian chain analysis. During 1986–2000, urban agglomeration/bare soil (8.79 ha/year) increased, whereas the natural vegetation cover increased during the period 2000–2015, particularly mangroves (9.81 ha/year). Assuming the dynamic observed, the mangroves will increase by 2070 (6% of its cover). However, an important increase is also expected for farmland (13% of its cover). It is, therefore, important to strengthen the actions and strategies around and within the MTBR for sustainable management of biological resources.

Keywords: Dahomey gap, future scenarios, land use/land cover, prospective analysis, protected area

1. Introduction

The land and its resources have been used to meet material, social, cultural, and spiritual needs of human beings [1]. In that process, human beings modified land uses through daily activities [2]. Conversion of natural forests and grasslands into farming and crop areas in order to meet the food demand of the ever-increasing world population is among the examples. Land use/land cover (LULC) change, as one of the main driving forces of global environmental change, is a key component in the sustainable development debate [3, 4]. LULC changes are aspects of global environmental change and affect ecosystem processes and services [2, 5, 6]. Those changes influence energy exchanges between land and atmosphere and affect climate, water and soil quality, biogeochemical cycles, biodiversity, and ecosystem services [7]. Increasing demand for agricultural, industrial, or urban areas compromises the ability of natural forests, waterbodies, and grasslands to support community's needs.

The rapid changes of LULC than ever before, particularly in developing countries, are often characterized by rampant urban sprawling, land degradation, or the transformation of forest land to farming, ensuing enormous cost to the environment [8]. In sub-Saharan Africa, several studies were conducted on mapping and valuation of ecosystem services in the context of LULC [9, 10]. Almost all studies indicate that the region is under severe pressure of degradation, with significant consequences for rural livelihoods [3–5, 11, 12]. Alterations of land cover and land use types result from human activities such as agricultural expansion, deforestation, and natural factors (drought, cyclone, etc.), and generate more or less sensitive consequences on the environment.

These observations related to changes in LULC come true in highly populated areas marked by contrasting climatic conditions and high demand for arable land and are particularly pointed out by several studies carried out in the Mono Transboundary Biosphere Reserve (MTBR) located in the Dahomey corridor on the southern border between Benin and Togo [11, 13–16]. The area is rich in biodiversity associated with different multi-functional ecosystems [16], but it has also been facing many anthropogenic pressures since few years. These include the uncontrolled exploitation of forest resources, fragmentation of habitats, and permanent search for arable land [11]. This situation puts great pressure on the dynamics and conversion of LULC. The conversion, including changes of forest and/or woodlands to agricultural lands, has negative impacts on climate, terrestrial carbon stores, loss of biodiversity [5, 6, 17], fragmentation of wildlife habitats, and disruption of ecological and hydrological processes [18].

Facing that situation and in view of the uncertainties surrounding the future of forest resources and the specific ecosystems of the MTBR, territorial prospective analysis approaches should be adopted to provide specific insights and elements for thoughts on the possible room for maneuver over a long period and at different horizons for a balanced and sustainable management of the forest resources and biodiversity of this reserve in line with the socioeconomic and environmental challenges of the region. Exploring the possible future development of land occupations and uses in the MTBR remains an effective means of identifying areas at stake for the conservation of natural resources and biodiversity and assessing the influence of management policies and strategies at different spatiotemporal scales on land use [19–21].

This study aims to provide scientific evidence to better understand and project future changes in LULC in the MTBR at different spatial and temporal scales. Based on remote sensing technologies and satellite data coupled with dynamic and spatially explicit modeling methods, this chapter aimed at: (i) analyzing the dynamics of land-use patterns in the period 1986 to 2015 for a better understanding of the trends in the evolution of the natural landscape and (ii) establishing a future scenario (2015–2070) changes in each land cover class. This research is unique as the modeling of land use dynamics in the MTBR will make it possible to follow the evolutionary trend of the landscape and to find acceptable rules for preserving natural resources, particularly forest resources and biodiversity in the reserve.

2. Materials and methods

2.1 Study area

The Mono Transboundary Biosphere Reserve (MTBR) is located at the southern border between Benin and Togo (6°8′52.8″–7°3′41.8″ North latitude and 1°24′18.2″–1°30′0.0″ East longitude) and covers an area of 345.22 km^2 (**Figure 1**). The reserve is located in the Dahomey gap, a corridor characterized by mosaics of dense semi-deciduous forests, Guinean savannas, marshy meadows, marshes, mangroves, and water plans, and mosaics of crops and fallows [16]. The reserve is characterized by a tropical humid climate with a succession of four seasons per year, two dry seasons (November to March and July to September) and two rainy seasons (March to July and September to November). Rainfall varies between 850 mm and 1250 mm per year, with an average monthly rainfall of about 222.57 mm during the long rainy season and 88.30 mm during the short rainy season (October). The average maximum temperature is 31.25°C between December and April, and the minimum temperature

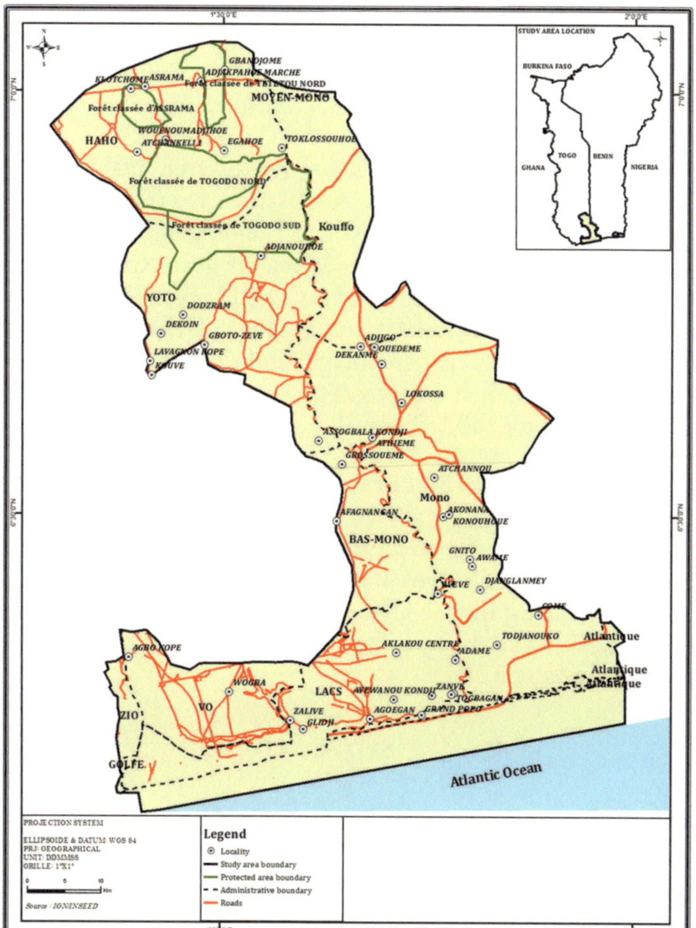

Figure 1.
Location of the Mono Transboundary Biosphere Reserve.

is 28° C between July and September. The area is home to different ecosystems (marine, terrestrial, and lagoon). The Mono River is the main river around which the reserve is built. Approximately two million people are riverine to the reserve, with 80% depending largely on the ecosystem services provided by the reserve (small-scale farming, small-scale fishing, and exploitation of wood and charcoal [22].

2.2 Land use land cover (LULC) maps

Two data sources were used to establish the baseline and the analysis of the LULC dynamics of the reserve. These include two Landsat satellite images (TM (1986) and ETM + (2000)) and a Sentinel 2A satellite image (2015 being the reference year). The scenes were chosen during the dry season with low cloud cover [23]. The interpretation was aided by additional data sources including the administrative maps of Benin and Togo, the GPS data from the field, and Google Earth Pro.

The radiometric correction of Landsat TM, ETM +, and Sentinel 2A images was used to correct for atmospheric bias and change from pixel value to digital count as a reflectance value. This operation is completed by mosaicking the two Sentinel 2A image scenes in order to obtain a single scene that can be used to extract easily the study area. The color composition of bands 4-5-7 of TM and ETM + images and bands 4-3-2 of Sentinel 2A image was chosen by selecting training sites because they present the best discrimination of LULC types [24]. About 100 plots representing all types of LULC chosen according to their spatial distribution on TM and ETM + color compositions of bands 4-5-7 and bands 4-3-2 of Sentinel 2A image were identified and delineated.

The spectral properties were used to classify the different LULCs of the image into thematic classes based on the supervised classification (due to a good knowledge of the study area) using the maximum-likelihood algorithm. The accuracy of the classifications was evaluated using a confusion matrix or contingency table obtained from field truth data and a representative of each LULC class. The validation of the classification was based on the calculation of two indices: the overall accuracy (the proportion of well-ranked pixels in percentage) and the Kappa index (the ratio between the well-ranked pixels and the total pixels surveyed) [25]. In addition, the field truth data were used for validation.

2.3 Land use/land cover dynamic analysis

Quantitative analysis of changes over the entire study period was carried out in order to identify the different changes in LULC classes based on change detection matrix resulting from the comparison between the pixels of the classifications of two dates [26]. This analysis was done by calculating the rate of change (Rc) used in LULC studies [27, 28] as follows:

$$Rc = \left[(\mathrm{S2}/\mathrm{S1})1/\mathrm{d} - 1\right] \times 100 \qquad (1)$$

(where: Rc = rate of change (%); S1 = area of the LULC class of the date d1; S2 = area of the class of the date d2 (d2 > d1) et d = number of years between the two dates). Positive values indicate a "progression," whereas negative values indicate a "regression." Values close to zero indicate a relative "stability" of the class.

The average annual rate of forest degradation [29] was evaluated using the following formula:

$$ARD = (S2 / S1) / d \times 100 \tag{2}$$

(where ARD = average annual rate of degradation (%); S2 = Total area of forest lost; S1 = Initial area of forest and d = number of years between the two dates).

The transition matrix was elaborated by superposing the LULC maps of 1986, 2000, and 2015 with the "Intersect polygons" algorithm of the Geoprocessing extension using ArcGIS 10.0. The transition matrix was used to highlight the different changes in LULC between two dates [30]. The matrix values were standardized to obtain annualized changes and to make comparisons. To annualize the matrix values, each probability matrix was used separately to compute the matrix's eigenvectors and eigenvalues using the diagonalization method [31].

2.4 Futures scenarios

The standard annualized transition matrices were used to further predict the proportion of each land cover class at any one time based on a Markovian chain model. Two different scenarios were assumed corresponding to each of the two Markovian matrices (1986–2000 and 2000–2015). The area expected for 2015 scenarios based on the 1986–2000 period was compared with the area of 2015 from the 2015 map using a chi-square (χ^2) test for the model validation.

3. Results

3.1 Land cover maps

The results of the processing images of the year 2015 indicated an overall good accuracy (89.84%) and an estimated Kappa index of 0.88 with nine LULC units (**Table 1**; **Figure 2**) including forest, savannas, mosaic of crops and fallows, wetlands, plantations, urban agglomerations, and bare soil. Forests were composed of dense semi-deciduous forests, woodland, and gallery forests with an area of 15,740.91 ha

Land cover/land use classes		Area (ha)	Percentage (%)
Forests (dense, semi-deciduous, woodlands, and gallery forest)		15,740.91	4.55
Savannas on drained soil		88,917.48	25.71
Wetlands	Floodplain savannas of *Mitragyna inermis*	41,125.77	11.89
	Marshy meadows	15,092.73	4.36
	Mangroves	25,941.87	7.50
	Water body	41,979.51	12.14
Plantations		27,113.13	7.84
Mosaic of crops/fallows		80,599.05	23.31
Urban agglomeration/bare soil		9249.03	2.67

Table 1.
Land use land cover classes in the Mono Transboundary Biosphere Reserve in 2015.

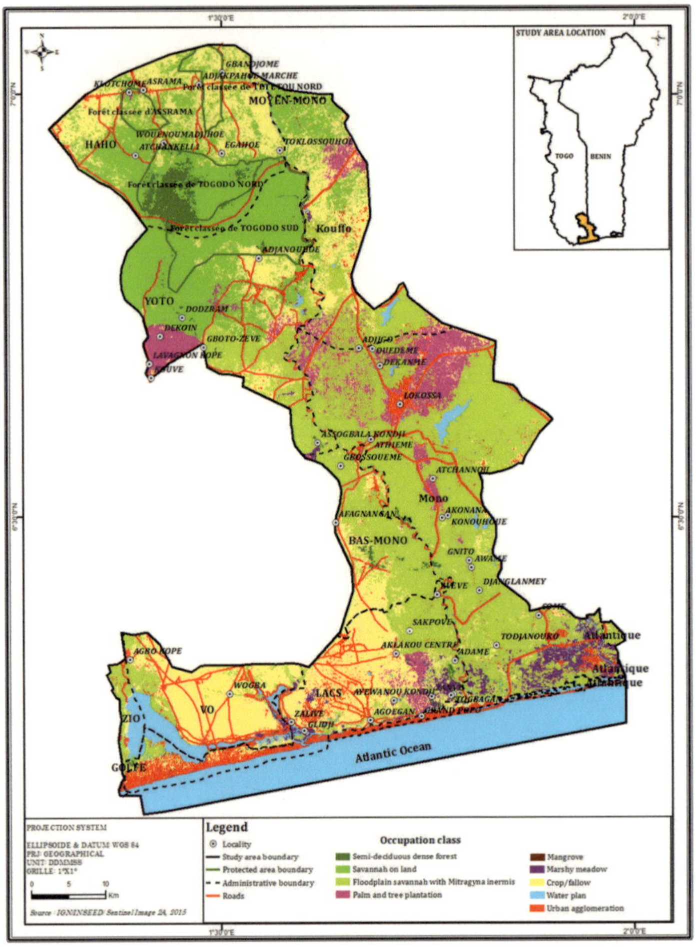

Figure 2.
Reference situation map of LULC in the Mono Transboundary Biosphere Reserve in 2015.

(4.55% of the reserve); these ecosystems were in the form of fragmented islands dispersed within the reserve.

Savannas on drained soil had an area of 88,917.48 ha (25.71% of the reserve), holding tree and shrub savannas. Wetlands covered an area of 124,139.88 ha (35.90% of the reserve) and included mangroves, floodplain savannas dominated by *Mitragyna inermis*, marshy meadows, and water. The majority of wetlands and their associated plant communities were mostly located in the southern half of the reserve. Within these wetlands, mangroves that constitute particular ecosystems occupied an area of 25,941.87 ha (7.50% of the reserve area).

Plantations with an area of 27,113.13 ha (7.84% of the reserve) were composed of *Tectona grandis, Khaya senegalensis, Eucalyptus* sp., *Elaeis guineensis,* and *Cocos nucifera*. Mosaic of crops and fallows with a total area of 80,599.05 ha (23.31% of the reserve) consisted of areas of crops and areas previously cultivated and abandoned (fallows) or invaded by exotic species.

Urban agglomerations and bare soil with an area of 9249.03 ha (2.67% of the reserve) included towns and villages and areas with very low vegetation cover, including quarries (sand and gravel) and rocky outcrops.

3.2 Changes in land use/land cover

The proportions of the nine LULC types changed considerably from 1986 to 2015 (**Table 2**). In 1986, floodplain savanna of *Mitragyna inermis*, savannas on drained soil and mosaic of crops, and fallows were the dominant land cover types (**Table 2**; **Figure 3**). In 2000, the land cover types were dominated by agglomeration and dry savannas, whereas in 2015, savannas on drained soil and farmland were the dominant land cover types. The cover of forests and floodplain savannas of *Mitragyna inermis* decreased in the periods 1986–2000, whereas other land uses increased except farmland, which remained stable. In the period 2000–2015, the cover of floodplain

Land cover class		Year 1986		Year 2000		Year 2015	
		Area (ha)	%	Area (ha)	%	Area (ha)	%
Forests		18,346.95	5.31	11,384.73	3.29	15,740.91	4.55
Savannas on drained soil		53,481.15	15.47	65,298.96	18.89	88,917.48	25.71
Mosaic of crops and fallows		55,029.69	15.91	51,973.65	15.03	80,599.05	23.31
Wetlands	Floodplain savannas of *Mitragyna inermis*	117,954.27	34.11	55,974.87	16.18	41,125.77	11.89
	Swamp grasslands/ Marshy meadows	18,021.51	5.21	23,800.05	6.88	15,092.73	4.36
	Mangroves	4721.4	1.36	6369.03	1.84	25,941.87	7.50
	Water body	40,721.04	11.77	41,912.37	12.12	41,979.51	12.14
Plantations		16,650.45	4.82	21,235.41	6.14	27,113.13	7.84
Urban agglomeration/bare soil		20,833.02	6.03	67,810.41	19.61	9249.03	2.67
Total		**345,759.48**	**100**	**345,759.48**	**100**	**345,759.48**	**100**

Table 2.
Land use/land cover classes used in the analysis of change (area in ha).

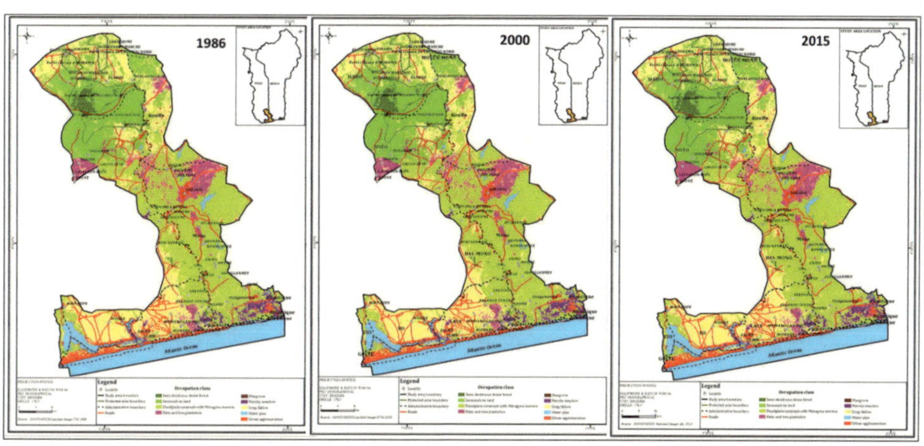

Figure 3.
Dynamic of land use/land cover in the Mono Transboundary Biosphere Reserve from 1986 to 2015.

savannas of *Mitragyna inermis*, swamp grassland/marshy meadow, and urban agglomeration/bare soil decreased, while the others increased except for water body that remained stable. In both periods, the cover of floodplain savannas of *Mitragyna inermis* decreased, while the cover of savannas on drained soil, mangroves, and plantations increased.

The transition matrices of the observed time periods 1986–2000 and 2000–2015 (**Table 3**) helped to derive the probability of change (**Table 4**). During the period 1986–2000, water body and savannas on drained soil showed large persistence (99.9% and 97.8% per year, respectively) as well as farmland and urban agglomeration/bare soil (96.5% and 96.0%, respectively) (**Table 3**). The forest cover converted to mangroves (0.1%), floodplain savannas of *Mitragyna inermis* (1.4%), savanna on drained soil (1.2%), swamp grassland (0.3%), plantations (0.6%), farmland (0.7%), and urban agglomeration/bare soil (1.1%). The floodplain savannas of *Mitragyna inermis* mainly regressed into savannas on drained soil (0.5%), swamp grassland (0.6%), plantations (0.6%), farmland (0.5%), urban agglomeration/bare soil (2%), and water body (0.1%). However, it progressed in forests (0.3%) and mangroves (0.2). The mangroves also regressed into floodplain savannas of *Mitragyna inermis* (1.8%), savannas on drained soil (0.3%), swamp grassland (1.8%), plantations (0.5%), farmland (0.1%), and urban agglomeration/bare soil (0.6%). However, it progressed into forest (0.9%).

In the period 2000–2015, water body had a large annual persistence (99.8%) followed by farmland (97.9%). Forest cover was regressed into mangroves (0.6%), savanna on drained soil (2.2%), floodplain savannas of *Mitragyna inermis* (1.1%), swamp grassland (0.2%), plantations (0.5%), and farmland (0.3%). Floodplain savannas of *Mitragyna inermis* were mainly regressed in savannas on drained soil (2.5%), swamp grassland (0.1%), plantations (1.7%), farmland (0.7%), and water (0.1%). However, it progressed into mangroves (0.4%) and forests (0.3%). Mangroves were regressed into savannas on drained soil (2.1%), floodplain savannas of *Mitragyna inermis* (1.5%), swamp grassland (0.2%), plantations (0.4%), farmland (1%), and urban and agglomeration/bare soil (0.2%). However, it progressed into forests (0.3%).

3.3 Land use/land cover degradation or conservation rates

During the first period, 1986–2000, the highest rate of degradation (**Table 5**) was observed for floodplain savannas of Mitragyna inermis (61,979.4 ha lost) and forests (6962.22 ha). The other LULC had increased with the highest increase for urban agglomeration/bare soil (46,977.39 ha). In the second period, 2000–2015, urban agglomeration/bare soil had a high annual rate of degradation (58,561.38 ha) in addition to floodplain savannas of Mitragyna inermis (14,849.10 ha). The other LULC had increased with the highest increase for mangroves (19,572.84 ha).

3.4 Future LULC changes forecasting

Future land cover changes will depend upon the previously observed dynamics for the time period considered (1986–2000 and 2000–2015). Based on the observed dynamics in the first period (1986–2000), the area of forest and floodplain savannas of *Mitragyna inermis* is expected to decrease by 3.5% and 25.5% of the area recorded in 1986 by 2070 (**Figure 4**). The area of savannas on drained soil, mosaic of crops and fallows, swamp grasslands, mangroves, water, and urban agglomeration/bare soil will increase respectively by 8.4%, 3%, 1.3%, 0.1%, 2.4%, and 13.8% of the areas recorded in 1986 by 2070.

	Forest	Savannas on drained sol	Floodplain savannas of Mitragyna inermis	Swamp grasslands	Mangroves	Plantations	Water	Mosaic of crops and fallows	Urban agglomeration/bare soil
1986–2000									
Forests	4351.41	3099.33	3680.46	809.01	375.3	1450.08	67.86	1767.69	2745.81
Savannas on drained sol	762.21	37075.95	1384.11	3370.32	320.04	516.87	0.45	4108.59	5942.61
Floodplain savannas of *Mitragyna inermis*	4416.21	9052.02	39273.93	10028.07	3205.62	9458.55	979.38	7802.28	33738.21
Swamp grasslands	378.18	5544.54	1464.66	6321.15	503.37	358.92	301.41	908.1	2241.18
Mangroves	598.95	210.42	1201.86	1179.54	656.64	339.48	24.57	95.76	414.18
Plantations	463.14	1132.29	4792.41	16.29	230.85	4801.14	4.14	3307.32	1902.87
Water body	1.53	8.64	305.64	36.27	5.94	0.09	40121.64	2.07	239.22
Mosaic of crops and fallows	293.13	7333.92	2790.45	851.49	643.14	3431.34	11.25	28390.32	11284.65
Urban agglomeration/bare soil	119.97	1841.85	1081.35	1187.91	428.13	878.94	401.67	5591.52	9301.68
2000–2015									
Forests	3131.01	3686.13	1799.28	393.84	1074.42	769.5	17.73	457.02	55.8
Savannas on drained sol	2940.39	20812.59	11491.65	9608.04	8335.53	584.37	47.79	10969.29	509.31
Floodplain savannas of *Mitragyna inermis*	3745.8	21,321	5903.19	1210.68	3187.17	14104.17	668.61	5465.16	369.09
Swamp grasslands	775.71	6690.06	7322.22	2486.88	3788.37	46.71	165.96	1989	535.14
Mangrove	300.96	2027.07	1457.01	162.18	886.14	403.29	27	928.62	176.76

	Forest	Savannas on drained sol	Floodplain savannas of Mitragyna inermis	Swamp grasslands	Mangroves	Plantations	Water	Mosaic of crops and fallows	Urban agglomeration/bare soil
Plantations	543.69	6010.11	1240.92	31.23	671.22	5567.94	3.06	6847.74	319.5
Water body	83.16	174.69	457.47	248.13	288.99	6.93	40447.8	25.11	180.09
Mosaic of crops and fallows	228.15	7298.28	3402.9	256.68	2795.13	1197.63	20.07	35503.2	1271.61
Urban agglomeration/bare soil	3992.04	20897.55	8051.13	695.07	4914.9	4432.59	581.49	18413.91	5831.73

Table 3.
Land use/land cover transition matrix (area in ha) for the considered time period (1986–2000–2015).

	Forests	Savannas on drained sol	Floodplain savannas of Mitragyna inermis	Swamp grasslands	Mangroves	Plantations	Water body	Mosaic of crops and fallows	Urban agglomeration/bare soil
1986–2000									
Forests	0.946	0.012	0.014	0.003	0.001	0.006	0.000	0.007	0.011
Savannas on drained sol	0.001	0.978	0.002	0.005	0.000	0.001	0.000	0.005	0.008
Floodplain savannas of *Mitragyna inermis*	0.003	0.005	0.952	0.006	0.002	0.006	0.001	0.005	0.020
Swamp grasslands	0.001	0.022	0.006	0.954	0.002	0.001	0.001	0.004	0.009
Mangroves	0.009	0.003	0.018	0.018	0.939	0.005	0.000	0.001	0.006
Plantations	0.002	0.005	0.021	0.000	0.001	0.949	0.000	0.014	0.008
Water body	0.000	0.000	0.001	0.000	0.000	0.000	0.999	0.000	0.000
Mosaic of crops and fallows	0.000	0.010	0.004	0.001	0.001	0.004	0.000	0.965	0.015
Urban agglomeration/ bare soil	0.000	0.006	0.004	0.004	0.001	0.003	0.001	0.019	0.960
2000–2015									
Forests	0.952	0.022	0.011	0.002	0.006	0.005	0.000	0.003	0.000
Savannas on drained soil	0.003	0.955	0.012	0.010	0.009	0.001	0.000	0.011	0.001
Floodplain savannas of *Mitragyna inermis*	0.004	0.025	0.940	0.001	0.004	0.017	0.001	0.007	0.000
Swamp grasslands	0.002	0.019	0.021	0.940	0.011	0.000	0.000	0.006	0.001
Mangroves	0.003	0.021	0.015	0.002	0.943	0.004	0.000	0.010	0.002
Plantations	0.002	0.019	0.004	0.000	0.002	0.951	0.000	0.021	0.001
Water body	0.000	0.000	0.001	0.000	0.000	0.000	0.998	0.000	0.000

	Forests	Savannas on drained sol	Floodplain savannas of Mitragyna inermis	Swamp grasslands	Mangroves	Plantations	Water body	Mosaic of crops and fallows	Urban agglomeration/bare soil
Mosaic of crops and fallows	0.000	0.009	0.004	0.000	0.004	0.002	0.000	0.979	0.002
Urban agglomeration/ bare soil	0.004	0.021	0.008	0.001	0.005	0.004	0.001	0.018	0.939

Table 4.
Annual probability matrices for the considered time period (1986–2000–2015).

Land cover class	1986–2000	2000–2015
Forests	3.35	−2.18
Savannas on drained soil	−1.44	−2.08
Mosaic of crops and fallows	0.41	−2.96
Floodplain savannas of *Mitragyna inermis*	5.18	2.03
Swamp grasslands	−2.01	2.99
Mangroves	−2.16	−9.81
Water	−0.21	−0.02
Plantations	−1.75	−1.64
Urban agglomeration/bare soil	−8.79	12.43

Table 5.
Annual rate of degradation and conservation of land use/land cover (% lost ha/year).

Assuming the dynamics recorded in the second period (2000–2015), the area of land covered by floodplain savannas of *Mitragyna inermis*, swamp grassland, water, and urban agglomeration/bare soil will decrease by 4.3%, 2.1%, 0.5%, and 17.8% considering their cover in 2000, respectively, while the areas covered by forests, savannas on drained soil, mosaic of crops and fallows, mangroves, and plantations will increase by 0.6%, 4.8%, 13%, 6%, and 0.4% of their cover in 2000, respectively.

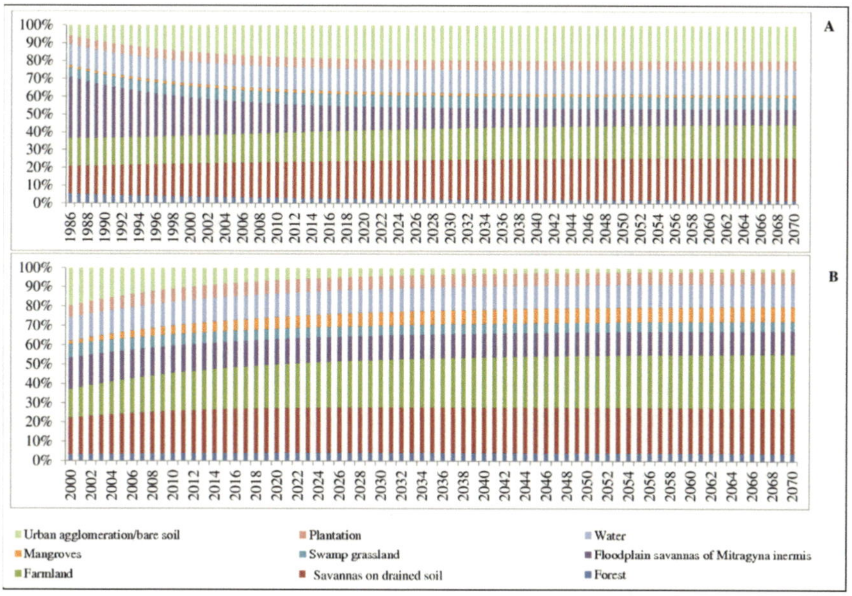

Figure 4.
Simulation of the evolution of the nine land cover classes under two future scenarios (dynamics observed during the periods 1986–2000 and 2000–2015).

4. Discussion

Main findings from this study were that natural vegetation (closed forest formation, mangrove forest, flooded savanna of Mitragyna, savannas on drained soil, swamp grassland) converted into agricultural and nonvegetated areas (mosaic of crops and fallows, urban agglomeration/bare soil, and plantations). These changes in LULC confirmed the dynamic of Mono Transboundary Biosphere Reserve [11, 32, 33].

The Mono Transboundary Biosphere Reserve (MTBR) holds an important wetland protected by the Ramsar convention. Before the year 2000, only natural vegetation (forest and floodplain savannas of *Mitragyna inermis*) was observed to be degraded, while after the year 2000, urban agglomeration/bare soil was mainly degraded, when important reconstitution was observed for natural vegetation (forests, savannas on drained soil, and mangroves). The year 2000 was marked by the ratification of the Ramsar convention by Benin. In the case of Togo, the Ramsar convention was ratified since 1995. Prior to this period, there was no restriction on the use of the reserve resources that were subject to important overexploitation, as confirmed by the exceptional increase of urban agglomeration/bare soil in the period 1986–2000. Later in 2000, several project activities followed the ratification of the Ramsar convention that contributed to the restoration of the natural vegetation, mainly the mangroves.

The MTBR is the only place in Dahomey Gap where mangroves remain natural. The mangroves provided ecosystem services including support for aquaculture and fishery activities, salt extraction, fuelwood, and agriculture [34–36]. Mangroves also provide ecological, socioeconomic, and climate regulation roles [37–39]. Thus, human beings remain the main beneficiaries in terms of self-consumption and the improvement of their income. The multiple ecosystem goods and services provided by the mangroves are among the main reason for the designation of the MTBR in 2017. This reserve is sustaining the conservation of mangroves as its cover had significantly increased in the period 2000–2015.

The future scenarios predict an important loss of natural vegetation (forests and floodplain savannas of *Mitragyna inermis*) and a significant increase in urban agglomeration/bare soil, assuming the dynamic recorded in the first period (1986–2000). In the second period, natural vegetation, mainly mangroves, will increase, while important loss will be observed for urban agglomeration/bare soil. Based on the progress observed after the year 2000 in the restoration of the natural vegetation, it is hopefully expected that the dynamic observed in the period 2000–2015 will prevail in the future. Moreover, the recent designation of MTBR as UNESCO biodiversity reserve confirms the need to sustain the conservation of this important biodiversity.

More actions including awareness-raising and sustainable management are needed to reduce the cover of farmland that will progress by 2070, assuming the dynamic of the period 2000–2015. The management of the reserve must be participatory based on gender approach in order to prevent the population from illegally re-introduction in the reserve. The successful management of the reserve also requires local interventions coordinated across ecologically appropriate spatial scales, and best guided by frequent and synoptic sampling and monitoring through the results of multidisciplinary research [40, 41].

The Markovian model used to predict the dynamic of LULC is useful for exploratory analysis and for depicting contrasting scenarios [41]. The model is not spatially explicit and assumes homogeneity of the transition probabilities over time

[41, 42]. Thus, spatially explicit model should be used in future on changes in LULC analysis to understand the LULC dynamics locations and pathways in the MTBR. Future similar studies should take into account the limits observed in the model used in this study.

5. Conclusion

The Mono Transboundary Biosphere Reserve (MTBR) has contributed to the restoration of natural vegetation since the year 2000, that is, characterized by the ratification of Ramsar convention by Benin and Togo with the aims of the conservation and sustainable use of wetlands. The current study was designed to assess LULC dynamics from 1986 to 2015 and to predict future scenarios in the Mono Transboundary Biosphere Reserve (MTBR). The analysis of the dynamics of change in LULC revealed the different processes of evolution within the landscape during the period 1986–2015. These changes mainly concern the regression of natural ecosystems such as forests and wooded savannas, whereas low-cover land occupancies (mosaics of crops/fallows and urban agglomerations/bare soil) have been gradually increasing.

Despite the changes and conversions observed during the period of this study (1986 to 2015), the area remained largely covered by natural vegetation and still has good potential for biodiversity conservation. The MTBR is the only place in Dahomey Gap where mangroves remain natural. These mangroves provided ecosystem services including support for aquaculture and fishery activities, salt extraction, fuelwood, and agriculture. These mangrove ecosystems also provide ecological, socioeconomic, and climate regulation roles, and the multiple ecosystem goods and services provided by the mangroves are among the main reason for the designation of the MTBR in 2017.

The simulation of future land use dynamics in this study is part of the need to understand the functioning of LULC in the area of the reserve. Based on the observed dynamics in the first period (1986–2000), the area of forest and floodplain savannas of *Mitragyna inermis* is expected to decrease by 3.5% and 25.5% of the area recorded in 1986 by 2070. The area of savannas on drained soil, mosaic of crops and fallows, swamp grasslands, mangroves, water, and urban agglomeration/bare soil will increase, respectively, by 8.4%, 3%, 1.3%, 0.1%, 2.4%, and 13.8% of the areas recorded in 1986 by 2070.

The future scenario predicts the conservation of the natural vegetation mainly mangroves assuming the dynamic recorded in the period 2000–2015. By describing the possible evolutions of the LULC on the basis of prospective scenarios, it becomes possible to initiate a reflection on possible adaptation strategies to adjust natural and human systems to a new environment. It is very important to strengthen the conservation of the reserve with activities that support the Ramsar convention on wetlands and monitor the implementation of the management plan of the reserve in order to reduce the cover of farmlands that are expected to increase by 2070. Thus, the MTBR will be the potentially good for the conservation of biodiversity for the future generation. Thus, more actions including awareness-raising and sustainable management are needed to reduce the cover of farmland that will progress by 2070, assuming the dynamic of the period 2000–2015. The management of the reserve must be participatory and based on a gender approach in order to prevent the population from illegally re-introduction in the reserve.

Acknowledgements

This study received financial support from:

- The Central and West African Forest Space Observation Project (OSFACO) of Research Institute for Development (IRD) and French Agency for Development (AFD);

- The Mono Delta Transborder Biosphere Reserve Project between Togo and Benin (ProMono) of the German international cooperation agency for international development (Deutsche Gesellschaft für Internationale Zusammenarbeit - GIZ).

Conflict of interest

The authors declare no conflicts of interest.

Author details

Kossi Adjonou[1*], Elie A. Padonou[2,3], Rodrigue Idohou[4,5], Moustapha A. Kolawolé[3,4], Issa Adbou-Kerim Bindaoudou[6], Salako Valère[4], Fiacre Ahononga[7], Romain Glèlè Kakaï[4] and Kouami Kokou[1]

1 Laboratory of Forestry Research, Faculty of Science, University of Lome, Lome, Togo

2 School of Tropical Forestry, National University of Agriculture, Ketou, Republic of Benin

3 Laboratory of Applied Ecology, Faculty of Agronomic Sciences, University of Abomey-Calavi, Cotonou, Republic of Benin

4 Laboratory of Biomathematics and Forest Estimation, Faculty of Agronomic Sciences, University of Abomey-Calavi, Cotonou, Republic of Benin

5 School of Plant and Seed Production and Management, National University of Agriculture, Ketou, Republic of Benin

6 University Center for Research and Application in Remote Sensing, University of Félix Houphouët-Boigny, Abidjan, Republic of Côte d'Ivoire

7 Forest Biology and Ecological Modeling Research Unit (UR-BioME), Faculty of Agronomy, University of Parakou, Parakou, Republic of Benin

*Address all correspondence to: kossiadjonou@hotmail.com

References

[1] Birhane E, Ashfare H, Fenta AA, Hishe H, Gebremedhin MA, Hailemariam GW, et al. Land use land cover changes along topographic gradients in Hugumburda national forest priority area, northern Ethiopia. Remote Sensing Applications: Society and Environment. 2019;**13**:61-68

[2] Shiferaw H, Bewket W, Alamirew T, Zeleke G, Teketay D, Bekele K, et al. Implications of land use/land cover dynamics and Prosopis invasion on ecosystem service values in Afar region, Ethiopia. Science of the Total Environment. 2019;**675**:354-366

[3] Gerssen-Gondelach S, Wicke B, Faaij A. Assessment of driving factors for yield and productivity developments in crop and cattle production as key to increasing sustainable biomass potentials. Food and Energy Security. 2015;**4**(1):36-75. DOI: 10.1002/fes3.53

[4] Zoungrana BJ-B, Conrad C, Thiel M, Amekudzi LK, Dapola Da E. MODIS NDVI trends and fractional land cover change for improved assessments of vegetation degradation in Burkina Faso, West Africa. Journal of Arid Environments. 2018;**153**:66-75

[5] Sibanda N, McKenna A, Richmond A, Ricke SC, Callaway T, Stratakos AC, et al. A review of the effect of management practices on campylobacter prevalence in poultry farms. Frontiers in Microbiology. 2018;**24**(9):1-9. DOI: 10.3389/fmicb.2018.02002

[6] Dube T, Mutanga O. Investigating the robustness of the Landsat-8 sensor derived texture parameters in estimating plantation forest species aboveground biomass in Kwa Zulu-Natal, South Africa. ISPRS Journal of Photogrammetry and Remote Sensing. 2015;**108**:12-32

[7] Lambin EF, Geist HJ. Global land-use and land-cover change: What have we learned so far? In: Annual NASA LCLUC Science Team Meeting University of Maryland Inn and Conference Center, Adelphi, MD; 2002. pp. 27-30

[8] Hirsch AL et al. Modelled biophysical impacts of conservation agriculture on local climates. Global Change Biology. 2018;**24**(10):4758-4774. DOI: 10.1111/gcb.14362

[9] Arowolo O, Deng X, Olatunji A, Obayelu E. Assessing changes in the value of ecosystem services in response to land-use/land-cover dynamics in Nigeria. Science of the Total Environment. 2018;**636**:597-609

[10] Tolessa TM, Senbeta F, Biru MK. The impact of land use/land cover change on ecosystem services in the central highlands of Ethiopia. Ecosystem Services. 2017;**23**:47-54. DOI: 10.1016/j.ecoser.2016.11.010

[11] Adjonou K, Bindaoudou IA-K, Segla KN, Idohou R, Salako KV, Glele-Kakaï R, et al. Land use/land cover patterns and challenges to sustainable management of the mono transboundary biosphere reserve between Togo and Benin, West Africa. International Journal of Biological and Chemical Sciences. 2020;**14**(5):1734-1751

[12] IPBES: Summary for policymakers of the assessment report on land degradation and restoration of the Intergovernmental Science-Policy Platform on Biodiversity and Ecosystem Services. In: Scholes R, Montanarella L, Brainich A, Barger N, ten Brink B, Cantele M, editors. Bonn, Germany: IPBES Secretariat; 2018. p. 44

[13] Konko Y, Okhimambe A, Nimon P, Asaana J, Rudant JP, Kokou K. Coastline change modelling induced by climate change using geospatial techniques in Togo (West Africa). Advances in Remote Sensing. 2020;**9**:85-100. DOI: 10.4236/ars.2020.92005

[14] Agbessi GE, Ouedraogo M, Camara M, Segniagbeto H, Houngbedji MB, Kabre AT. Distribution spatiale du singe à ventre rouge, Cercopithecus erythrogaster erythrogaster Gray et les menaces pesant Sur sa conservation durable au Togo. International Journal of Biological and Chemical Sciences. 2017;**11**(1):157-173

[15] Hougbédji BM, Djossa BA, Adomou AC, Dakpogan C, Sinsin B, Mensah GA. Conservation status of the Redbellied guenon (Cercopithecus erythrogaster erythrogaster) in the West Dahomey gap in southwestern Benin and the adjacent Togodo Forest reserve, South Togo. African Primates. 2012;**7**(2):184-192

[16] Kokou K, Sokpon N. Les forêts sacrées du couloir du Dahomey. Bois et Forêts des Tropiques. 2006;**288**(2):15-23

[17] Muriuki GW, Seabrook L, Mcalpine C, Baxter GS. Land cover change under unplanned human settlements: A study of the Chyulu Hills squatters, Kenya. Landscape and Urban Planning. 2011;**99**(2):154-165

[18] Liu YI, Chang MV, Li HE, Barolo S, Chang JL, Blauwkamp TA, et al. The chromatin remodelers ISWI and ACF1 directly repress wingless transcriptional targets. Developmental Biology. 2008;**323**(1):41-52

[19] Agbanou T, Paegelow M, Toko II, Tente B. Modelisation Des Changements D'occupation Des Terres En Region Soudanienne Au Nord-Ouest Du Benin. European Scientific Journal. 2018;**14**(12):248-266. DOI: 10.19044/esj.2018.v14n12p248

[20] Abdus S, Xiangzheng D, Siqi J, Dongdong C. Scenario based simulation on dynamics of land-use-land-cover change in Punjab Province, Pakistan. Sustainability. 2017;**9**:1285 17 p

[21] Vacquié L. Modélisation prospective et échelles spatiales en montagne: application aux Pyrénées françaises. Géographie. Français: Université Toulouse le Mirail-Toulouse II; 2015 ffNNT: 2015TOU20014ff. fftel-01275936f

[22] World Bank. Réserve de Biosphère transfrontalière du Delta du Mono: Etude de cas 1. 2017. 5 p

[23] Clerici N, Bodini A, Eva H, Grégoire J-M, Dulieu D, Paolini C. Increased isolation of two biosphere reserves and surrounding protected areas (WAP ecological complex, West Africa). Journal for Nature Conservation. 2007;**15**(1):26-40

[24] Sarr MA. Cartographie des changements de l'occupation du sol entre 1990 et 2002 dans le nord du Sénégal (Ferlo) à partir des images Landsat. Cybergeo. European Journal of Geography, Environnement, Nature, Paysage. 2009;**47**:1-14. DOI: 10.4000/cybergeo.22707

[25] Skupinski G, Binthtran D, Weber C. Les images satellites Spot multi-dates et la métrique spatiale dans l'étude du changement urbain et suburbain – Le cas de la basse vallée de la Bruche (Bas-Rhin, France). Cybergeo: European. Journal of Geography. 2009;**63**:439. DOI: 10.4000/cybergeo.21995

[26] Girard MC, Girard CM. Traitement des données de télédétection. Paris, France: Dunod; 1999. p. 529

[27] FAO. Forest resources assessment 1990 - survey tropical forest cover studies of change processes. In: FAO Forestry Paper 130. Rome, Italie: Food and Agriculture Organization of United Nations; 1996 Available from: http://www.fao.org/docrep/007/w0015e/w0015e00.htm

[28] Achard F, Eva HD, Stibig HJ, Mayaux P, Gallego J, Richards T, et al. Determination of deforestation rates of the world's humid tropical forests. Science. 2002;**297**(5583):999-1002

[29] Kamungandu CM. Etudes de cas sur l'évaluation de la dégradation des forêts : La dégradation des forêts en République Démocratique du Congo. In: Evaluation des ressources forestières, Document de travail 169. Rome, Italie: FAO Département des forêts, Viale delle Terme di Caracalla; 2009. www.fao.org/forestry/fra

[30] Schlaepfer MA, Runge MC, Sherman PW. Ecological and evolutionary traps. Trends in Ecology and Evolution. 2002;**17**:474-480

[31] Çinlar. Introduction to Stochastic Processes. Englewood Cliffs, NJ: Prentice Hall; 1975

[32] Ouedraogo I, Tigabu M, Savadogo P, Compaore H, Oden PC, Ouadba JM. Land cover change and its relation with population dynamics in Burkina Faso, West Africa. Land Degradation and Development. 2010;**21**:453-462

[33] Houessou LG, Teka O, Toko II, Lykke AM, Sinsin B. Land use and land-cover change at "W" Biosphere Reserve and its surroundings areas in Benin Republic (West Africa). Environment and Natural Resources Research. 2013;**3**(2):87-101. DOI: 10.1016/j.jaridenv.2004.03.022

[34] Satyanarayana B, Mulder S, Jayatissa LP, Dahdouh-Guebas F. Are the mangroves in the Galle-Unawatuna area (Sri Lanka) at risk? A social-ecological approach involving local stakeholders for a better conservation policy. Ocean & Coastal Management. 2013;**71**:225-237

[35] Sinsin B, Assogbadjo AE, Tente B, Yo T, Adanguidi J, Lougbegnon T, et al. Inventaire floristique et faunique des écosystèmes de mangroves et des zones humides côtières du Bénin. Bénin: FAO & Laboratoire d'Écologie Appliquée; 2018

[36] Adanguidi J, Padonou EA, Zannou A, Houngbo SB, Saliou IO, Agbahoungba S. Fuelwood consumption and supply strategies in mangrove forests-insights from RAMSAR sites in Benin. Forest Policy and Economics. 2020;**116**:102192

[37] Ndour N, Dieng S, Fall M. Rôles des mangroves, modes et perspectives de gestion au Delta du Saloum (Sénégal). [VertigO] La revue électronique en sciences de l'environnement [En ligne]. 2011;**11**(3). DOI: 10.4000/vertigo.11515

[38] Pramova E, Locatelli B, Djoudi H. et Somorin O. Forests and trees for social adaptation to climate variability and change. WIREs Climate Change. 2012;**3**:581-596. DOI: 10.1002/wcc.195

[39] Locatelli B. Services écosystémiques et changement climatique [Doctoral dissertation]. Université Grenoble; 2013. p. 1

[40] Sounon BB, Sinsin B, Goura SB. Effets de la dynamique d'occupation du sol sur la structure et la diversité floristique des forêts claires et savanes du Bénin. Tropicultura. 2007;**25**(4): 221-227

[41] Piquer-Rodríguez M, Butsic V, Gärtner P, Macchi L, Baumann M, Gavier PG, et al. Drivers of agricultural land-use change in the argentine pampas and Chaco regions.

Applied Geography. 2018;**91**:111-122. DOI: 10.1016/j.apgeog.2018.01.004

[42] Padonou EA, Lykke AM, Bachmann Y, Idohou R, Sinsin B. Mapping changes in land use/land cover and prediction of future extension of bowé in Benin, West Africa. Land Use Policy. 2017;**69**:85-92

Chapter 4

Improving the Sustainability of Agriculture: Challenges and Opportunities

Gebeyanesh Worku Zerssa, Marta Hailemariam and Kirubel Teshome Tadele

Abstract

The agricultural practice is a foundation for all global development. Increasing its production and productivity may affect the land capacity in the future if not managed sustainably. Sustainable agriculture could be one way to preserve land use potential. However, several obstacles impede its implementation, such as high reliance on external inputs to boost short-term output, lack of innovative technology in developing countries, and climate change impacts. Despite these obstacles, a variety of tackling options have been proposed, like decreasing the excessive usage of artificial fertilizer and relying on locally available organic materials as sources of plant nutrients. Improving small-scale irrigation practices by managing their negative environmental effects in small-scale agriculture could also enhance sustainable agriculture. This chapter briefly overviews sustainable agriculture, its components, and the potential and obstacles to achieving overall sustainability in both developed and developing countries.

Keywords: organic fertilizer, small-scale farms, sustainable agriculture, conventional agriculture, food security

1. Introduction

Agriculture, which supplies all of the world's food and occupies 40% of the available land, is both the largest industry in the world and a major land use [1]. The economic growth of the world is heavily dependent on the agricultural sector. Developing countries continue to face the most pressing difficulties due to the increasing population and related food security. In the twentieth century, enhancing food production was only possible by increasing agricultural output with outside inputs like mineral fertilizers and pesticides [2–4]. Modern agricultural techniques built on the green revolution have led to a significant increase in grain productivity at the expense of depleting natural resources. Soil fertility and environmental resilience suffered significantly because of agriculture's externalization. Thus, it calls for different strategies that should train farmers to use their traditional knowledge to produce more grains with fewer outside inputs. The method is referred to as sustainable agriculture, which is currently essential.

The integrated usage of a variety of soil, nutrients, and pest management techniques including manure, crop residue, mixed cropping, and crop rotations has been encouraged in sustainable agriculture systems [5–8]. By minimizing soil degradation, these approaches increased soil quality, nutrient pools, climatic resilience, and ecosystem restoration, increasing the socioeconomic status of farmers. However, switching to exclusively organic management of agroecosystems is difficult due to the relatively lower supply of organic fertilizers. In order to improve soil quality and nutrient pools, integrated nutrient management (INM), which combines increased organic inputs into the soil with a balanced application of inorganic fertilizers, is encouraged [1, 9]. Briefly said the fundamental strategy of sustainable agriculture is that we must produce more while using fewer natural resources. Many new alternative practices, such as conservation agriculture and organic farming for soil management, water-saving agronomic practices, INM, biofertilizers, and precision agriculture, have been proposed to achieve the fundamental goals of sustainable agriculture.

There is no debate that conventional agriculture (CA) has high productivity, but it simultaneously generates environmental and social impacts of global concern [5, 10]. CA has an impact on the environment through greenhouse gas emissions, water quality decline, soil erosion, livelihoods, and food security [5, 6]. Currently, CA practices are contributing to the degradation of important ecological processes that support life on Earth. These practices are responsible for climate change, the degradation of the biosphere, the destruction of the land system, and the eutrophication of the oceans as a result of mineral fertilizers application [8, 11]. This chapter explores the viability of using sustainable agriculture practices in order to achieve global food and nutritional security sustainably [7, 12, 13]. Furthermore, it addresses the obstacles and possibilities for improving the practice in developed and developing countries. Disseminating sustainable agriculture methods to the field level through academic curricula, seminars, symposiums, and research is essential to achieving a brighter future.

2. Major components of sustainable agriculture

Agriculture could become sustainable with careful management of its components. The major components of sustainable agriculture are building healthy soil and preventing erosion, managing water wisely, increasing carbon sequestration, increasing resilience to extreme weather, and promoting biodiversity (**Figure 1**). In this chapter, the components related to soil ecosystem have received the most attention because it substantially impacts all other components and sustainable agriculture. Application of organic fertilizers like compost, green manure, vermicomposting, and cover crops supported by a careful rotation of crops are used in sustainable agriculture to maintain and enhance soil fertility. Maintaining healthy soil, increasing carbon sequestration, and resilience to extreme weather are interconnected and could be attained through these methods [8, 14]. Besides, locally accessible organic wastes could be transformed into plant nutrients, reducing the negative impact of artificial fertilizers on sustainable soil management. Developing guidelines to reuse different wastes as plant nutrients is crucial to reducing the use of synthetic fertilizer. The primary issues with artificial fertilizer use in industrialized countries are excessive application. However, low-rate applications are a problem in developing countries. Land resources and agricultural production are strongly impacted in both excessive

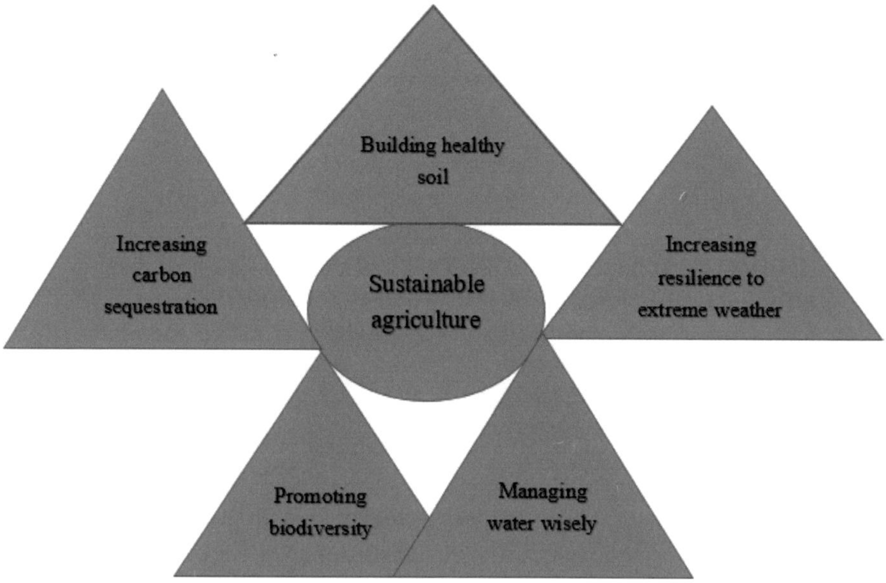

Figure 1.
Components of sustainable agriculture.

and low application scenarios. Supplementing with organic fertilizer made from waste materials through composting is essential to balancing the constraint caused by excessive and low application [9, 15]. Not only does building healthy soil boost productivity, but it also makes the soil more drought-resilient and increases carbon sequestration. As a result, it might be easier to adapt to a changing climate and reduce greenhouse gas emissions [16–18]. Increasing soil organic matter (SOM) content in the soils can increase water retention more at field capacity by improving bulk density and porosity and thus increase the plant available water capacity (PAWC) [19–21]. The availability of SOM material may affect how much PAWC increases. Thus, building up the SOM content of soils can make them as well as agroecosystems climate-resilient. Increasing soil resilience to drought could ensure optimum crop yield in dry seasons [20]; consequently, it improves sustained yield intensification.

3. Major challenges for achieving overall sustainability in agriculture

3.1 High use of mineral fertilizer and other chemical inputs

Due to the extensive use of synthetic chemical fertilizers and pesticides, the agricultural sector of developed countries is one of the most significant sources of environmental pollution [22–24]. To increase productivity per unit area, agricultural systems around the world use a lot of chemicals including fertilizers, insecticides, and herbicides [22]. These chemicals and fertilizers contribute to a number of issues, including soil, water, and air pollution, decreased input efficiency, decreased food quality, soil degradation, a lack of micronutrients in the soil, toxicity to various beneficial living organisms present above and below the soil surface, and decreased production. Additionally, overuse of synthetic nitrogen fertilizer may result in large atmospheric emissions of nitrous oxide [25].

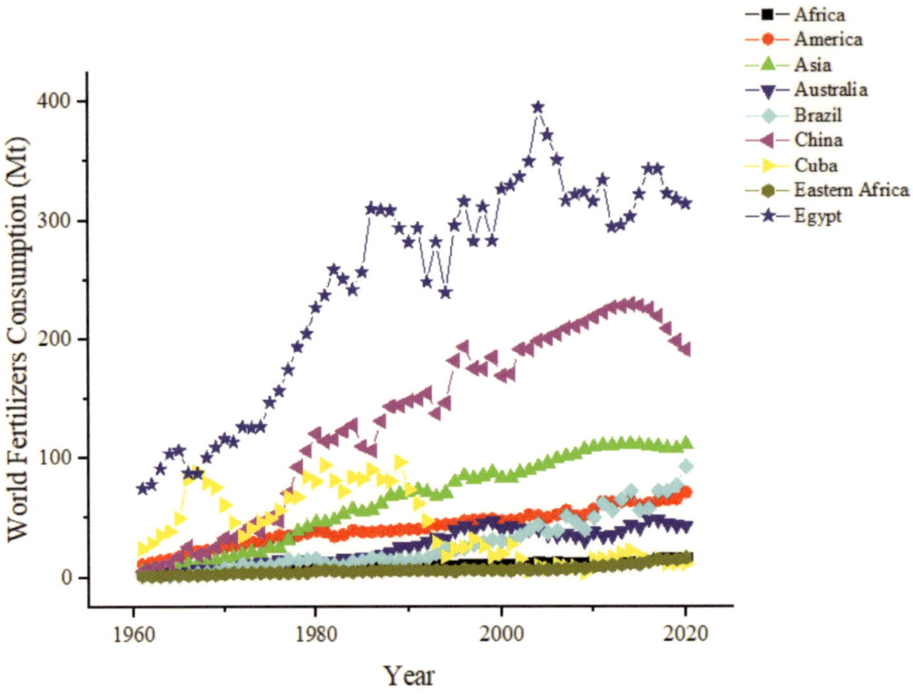

Figure 2.
World fertilizers consumption (Mt). Sources: IFA and FAOSTAT [26, 27].

The consumption of fertilizer worldwide has greatly increased since 1961 (**Figure 2**). Global research indicates that the production of synthetic N fertilizers that are added to crops has increased about sevenfold, whereas the yield production of crops has increased by almost 2.4 times [28, 29]. Furthermore, nearly 60% of all synthetic chemical fertilizer production was made up of nitrogen. The significant attention paid to this fertilizer significantly affects natural soil ecosystems, which in turn impacts sustainable agriculture. As a result, producing agricultural products that are chemical-free and high in nutrition is necessary for both human and animal use. To prevent the degradation of natural resources, the focus should be placed on producing high quality and quantity food [29]. Overall, using excess mineral fertilizer has a negative influence on sustainable agriculture.

3.2 Lack of advanced technology

Adoption of advanced technology by smallholder farmers can enhance their income and livelihood [30–32]. In most developing countries, agricultural practices are dominated by many traditional approaches. For instance, compared to other regions, the sub-Saharan African countries, which rely primarily on rain-fed agriculture, have been adversely affected by climate change and variability [33, 34]. Due to low adoption of advanced irrigation practices like drip irrigation and water harvesting, the region is highly susceptible to climate change and variability. Drip irrigation is a technology that conserves water and reduces water losses through drainage. This technology was developed in response to the incentives present in Israel, a country that suffers from a severe water scarcity problem and which made a concerted effort to develop water-conserving technologies [30]. It is critical to prioritize smallholders' needs in agricultural development programs in an area where they account for an estimated 80% of farms and generate the majority of the region's food [30].

3.3 Climate change impacts

Climate change and variability are the greatest challenging factors to sustainable agriculture (SA) in the world [16, 21]. Climate change and variability affect the cereal production system through irregular rainfall distribution, flooding, and increasing mean temperature [35]. Most developing countries are highly vulnerable to climate variability due to extremely high dependence on rain-fed agriculture, low development of irrigation schemes [16, 36, 37]. Vulnerability to climate variability is also exacerbated due to a lack of improved technologies, lack of effective early warning systems, and small and fragmented land size [35]. For instance, in Ethiopia, it is anticipated that agricultural production will decrease by 6–33% between 2030 and 2050 due to the effects of climate change and variability [14, 38]. This will cause food and nutrition insecurity and increases the loss of life in the country. The effects of climate change on agriculture will depend on the rate and severity of the change and how successfully farmers can adapt. The impact of climate change and variability is very evident in developing countries as compared to developed countries. In order to guarantee sustainable agriculture and food security, developing countries need to receive a lot more attention.

4. Opportunities to enhance sustainable agriculture

There are numerous potentials to expand sustainable agriculture worldwide. Some of the opportunities are region-specific, while others can be applied everywhere [11, 13, 30]. To feed the world's growing population without depleting the land's capacity and transfer for future generations, SA must be adopted. Some of them include focusing on INM, expanding the use of small-scale irrigation, and promoting the adoption of locally accessible organic nutrients like compost, vermicompost, biofertilizer, and biochar application.

4.1 Focusing on locally available organic resources

4.1.1 Compost application

Compost is a plant- and animal-derived organic material aerobically digested by mesophilic and thermophilic bacteria [15, 22]. Compost application in agriculture can enhance nutrients and organic matter in the soil. The improvement of SOM, soil humus, soil microbial biomass, enzyme activity, and resistance to pests and diseases are among the outstanding benefits of compost application [8, 39, 40]. Applying compost to the ground can boost the soil's capacity to store carbon, which in turn reduces the impact of global warming. Additionally, adding compost to soil can increase the cation exchange capacity of the soil and improve the availability of both macro and micronutrients for plant uptake. It can enhance the soil bulk density, porosity, and water-holding capacity, increasing plants' tolerance to water shortages. Due to a number of positive impacts, compost application may be suggested as a practical tool in sustainable agriculture. For instance, farmers could obtain compost more easily than inorganic fertilizer because they could make it by themselves from locally available waste resources; it could enhance all soil properties (i.e., physical, chemical, and biological) and could provide all essential plant nutrients for plants [8, 9, 22]. Compost has numerous advantages; therefore, farmers should combine it with other soil-management techniques to ensure sustainable crop production.

4.1.2 Vermicompost application

Earthworms are employed in the vermicomposting process to turn organic waste into a humus-like substance known as vermicompost. It is a mesophilic technique that makes use of bacteria and earthworms that are active between 10°C and 32°C. The process is faster than composting; because the material goes through the earthworm gut, thereby leading to the creation of earthworm castings [41, 42]. Vermicomposting, or worm composting, produces a rich organic soil amendment containing a diversity of plant nutrients and beneficial microorganisms. Vermicompost improves soil physicochemical properties of the soil and hence increases crop yields to improve the livelihood of the community. In recent years, various research studies have reported the significant role of vermicompost in crop production in different agroecological conditions. Economically, it is affordable for poor farmers, and it is environmentally suitable, making it efficient for sustainable crop intensification. Studies have shown that applying vermicompost leads to enhanced nutrient availability and positive effects on soil properties, productivity, profitability, and resilience [41, 43, 44].

4.1.3 Biofertilizer application

Biofertilizers are types of fertilizer that contain different microorganisms, which can enhance microbial activity in soil [45, 46]. They can convert the organic nitrogen into available forms for plant use such as nitrate and ammonia, improve soil porosity and improve the resistance of plants against pathogens. Biofertilizers are one of the methods used in organic agriculture practices. They are the most important biotechnology needed to enhance the expansion of organic farming, sustainable agricultural development, and alternative clean agriculture [46–48]. Biofertilizers are natural and organic fertilizers that help to maintain soil with all nutrients and living microorganisms needed for crop health [46, 49, 50]. Biofertilizers are energy-efficient, free pollution and rely on exploiting the ability of some microorganisms such as bacteria, algae, and fungi. Biofertilizers fix atmospheric nitrogen in the soil, root nodules of legume crops, and make it available into the plant [46, 47]. Biofertilizers are low-cost plant nutrient source, eco-friendly and has a complementary role with synthetic fertilizers. They are Rhizobium, Azotobacter, Azospirillum, Blue Algae Green, and Azola. They improve physical and chemical properties of soil such as water-holding capacity, and buffer capacity. Biofertilizers can improve the yield by 10–25% and minimize the use of inorganic N by 25–50 kg ha^{-1} without adversely affecting the soil and environment [45, 47, 51]. It ensures sustainable agriculture by boosting soil resilience, plant productivity, and soil quality.

4.1.4 Biochar application

Biochar is the carbon-rich organic matter that is obtained after heating biomass (corn, rice or wheat waste) in little or no oxygen through a process called pyrolysis [15, 52, 53]. The chemical, biological, and physical features of the soil are changed when biochar is applied as a soil amendment, which substantially impacts soil fertility.

Its effects as a soil amendment improve soil fertility and plant growth, which increases crop output [52–54]. The potential for biochar to increase soil fertility and health could lead to sustainable yield intensification. Many reports stated that biochar application to soils significantly affected crop productivity taking into account soil health and increasing water availability [53–55]. Biochar as soil conditioner reduces nutrient loss by decreasing leaching through increasing cation exchange capacity [54]. It increases water-holding capacity due to its porous structure. It can increase soil fertility of acidic soils, protects plants from diseases, promotes growth of soil microbes, and increase the soil carbon content. Biochar can be used for long-term storage of carbon in the soil, thus decreasing the amount of CO_2 released in the atmosphere [54, 56].

4.2 Integrated nutrient management

INM, which is a comprehensive strategy, including maintaining and continuously adjusting soil fertility and plant nutrient delivery to an optimum level [14, 57, 58]. In order to achieve and sustain maximum production without threatening the soil ecology, adopting INM is a must. It is based on the integration of biological, inorganic, and organic nutrient sources in a specific cropping system while considering regional variables. In addition to having a good impact on the soil nutrient condition, INM can improve SOM and improve water retention and storage. As a result, it can strengthen agricultural systems and enhances soil carbon sequestration. Using INM instead of applying mineral fertilizer in Nitisol increased maize production by up to 18% [9]. Thus, it strongly supports the concept of sustainable agriculture anywhere. Combining applications could boost a farm's economic resilience, particularly for poor farmers in developing countries who cannot afford enough mineral fertilizer. Due to their limited economic capacity, they are unable to afford the significantly rising price of mineral fertilizer. Therefore, due to its substantial benefits for sustainable agriculture, various researchers recommended the adoption of INM rather than sole application [9, 45, 59, 60].

4.3 Adopting small-scale irrigation

The adoption of small-scale irrigation farming as a sustainable agricultural practice could significantly influence ensuring food security [33, 34]. Adopting small-scale irrigated farming as a SA practice is crucial for dry-land farming systems because it guarantees crop production during the dry season. The production of various crops twice or three times a year and boosting the income of rural farm-households are two significant goals that can be achieved by small-scale irrigation. However, the use of small-scale irrigation farming is significantly influenced by the availability of irrigation equipment, access to quality water sources, and awareness of water-saving techniques like rainwater harvesting [31, 33, 34]. Practices that will facilitate the implementation of small-scale irrigation farming are essential since this will substantially impact agricultural income and enable smallholder farmers to adjust quickly to climate change and variability.

5. Conclusion

Food and nutrition security could result from sustainable agriculture without harming the environment for future generations. The goal of sustainable development may be achieved by comprehending its components and managing them appropriately. However, significant reliance on mineral fertilizers, a lack of innovative technologies, and climate change and variability are likely to have an impact on sustainable agriculture. Both developed and developing countries are impacted by the same variables. However, the intensity of the impact is high in developing countries due to low adaptation capacity. Focusing on locally available organic resources, INM, and increasing the use of small-scale irrigation can help to enhance the SA everywhere. These could increase agriculture productivity and ecosystem sustainability due to their high input use efficiencies, reduced use of synthetic fertilizers and pesticides, and improved soil resilience and quality in a changing climate. Effective agricultural policies based on locally developed sustainable agricultural practices, a review of extension services for better information dissemination, and farmer training are required to increase the adoption of sustainable agricultural practices in both developed and developing countries.

Author details

Gebeyanesh Worku Zerssa[1*], Marta Hailemariam[2] and Kirubel Teshome Tadele[3]

1 Department of Natural Resources Management, Jimma University, Jimma, Ethiopia

2 Department of Agricultural Economics and Agribusiness Management, Jimma University, Ethiopia

3 Department of Chemistry, College of Natural Science, Jimma University, Ethiopia

*Address all correspondence to: workugb2010@gmail.com

References

[1] Singh R, Singh H, Raghubanshi AS. Challenges and opportunities for agricultural sustainability in changing climate scenarios: A perspective on Indian agriculture. Tropical Ecology. 2019;**60**:167-185

[2] Tubiello F, Schmidhuber J, Howden M, Neofotis PG, Park S, Fernandes E, et al. Climate change response strategies for agriculture: Challenges and opportunities for the 21st century. In: Agriculture Rural Development Discussion Paper. 2008. pp. 42-103

[3] Urgesa AA, Abegaz A, Bahir AL, Antille DL. Population growth and other factors affecting land-use and land-cover changes in north-eastern Wollega, Ethiopia. Tropical Agriculture. 2016;**93**(4):298-311

[4] Mekuria W. The link between agricultural production and population dynamics in Ethiopia: A review. Advances in Plants & Agriculture Research. 2018;**8**(2):348-353

[5] DeLonge MS, Miles A, Carlisle L. Investing in the transition to sustainable agriculture. Environmental Science & Policy. 2016;**55**:266-273

[6] Mishra DBB, Nayak DKC. Organic farming for sustainable agriculture. Journal of Agriculture. 2004;**24**(2):25

[7] Mutyasira V, Hoag D, Pendell D, Yildiz F. The adoption of sustainable agricultural practices by smallholder farmers in Ethiopian highlands: An integrative approach. Cogent Food & Agriculture. 2018;**4**(1):1552439

[8] Brock C, Oltmanns M, Matthes C, Schmehe B, Schaaf H, Burghardt D, et al. Compost as an option for sustainable crop production at low stocking rates in organic farming. Agronomy. 2021;**11**(6):1078

[9] Zerssa GW, Kim DG, Koal P, Eichler-Löbermann B. Combination of compost and mineral fertilizers as an option for enhancing maize (Zea mays L.) Yields and mitigating greenhouse gas emissions from a Nitisol in Ethiopia. Agronomy. 2021;**11**(11):2097

[10] Darnhofer I, Bellon S, Dedieu B, Milestad R. Adaptiveness to enhance the sustainability of farming systems. A review. Agronomy for Sustainable Development. 2010;**30**:545-555

[11] Adimassu Z, Langan S, Johnston R. Understanding determinants of farmers' investments in sustainable land management practices in Ethiopia: Review and synthesis. Environment, Development and Sustainability. 2016;**18**(4):1005-1023

[12] Jensen ES, Bedoussac L, Carlsson G, Journet EP, Justes E, Hauggaard-Nielsen H. Enhancing yields in organic crop production by eco-functional intensification. Sustainable Agriculture Research. 2015;**4**(3):42-50

[13] Islam S. Conservation agriculture based sustainable intensification_ Increasing yields and water productivity for smallholders of the Eastern Gangetic Plains. Field Crops Research. 2019;**17**(1):25-42

[14] Zerssa G, Feyssa D, Kim DG, Eichler-Löbermann B. Challenges of smallholder farming in Ethiopia and opportunities by adopting climate-smart agriculture. Agriculture. 2021;**11**(3):192

[15] Agegnehu G, Nelson PN, Bird MI. The effects of biochar, compost and their

mixture and nitrogen fertilizer on yield and nitrogen use efficiency of barley grown on a Nitisol in the highlands of Ethiopia. Science of the Total Environment. 2016;**569-570**:869-879

[16] Nagothu US. Climate Change and Agricultural Development: Improving Resilience through Climate Smart Agriculture, Agroecology and Conservation. Routledge; 2016. ISBN 9781138364080

[17] Song Z, Gao H, Zhu P, Peng C, Deng A, Zheng C, et al. Organic amendments increase corn yield by enhancing soil resilience to climate change. The Crop Journal. 2015;**3**(2):110-117

[18] Smith JH, Nayak D, Albanito F, Balana B, Black H, Boke S, et al. Treatment of organic resources before soil incorporation in semi-arid regions improves resilience to El Nino, and increases crop production and economic returns. Environmental Research Letters. 2019;**14**(8):721-759

[19] Lal R. Soil organic matter and water retention. Agronomy Journal. 2020;**112**(5):3265-3277

[20] Kane DA, Bradford MA, Fuller E, Oldfield EE, Wood SA. Soil organic matter protects US maize yields and lowers crop insurance payouts under drought. Environmental Research Letters. 2021;**16**(4):044018

[21] Reidsma P, Wolf J, Kanellopoulos A, Schaap BF, Mandryk M, Verhagen J, et al. Climate change impact and adaptation research requires integrated assessment and farming systems analysis: A case study in the Netherlands. Environmental Research Letters. 2015;**10**(4):045004

[22] Abou-El-Hassan S, Abd Elwanis M, El-Shinawy MZ. Application of compost and vermicompost as substitutes for mineral fertilizers to produce green beans. Egyptian Journal of Horticulture. 30 Dec 2017;**44**(2):155-163

[23] Sun L, Ma Y, Li B, Xiao C, Fan L, Xiong Z. Nitrogen fertilizer in combination with an ameliorant mitigated yield-scaled greenhouse gas emissions from a coastal saline rice field in southeastern China. Environmental Science and Pollution Research. 2018;**25**(16):15896-15908

[24] Aulakh MS, Malhi SS. Interactions of nitrogen with other nutrients and water: Effect on crop yield and quality, nutrient use efficiency, carbon sequestration, and environmental pollution. Advances in Agronomy. 2005;**86**:341-409

[25] Han J, Shi J, Zeng L, Xu J, Wu L. Effects of nitrogen fertilization on the acidity and salinity of greenhouse soils. Environmental Science and Pollution Research. 2015;**22**(4):2976-2986

[26] IFA. International Fertilizer Association. Paris, France; 2022

[27] Food and Agriculture Organization of the United Nations. FAOSTAT Statistical Database. Rome: FAO; 2022

[28] Awaad H, Abu-Hashim M, Negm A. Mitigating Environmental Stresses for Agricultural Sustainability in Egypt. Vol. 16. Springer; 2021

[29] Seleiman MF, Hafez EM. Optimizing inputs management for sustainable agricultural development. In: Mitigating Environmental Stresses for Agricultural Sustainability in Egypt. Vol. 25, No. 1. 2021. pp. 487-507

[30] Adenle AA, Wedig K, Azadi H. Sustainable agriculture and food security in Africa: The role of innovative technologies and international organizations. Technology in Society. 2019;**58**:101143

[31] Amede T. Technical and institutional attributes constraining the performance of small-scale irrigation in Ethiopia. Water Resources and Rural Development. 2015;**6**:78-91

[32] Asfaw S, Shiferaw B, Simtowe F, Lipper L. Impact of modern agricultural technologies on smallholder welfare: Evidence from Tanzania and Ethiopia. Food Policy. 2012;**37**(3):283-295

[33] Adela FA, Aurbacher J, Abebe GK. Small-scale irrigation scheme governance - poverty nexus: Evidence from Ethiopia. Food Security. 2019;**11**(4):897-913

[34] Adugna E, Ermias A, Mekonnen A, Mihret D. The role of small scale irrigation in poverty reduction. Journal of Development and Agricultural Economics. 2014;**6**(1):12-21

[35] Kotir JH. Climate change and variability in Sub-Saharan Africa: A review of current and future trends and impacts on agriculture and food security. Environment, Development and Sustainability. 2011;**13**:587-605

[36] Berhane A. Climate change and variability impacts on agricultural productivity and food security. Climatology Weather Forecast. 2018;**6**(240):25

[37] Gezie M, Tejada MM. Farmer's response to climate change and variability in Ethiopia: A review. Cogent Food & Agriculture. 2019;**5**(1):161

[38] Zewdu E, Hadgu G, Nigatu L. Impacts of climate change on sorghum production in North Eastern Ethiopia. African Journal of Environmental Science and Technology. 2020;**14**(2):49-63

[39] Adugna G. A review on impact of compost on soil properties, water use and crop productivity. Academic Research Journal of Agricultural Science and Research. 2016;**4**(3):93-104

[40] Edwards S, Arefayne A. The impact of compost use on crop yields in Tigray, Ethiopia. International conference on organic agriculture and food security. FAO Rome December 2007. 2007

[41] Lim SL, Lee LH, Wu TY. Sustainability of using composting and vermicomposting technologies for organic solid waste biotransformation: Recent overview, greenhouse gases emissions and economic analysis. Journal of Cleaner Production. 2016;**111**:262-278

[42] Adhikary S. Vermicompost, the story of organic gold: A review. Plant and Soil. 2012;**6**:213-258

[43] Bekele A, Kibret K, Bedadi B, Yli-Halla M, Balemi T. Effects of lime, vermicompost, and chemical P fertilizer on selected properties of acid soils of Ebantu District, Western Highlands of Ethiopia. Applied and Environmental Soil Science. 2018;**2018**:1-13

[44] Rameshwar MY, Argaw A. Manurial value of khat waste vermicompost from Awday, Harar town, Ethiopia. International Journal of Recycling of Organic Waste in Agriculture. 2016;**5**(2):105-111

[45] Chen JH. The combined use of chemical and organic fertilizers and/or biofertilizer for crop growth and soil fertility. In: International Workshop on Sustained Management of the Soil-rhizosphere System for Efficient Crop Production and Fertilizer Use. Land Development Department Bangkok Thailand; 2006. pp. 1-11

[46] Mukhongo RW, Tumuhairwe JB, Ebanyat P, AbdelGadir AH, Thuita M, Masso C. Combined application of biofertilizers and inorganic nutrients

improves sweet potato yields. Frontiers in Plant Science[Internet]. 13 Mar 2017;**8**:541-604 [cited 2021 Jan 13]

[47] Schütz L, Gattinger A, Meier M, Müller A, Boller T, Mathimaran N, et al. Improving crop yield and nutrient use efficiency via biofertilization. A global meta-analysis. Frontiers in Plant Science. 2018;**8**:2204

[48] Vessey JK. Plant growth promoting rhizobacteria as biofertilizers. Plant Soil. 2003;**255**:571-586

[49] Schenck zu Schweinsberg-Mickan M, Müller T. Impact of effective microorganisms and other biofertilizers on soil microbial characteristics, organic-matter decomposition, and plant growth. Journal of Plant Nutrition and Soil Science. 2009;**172**(5):704-712

[50] Osman MEH, El-Sheekh MM, El-Naggar AH, Gheda SF. Effect of two species of cyanobacteria as biofertilizers on some metabolic activities, growth, and yield of pea plant. Biology and Fertility of Soils. 2010;**46**(8):861-875

[51] Al-Suhaibani N, Selim M, Alderfasi A, El-Hendawy S. Integrated application of composted agricultural wastes, chemical fertilizers and biofertilizers as an avenue to promote growth, yield and quality of maize in an arid agro-ecosystem. Sustainability. 2021;**13**(13):7439

[52] Oni BA, Oziegbe O, Olawole OO. Significance of biochar application to the environment and economy. Annals of Agricultural Science. 2019;**64**(2):222-236

[53] Verheijen F, Jeffery S, Bastos AC, Van der Velde M, Diafas I. Biochar application to soils. Critical Scientific Review of Effects on Soil Properties, Processes and. Functions EUR. 2010;**24099**(162):2183-2207

[54] Agegnehu G, Bass AM, Nelson PN, Bird MI. Benefits of biochar, compost and biochar–compost for soil quality, maize yield and greenhouse gas emissions in a tropical agricultural soil. Science of the Total Environment. 2016;**543**:295-306

[55] Akinnuoye-Adelabu DB, Steenhuisen S, Bredenhand E. Improving pea quality with vermicompost tea and aqueous biochar: Prospects for sustainable farming in Southern Africa. South African Journal of Botany. 2019;**123**:278-285

[56] Agegnehu Jenberu G. Biochar, compost and biochar-compost: Effects on crop performance, soil quality and greenhouse gas emissions in tropical agricultural soils [PhD Thesis]. James Cook University; 2017

[57] Abraham RR, Joseph K, Joseph P. Effect of integrated nutrient management on soil quality and growth of Hevea brasiliensis during the immature phase. Rubber Science. 2015;**28**:159-167

[58] Agegnehu G, vanbeek C, Bird MI. Influence of integrated soil fertility management in wheat and tef productivity and soil chemical properties in the highland tropical environment. Journal of Soil Science and Plant Nutrition. 2014;**14**(3):532-545

[59] Chivenge P, Vanlauwe B, Six J. Does the combined application of organic and mineral nutrient sources influence maize productivity? A meta-analysis. Plant and Soil. 2011;**342**(1-2):1-30

[60] Zerssa GW, Koal P, Eichler-Löbermann B. Fertilizer management strategy to reduce global warming potential and improve soil fertility in a Nitisol in Southwestern Ethiopia. Chemical Processing. 2022;**10**(1):51

Chapter 5

Integrated Effect of the Payment for Forest Environmental Services (PFES) in Vietnam

Vien Tran Duc, Son Cao Truong, Lam Nguyen Thanh, Van Dinh Thi Hai, Huong Le Thi Thu and Thorkil Casse

Abstract

Payment for forest environmental services (PFES) has become an effective management tool for forest resources in the world, especially in developing countries such as Vietnam. The Vietnamese PFES policy has been institutionalized and implemented since 2010, contributing to forest protection and improving the livelihoods of people who depend on forests. In this chapter, the PFES policy was analyzed, followed by the evaluation of the effectiveness of a PFES program applied in the Ba Be district, Bac Kan province, Vietnam in three aspects: environment, economy, and society. Finally, we synthesize the combined effectiveness of the PFES program in Vietnam and offer solutions to improve and promote the PFES policy in Vietnam and developing countries around the world.

Keywords: babe district, evaluation, integrated effect, payment for forest environmental services (PFES), policy

1. Introduction

Payment for environmental services is understood as a mechanism to convert external/nonmarket values of the environment into actual funding to motivate those providing these ecosystem services (ES). In other words, payment for environmental services applies the benefit pays principle (BPP) to mobilize funds for environmental protection activities. Currently, payment for environmental services is being widely applied globally because this tool effectively protects environment and brings economic benefits to people.

In Vietnam, the program of payment for forest environmental services (PFES) was officially institutionalized through Decree No. 99/2010/ND-CP on "Payment for forest environmental services". After being promulgated, this policy has received great consensus from stakeholders and brought positive environmental and socio-economic effects. However, whether this policy has really become a new driving force for the protection and sustainable development of forests requires detailed evaluation. At the Conference summarizing Vietnam's PFES program after ten years of implementation, scientists and managers all agreed that Vietnam currently lacks an effective evaluation mechanism for the national program of PFES [1].

According to experts in the field of assessment of environmental services payment programs, there are three main terms used: *"Evaluate the results of the implementation of the policy" and "evaluate the implementation process of the policy"* and *"evaluate the effectiveness of the policy"*. Which, the reviews of the program of payment for forest environmental services in Vietnam mainly focus on the first two aspects, while the third aspect has not been given due attention [2]. Sharing the same view, Ngai [3] said that Vietnam's state agencies mainly focus on the evaluation process of "Evaluating the implementation process" of PFES programs. In contrast, evaluations of the effectiveness and actual impacts of PFES programs on people's lives (social efficiency), benefits of economic (economic efficiency), and the effectiveness of forest protection (environmental efficiency) in fact have not been noticed. Faced with that situation, scientists and managers in Vietnam all agree that it is necessary to develop a method to evaluate the effectiveness of PFES programs in Vietnam. In this chapter, we introduce a method to evaluate the combined effectiveness of PFES programs based on a sustainable development approach (considering the program's sustainability based on three aspects of economy, society, and environment) with a case study in Ba Be district, Bac Kan province, Vietnam.

2. Overview of PFES policy in Vietnam

2.1 The process of developing PFES policy in Vietnam

In 2004, the revised Law on Forest Protection and Development was approved by the National Assembly of Vietnam, which affirmed the important role of forests in providing environmental services such as limiting soil erosion, regulating water sources and climate, biodiversity conservation, and landscape preservation for tourism and recreational activities. Then, in 2007, Vietnam's Forestry Development Strategy for the period 2006–2020 was approved. The important task was identified as *"mobilizing revenue from PFES payments for forest protection and development activities and improving people's livelihoods"*. On the other hand, the Strategy also set out the important task of fully assessing the economic values of forest environmental services. These were considered two important legal documents laying the foundation for the development and implementation of the policy on PFES in Vietnam.

In 2008, the Government of Vietnam established the National Forest Protection and Development Fund (According to Decree No. 05/2008/ND-CP). The main task of the Fund is to act as an intermediary connecting forest environmental services suppliers and users in Vietnam. In addition, on April 10, 2008, the Prime Minister of Vietnam signed Decision No. 380/QD-TTg on the pilot implementation of the PFES policy in two provinces, Son La and Lam Dong. After only two years of implementing pilot projects on PFES, in 2010, the Government of Vietnam issued Decree No. 99/2010/ND-CP on implementation of PFES nationwide. This was considered an important event in the process of implementing payment for forest environmental services in Vietnam. With this Decree, Vietnam became one of the first countries in Asia to institutionalize the implementation of PFES on a national scale [4]. In the process of implementation due to the identification of payers for environmental services, payment levels, and beneficiaries. The Government of Vietnam has issued Decree 147/2016/ND-CP to amend a number of provisions in Decree No. 99/2010/ND-CP to be more appropriate. The process of amending Vietnam's forest protection policy continues with the promulgation of the Law on Forest Protection and Development 2017 on November 15, 2017, and Decree No. 158/2018 on November 16, 2018, guiding the implementation of the Law on Forest Protection and Development 2017. Both of these documents continue to specify the contents of PFES to solidify the legal basis for the implementation of PFES in Vietnam. Besides, Vietnam's Law on Environmental Protection 2020 also stipulates to encourage the implementation of payment for environmental services as an economic tool to protect the environment.

Presently, Vietnam has basically completed the legal basis for implementing payment programs for forest environment services nationwide.

2.2 Review of past PFES experiences in Vietnam

In 2008–2010, USAID and the German Development Agency (GIZ) assisted the Ministry of Agriculture and Rural Development to develop a pilot project on PFES in Vietnam and suggest potential buyers and providers of ES [5, 6]. Lam Dong and Son La provinces hosted the pilot projects. The main buyers included primarily hydropower plants, and it was intended that local farmers should protect the forests as service providers or receivers. With one exception [7], we selected peer-reviewed articles or CIFOR publications released in 2010 or later to gain insights into how scholars evaluate PFES achievements in Vietnam.

Scholars agree that the pilot phase's process was seemingly hasty because of the lack of rigorous evaluation and highly optimistic in forecasting an increase in revenues to $ 2 billion in 2020 [8]. Several studies before the issuance of the final Decree 99 were not reflected in the final decision [9].

A fundamental question is, therefore, whether the Vietnamese PFES experience appears to be a success. The answer probably depends on the criteria applied (environmental, economic, or social) and mainly on the conceived 'pureness' of the Vietnamese version according to economic principles.

Vien et al. [10] refer to two fundamental weaknesses in a PFES scheme from Bac Kan province: the ES receivers are not the services' direct users. The payment differs from the social cost or opportunity cost of forest protection. Wunder et al. [7] mentioned to rename the PES experience a nonstarter in Vietnam because few environmental services are provided (they emphasize hydropower plants and watershed protection). Few entities buy the services and there is an absence of private land ownership. Despite the pessimistic forecasting and, as pointed out by McElwee et al. [5], Wunder et al. [7] were proven wrong because PFES became a relative success in Vietnam, with a cumulative annual user fee of US$100 million. Suppose the scenario in which PFES ultimately serves to collect taxes and subsidize forest authorities [8]. In that case, Wunder et al. [7] 's criticism conveys more an intellectual claim that the Vietnamese PFES falls short of adhering to theoretical economic principles. The reality is that PES schemes transfer funds to the state outside the regular government budget, and the amount is not negligible.

One of the social objectives of the PES is to contribute to poverty alleviation. Households with limited access to the forest should participate in the program with the broader purpose of poverty reduction [11].

In an earlier evaluation of the Vietnamese PFES experience, Pham et al. [4] conclude that each household receives only a small amount, which is counter to increasing efficiency. Simultaneously, the system does not account for resource quality and thus lacks incentives to protect the forest. Despite data paucity, To et al. [8] followed the same line of argument by stating that no agency has produced data to show that poorer households received a higher share of total PFES payments. In support of this argument, Doung and De Groot [12] state that the direct contribution of PFES to poverty alleviation is small compared with the average household income, based on estimations from samples in three provinces. In contrast, Phan et al. [13] studied two groups of households in Lam Dong province, one participating in a PFES scheme and the other not, concluding a significant difference in 2008, with nonparticipating households reporting income levels twice as high. Later, the difference in income disappeared (2014).

Furthermore, households considered payments to be too low relative to their living costs. In certain villages, income opportunities other than PFES payments are limited. McElwee et al. [5] refer to many contradictory cases, making an overall conclusion on social objectivity at the national level virtually impossible.

The economic aspects of PFES encompass different angles, as either significant financial support to the forest sector or support for poor households (see above). If the Vietnamese government envisaged PFES payments to reach a $ 2 billion level in 2020, the PFES experience was a disappointment. Nevertheless, the current annual level of $ 100 million from PFES schemes appears significant compared with the forestry sector's central government budget. According to data from the Vietnam Administration of Forestry [14], the total payment for forest environmental services in the 2008–2018 period in Vietnam was VND 10,000 billion (an average of VND 1300 billion/ $56,000/ year). This amount accounts for 16% of Vietnam's total forest protection budget.

Did PFES assist in saving the forest cover or at least slow the transformation of the primary forest into plantations? [15] Decree 99 refers to an 'improved forest, 'but falls short of specifying what the condition implies and how to monitor progress [16].

In light of this, forest protection is one of PFES's primary objectives; surprisingly, few studies have been conducted to bring evidence to the environmental debate. Two studies represent an exception. Phan et al. [17], using a district-based satellite image interpretation of Lam Dong province, showed an increase in forest cover from 2010 to 2014. Arriving at a similar conclusion, Duong and De Groot [12] find that forest protection has become more effective due to the implementation of a PES scheme in three different provinces. However, only this single study from Lam Dong used forest cover data from satellite images and then one district. A national-level conclusion is not possible at this stage. The last study by Duong and De Groot [12] argued that forest protection had been very successful due to PES as a result of regular official visits to forest areas and threats of severe consequences in case of noncompliant behavior. Even if this statement is correct, the risk of leakage has not vanished. Farmers can clear forests in one area for agricultural production and receive PFES money for another protected forest area [18].

Fairness and transparency are essential in PFES schemes, and, usually, studies on this topic should be abundant. However, only two studies in our sample concentrate on these aspects, while others briefly refer to the discussion. Perceived fairness of payment distribution is at the core of Loft et al.'s [19] analysis. Households preferred an equal share with only a minority in favor of payments based on work efforts (Dien Bien province). Local people rejected the initial idea of differentiation of payments according to forest conditions (primary, secondary, and degraded forest) using a weighting system (K1–K3 coefficients) and opted for a flat rate.

In a study of three different PFES schemes in Thua Thien-Hue province, Hass et al. [20] found considerable differences. Households entered lucrative contracts with the national park, whereas other PFES schemes involved low payment. The authors focused more on the lack of transparency in selecting households than on the difference between the degrees of voluntarism among PFES schemes (our theme in this article). The government must ensure clarity in all PFES payment steps, from verification of forest area to payments to receivers [4]. Whether fairness in terms of payments based on performance equals equity is the concern of Pham et al. [21]. The authors conclude that 'equal distribution' among all villagers discourages any attempt to reach efficient local forest management.

Although the present literature review helped us situate the debate, we are unable to present an ultimate answer for Vietnamese ventures in regard to environmental payments, partly because any assessment depends on the criteria (ecological, social, or economic objectives) and partly because even within a limited scope and focusing on one of the requirements only, scholars seem to disagree. Most observers support the view that PFES programs in Vietnam differ from basic payment principles because authorities define mechanisms and compel service providers' participation. Scholars agree that payments appear inferior to opportunity costs or previous forest protection programs (Program 661) [21–23].

3. Study area

Study based on Ba Be District, Bac Kan province, a mountainous area located in the northern of Vietnam. Ba Be has 68,412 hectares in total, mean annual temperature ranges from 21.98 to 23.61°C, total sunshine hours in a year is around 1283–1577 hours, annual precipitation is from 1151.3 to 1699.2 mm, and the annual humidity is 85–86%. In 2019, the total population of this district was 47,415 persons, with an approximate

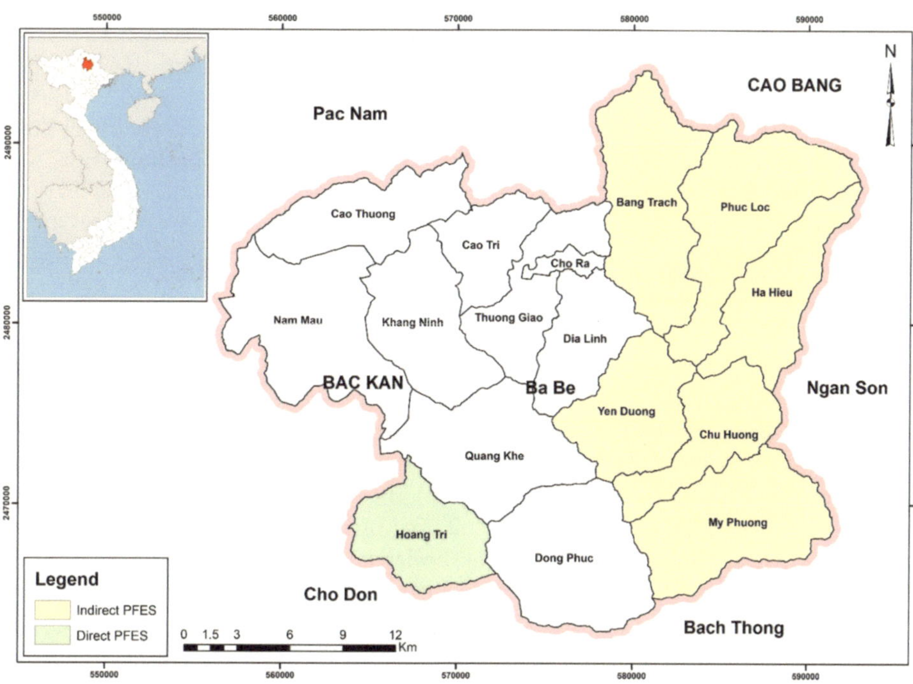

Figure 1.
Ba Be district— The area covered in this study shown on a map of Vietnam.

population density of 70 persons per km^2. There are four main ethnic groups living in this district: Tay, Dao, Kinh, and H'Mong groups. In comparison to other districts, Ba Be has slow economic growth, depends deeply on the agroforestry sector (taking 50% of total GDP), has a low annual income per capita (10 million VND per person), and high rate of poverty in comparison to the average rate of Vietnam (18.04% poor households in total) (**Figure 1**) [24].

Ba Be district has a large forest area of 68,412 hectares with forest coverage reaching 65%, especially in the district with Ba Be National Park which has high biodiversity and conservation value, so Ba Be receives interest and support from the State and many NGOs for forest conservation and development. Currently, in the district, there are many projects being implemented such as 3PAD, REDD+, UN-REDD, and so on. Since 2013, the PFES program has been implemented in Bac Kan province in general and in Ba Be district between Na Hang and Chiem Hoa hydro-power plants and forest owners in Ba Be district. With the above conditions, it can be seen that the Ba Be district is an appropriate place to conduct research to evaluate the actual effectiveness of the PFES program in Vietnam.

4. Study methods

4.1 Study data sources

The data used to evaluate the integrated effectiveness and analyze the actual impacts of the PFES program in Ba Be were collected from two specific sources as follows:

- Statistical data on the operation of the PFES program in the period 2013–2018 collected from the authorities in Ba Be district, Bac Kan province.

- Data from the questionnaire survey in 2016 and 2017 of 259 households in the study area, including 117 households participating and 142 households not participating in the PFES program.

4.2 Criteria for evaluating the effectiveness of the PFES program

Vietnam's PFES policy toward sustainable development of three pillars in the forestry sector: economic, social and environmental fields [25]. On that basis, we have built a set of criteria to evaluate the combined effectiveness of PFES program with 15 indicators. In which the economic aspect was evaluated based on four indicators (symbols Ec1, Ec2, Ec3, and Ec4), the social aspect was evaluated through six indicators (symbols So1, So2, So3, So4, So5, and So6) and the environmental aspect was assessed in five indicators (symbol En1, En2, En3, En4, and En5) (**Table 1**).

All these 15 criteria were synthesized and selected from the reality of the evaluation of PFES programs in the world and Vietnam. Specifically, four economic criteria (Ec1, Ec2, Ec3, and Ec4), 5 environmental criteria (En1, En2, En3, En4, and En5), and three social criteria (So1, So2, and So4) were used by the Vietnam Administration of Forestry during the evaluation of PFES programs [25]. Meanwhile, the remaining three social criteria (So3, So5, and So6) have been mentioned by scientists around the world when considering and evaluating PFES programs [26–28].

Aspect	Symbols	Indicator	Indicator description
Economic	Ec1	Average price paid (Million VND/ha/year)	Total amount received from PFES program for one hectare of forest in a year
	Ec2	Percentage of funds contributed to the local environmental protection budget (%).	Ratio between the total amount of PFES received/total annual environmental protection budget. In which, the environmental protection budget was calculated at 1% of the Babe's GDP.
	Ec3	Percentage of funds contributed to the forestry sector (%)	Ratio between the total amount of PFES received/total income of the forestry sector in Ba Be district.
	Ec4	Percentage of funds contributed to forest protection activities (%)	% of money directly used for forest protection activities from the total amount received in PFES program.
Social	So1	Percentage of poor households participating in the PFES program	Ratio of the poor to the total number of participants in the PFES program.
	So2	Percentage of ethnic minorities participating in the PFES program	Ratio of ethnic minorities to the total number of participants in the PFES program.
	So3	Social conflict	The change in the relationship between members of the community and between communities in the same locality when there was a PFES program.
	So4	Awareness of forest protection	People's awareness of the importance of forests, forest protection activities and environmental services of forests.
	So5	Fairness in PFES program	Ensure fairness among members, groups of people/communities in participating in activities of the PFES program.
	So6	Transparency in PFES program	The disclosure of activities, information, rights and responsibilities of stakeholders in the PFES program.
Environment	En1	Proportion of forest area protected under the PFES program (%)	Ratio of forest area participating in the PFES program to the total forest area of Ba Be district.
	En2	Forest quality	Divided by forest classification of Vietnam Administration of Forestry (Rich forest, medium forest, poor forest, depleted forest, restored forest)
	En3	Forest cover	The ratio of total forest area participating in the PFES program/total natural land area of Ba Be district.
	En4	Quality of forest protection activities	The quality of forest protection activities was determined based on criteria such as forest protection organization, forest patrol frequency; number of people participating in forest protection
	En5	Number of illegal deforestation cases	The increase and decrease in illegal logging cases before and after the PFES program

Table 1.
Criteria for evaluating the effectiveness of PFES program.

4.3 Evaluation of the integrated effectiveness the of PFES program

4.3.1 Scoring method

The combined effectiveness of the PFES program was evaluated by the weighted scoring method. The efficiency of the PFES program will be divided into seven levels according to a 10-point scale, specifically as shown in **Table 2**.

The Integrated Effectiveness Score (IES) was calculated on the basis of three economic, social, and environmental dimensions according to the following formula:

$$IES = EcS^* W_{Ec} + SoS^* W_{So} + EnS^* W_{En} \quad (1)$$

In which:

- IES = The Integrated Effectiveness Score of PFES
- EcS = Economic Effectiveness Score of PFES; SoS = Social Effectiveness Score of PFES; EnS = Environmental Effectiveness Score of PFES.
- W_{Ec}, W_{So}, and W_{En} are the weights of economic, social, and environmental aspects, respectively.

The weights of economic, social, and environmental sectors are taken according to the following three scenarios:

- **Scenarios 1:** From a sustainable development point of view, the weights in all three aspects were the same (Not prioritizing any aspect) then: $W_{Ec} = W_{So} = W_{En} = 33.33\%$.
- **Scenarios 2:** Prioritizing forest protection activities (prioritizing environmental aspects) then the specific weights are: $W_{Ec} = 25\%$, $W_{En} = 50\%$, $W_{So} = 25\%$.
- **Scenarios 3:** Consulted with forest managers and local authorities (Ba Be district), then: $W_{Ec} = 65\%$, $W_{En} = 20\%$, and $W_{So} = 15\%$.

Rating level	Rank
Very good	9.0–1.0
Good	8.0–8.9
Pretty good	7.0–7.9
Above average	6.0–6.9
Average	5.0–5.9
Weak	4.0–4.9
Poor	0–3.9

Table 2.
Integrated effectiveness rating scale of the PFES program.

Analysis of scenarios contributes to the change in the overall effectiveness of the PFES program. On that basis, to flexibly adjust the activities of the PFES programs to suit the actual situation of the locality. This has important implications when applying the integrated efficiency assessment system of the PFES program in other localities in the future.

4.3.2 Calculation method for the EcS, SoS, and EnS

Scores for each economic, social, and environmental aspect were calculated based on the evaluation indicator. The score of each aspect was divided equally among the evaluation indicators with equal weight. Specifically, the economic aspect has four indicators, so the maximum score for each indicator was 2.5 points; the social aspect has eight indicators so the maximum score of each indicator was 1.25 points; the environmental aspect has five indicators so the maximum score of each indicator was 2.0 points. The scoring of the indicators was based on the classification of the people and the actual results obtained from the PFES program (**Table 3**).

The basis for evaluating scores for each criterion was described in detail in **Table 4**.

Aspect	Indicator	Indicator score	Evaluation level of indicator			
			Good	Pretty good	Average	Poor
Economic	Ec1	2.5	2.5 (100% of indicator score)	1.875 (75% of indicator score)	1.75 (50% of indicator score)	0.825 (25% of indicator score)
	Ec2	2.5				
	Ec3	2.5				
	Ec4	2.5				
	Total EcS	**10**	**The maximum total score of four indicators**			
Environment	En1	2.0	2.0 (100% of indicator score)	1.5 (75% of indicator score)	1.0 (50% of indicator score)	0.5 (25% of indicator score)
	En2	2.0				
	En3	2.0				
	En4	2.0				
	En5	2.0				
	Total EnS	**10**	**The maximum total score of five indicators**			
Social	So1	1.67	1.67 (100% of indicator score)	1.25 (75% of indicator score)	0.84 (50% of indicator score)	0.42 (25% of indicator score)
	So2	1.67				
	So3	1.67				
	So4	1.67				
	So5	1.67				
	So6	1.67				
	Total SoS	**10**	**The maximum total score of five indicators**			

Table 3.
Scoring scale to assess the effectiveness of the PFES program.

Aspect	Indicator	Evaluation level description (Good, Pretty good, Average, and Poor)
Economic	Ec1	Good ≥200,000 VND/ha/year; Pretty good: from 100,000 to 200,000 VND/ha/year; Average: from 50,000 to 100,000 VND/ha/year; Poor <50,000 VND/ha/year (The contract level for forest protection in Vietnam is 200,000 VND/ha/year used as the basis for classification)
	Ec2	Good >75% of environmental protection budget; Pretty good: from 50 to 75% of the environmental protection budget; Average: from 25 to 50% of the environmental protection budget; Poor: < 25% of the environmental protection budget (In which environmental protection budget = 1% of local GDP, calculated according to the proportion of funding for national environmental protection of Vietnam.)
	Ec3	Good >75% of the total; Pretty good: from 50 to 75% of the total; Average: from 25 to 50% of the total; Poor <25% of the total. (Total = Total amount of payment received in the PFES program)
	Ec4	Good >75% of the total; Pretty good: from 50 to 75% of the total; Average: from 25 to 50% of the total; Poor <25% of total (Total = Total local forestry budget)
Environment	En1	Good >75% of the total; Pretty good: from 50 to 75% of the total; Average: from 25 to 50% of the total; Poor <25%the of the total. (Total = Total forest area of the locality)
	En2	Good >50%; Petty good >40–50%; Average: >30–40%; Poor <30% (Calculated according to the coverage of the paid forest area divided by the total natural area of the locality)
	En3	Rich forest = 5 scores; Medium Forest = 4 scores; Poor forest = 3 scores; Depleted forest = 2 scores; Restored forest = 1 score. Total forest quality score = 5*% rich forest +4*% medium forest +3*% Poor forest +2*% Depleted forest +1*%Restored forest. Total forest quality score from 1.0 to 2.0 = poor; from 2.1 to 3.0 = Average; 3.1–4.0 = Pretty good; 4.1–5.0 = Good
	En4	According to the results of the people's classification based on the survey (Good up = 3 Scores; No change = 2 scores; Reducing = 1 score) If evaluation score from 1.0 to 1.5 = Poor; from 1.6 to 2.0 = Average; 2.1–2.5 = Pretty good; 2.6–3.0 = Good
	En5	Good = Do not have; Pretty good = Reducing; Average = No Change; Poor = Increasing
Social	So1	Good >15%; Pretty good: from 10 to 15%; Average: from 5 to 10%; Poor <5% (The poverty rate of Ba Be district was 20%, which was used as a basis to spend the classification levels)
	So2	Good >75%; Pretty good: from 50 to 75%; Average: from 25 to 50%; Poor <25%.
	So3 So4	According to the results of the people's classification based on the survey (Good up = 3 scores; No change = 2 scores; Reduce = 1 score) Rating: from 1.0 to 1.5 scores = Poor; from 1.6 to 2.0 score = Average; from 2.1 to 2.5 scores = Pretty good; from 2.6 to 3.0 scores = Good
	So5 So6	Based on people's assessment of the indicator of fairness and transparency when implementing the payment program according to five evaluation levels. If score evaluation at level 1 and 2 = Poor, level 3 = Average, level 4 = Pretty good, and level 5 = Good

Table 4.
Detailed description of the basis of classification of evaluation indicator.

5. Results

5.1 PFES program in Ba Be

5.1.1 Formation process

The PFES program started to be implemented in Ba Be district in particular and Bac Kan province in general in 2013 in the spirit of Decree No. 99/ND/CP. However, due to many difficulties in preparing administrative procedures, it was not until 2015 that the payment activity was implemented for the first time. In this payment, the amount received by forest owners is the payment for all 3 years from 2013 to 2015. Since 2015, due to the completion of procedures and necessary conditions, the program has stabilized and paid once a year at the end of the year.

5.1.2 Stakeholders

5.1.2.1 Forest environmental services suppliers – Forest owners

PFES suppliers are forest owners (households, organizations, and individuals) in Ba Be district. Accordingly, Ba Be district currently has a total of 44,762.20 ha of forest

Number of household	**Unit**	**Rank**	**Mean ± SD**
Number of household members	Person	1–8	4.83 ± 1.60
Household income	million VND/year	2.70–312.75	57.08 ± 53.06
Land ownership			
Total area	Ha	0.11–160.82	4.67 ± 15.12
Agricultural land		*0.04–8.00*	*0.82 ± 1.18*
Forest land		*0.1–52.00*	*2.93 ± 5.35*
Ethnic composition	Kinh	Household	3
		%	*2.56*
	Tày	Household	61
		%	*52.14*
	Dao	Household	52
		%	*44.44*
	Other	Household	1
		%	*0.86*
Economic sectors	Poor	Household	30
		%	*25.86*
	Nonpoor	Household	86
		%	*74.14*

Note: The italic value is a part of the vertical value (Smaller item).

Table 5.
Characteristics of forest owners who are households in the PFES program.

allocated to different forest owners, including Ba Be National Park manages 7478.90 ha (16.71%), Ba Be Forest Enterprise manages 1190.60 ha (2.66%), households/individuals manage 18,783.40 ha (41.96%), village communities manage 6641.90 ha (14.84%) and the remaining 10,667.50 ha (23.83%) has not yet been contracted, so it is temporarily managed by the People's Committees of communes [24]. Forest management forms in Ba Be district are quite diverse, including state management (Ba Be National Park, People's Committees of communes), state enterprises (Ba Be Forest Enterprise), community management (Community/villages), and private management (Households/individuals) (**Table 5**).

5.1.2.2 Users of Forest environmental services

Tuyen Quang Hydropower Company and Chiem Hoa Hydropower Plant are users of the water source on Nang River basin to produce electricity and are identified as PFES users (Forest environmental services purchasers). However, they do not directly deal with forest owners but entrust the responsibility to the Vietnam Fund for Forest Protection & Development to do the transaction. In this program, neither the forest environmental service provider (Forest Owners) nor the forest environmental service user (Hydropower Plants/Companies) is the one to decide on the price paid, but the government is the one to decide this pay rate.

5.1.3 Payment mechanism

5.1.3.1 Cash flow

Annually, based on the output of electricity produced, Tuyen Quang Hydropower Company and Chiem Hoa Hydropower Plant contributed money to the Fund for Protection and Development of Vietnam with the unit price of 20 VND/KWh (Decision 99/2010/ND-CP), this payment has increased to 36 VND/KWh from 2018 (According to Decree 156/2018/ND-CP). The total amount of contribution was retained by the fund 0.5% as a management fund, and the remaining 99.5% of the amount was transferred to the Bac Kan Forest Protection and Development Fund. The Bac Kan Forest Protection and Development Fund was entitled to 5% of the management fee and 10% of the contingency fund (total of 15%), the remaining 85% of the amount was transferred directly to the forest owners (**Figure 2**). This form of payment is called indirect because the payment must be through a third party, the Forest Protection and Development Fund, at all levels.

5.1.3.2 Price paid

The rate of payment to forest owners under the PFES program was calculated according to the following formula:

$$\text{Total Payments} = S^{*} P^{*} K \tag{2}$$

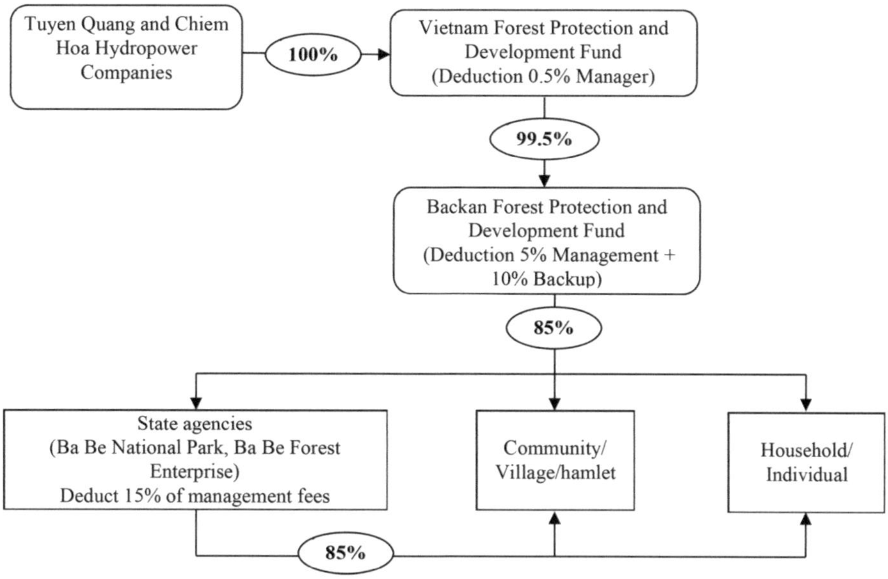

Figure 2.
Cash flow in the Ba Be PFES program.

In Which:

- S: forest area receiving payment (Ha)
- P: price paid for 1 hectare of forest (VND/ha)
- K = K1*K2*K3*K4. The coefficient was determined according to the criteria of forest quality (K1), forest type (plantation/natural forest) (K2), forest origin (K3), and difficulty level in forest protection (K4). However, at the time of the study, the K coefficient in Bac Kan province, in general, and Ba Be district, in particular, is agreed to be K = 1 for all forest areas providing environmental services.

5.1.3.3 Dossier appraisal

In order to receive money from the PFES program, forest owners must prepare a forest owner dossier, including a self-declaration of the forest area providing environmental services; commitment to protect and manage forest area providing environmental services; self-declaration of results of protection of forest areas providing environmental services. The forest owner dossier was submitted to the Bac Kan Forest Protection and Development Fund at the end of January every year. The Bac Kan Forest Protection and Development Fund will be responsible for appraising the dossier and conducting the actual acceptance test to accurately determine the area and quality of the forest. Applications that meet the Fund's requirements will receive payments in November or December each year (**Figure 3**).

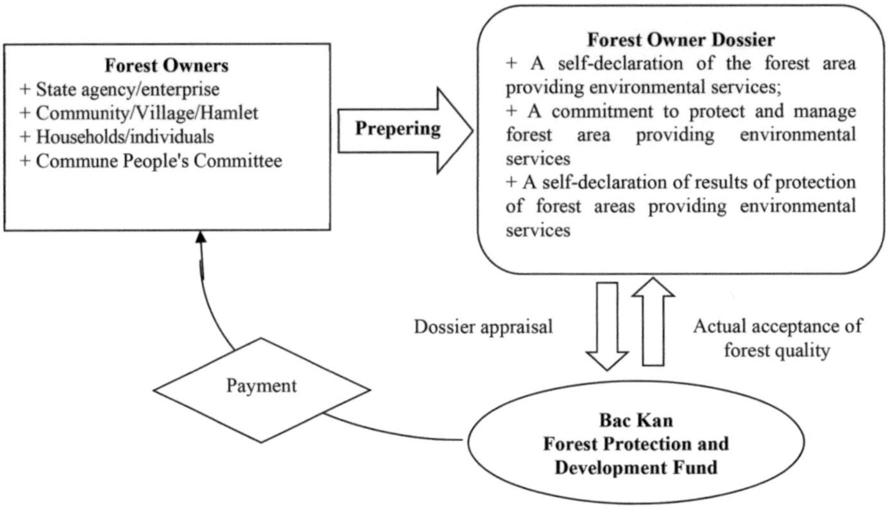

Figure 3.
The process of application assessment and payment in the PFES program.

5.2 Evaluating the effectiveness of the PFES program

5.2.1 Score of the evaluation indicator

Specific scores for each evaluation indicator are shown in **Table 6**. Accordingly, the scores of three economic, social, and environmental aspects were 5.63 points, 7.51 points, and 7.5 points, respectively. Thus, the economic efficiency of the PFES program was only average, while the social and environmental effects were evaluated equally and at a pretty good level.

Indicator	Unit	Evaluation		
		Value	Level	Score
Ec1	1000 VND/ha/year	67	Average	1.25
Ec2	%	44.71	Average	1.25
Ec3	%	2.01	Poor	0.625
Ec4	%	84.58	Good	2.5
Total EcS				**5.63**
So1	%	29.82	Good	1.67
So2	%	97.42	Good	1.67
So3	Score	2.32 ± 0.62	Pretty good	1.25
So4	Score		Pretty good	1.25
So5	Score	3.29 ± 0.11	Average	0.84
So6	Score	3.34 ± 0.12	Average	0.84

Indicator	Unit	Evaluation		
		Value	Level	Score
Total SoS				**7.51**
En1	%	80.15	Good	2.00
En2	Score	2.9	Average	1.00
En3	%	52.44	Good	2.00
En4	Score	2.41 ± 0.66	Pretty good	1.50
En5	%	27.59	Average	1.00
Total EnS				**7.50**

Table 6.
Score of three economic, social, and environmental aspects of the PFES program.

5.2.2 Integrated effectiveness of the PFES program

The results of calculating the IES of the PFES program under the three scenarios are presented in **Table 7**. The IES of the program achieved the highest score in the second scenario – Sustainable Development Scenario with a score of 7.03 (Pretty Good). In the remaining two scenarios, the IES was only above average with 6.88 points and 6.28 points for the first scenario and third Scenario, respectively.

IES analysis under different scenarios to recommend managers to select/adjust the evaluation weights of three economic, social and environmental aspects in actual situation of the locality or with predefined management objectives. This creates flexibility in the performance assessment of PFES programs. As for the program of Ba Be district is one of the poorest districts of Vietnam. Besides, the local people are mainly ethnic people living in the forest. Therefore, in the selection of scenarios to evaluate the PFES program should pay attention to social issues, especially issues such as poverty reduction, participation of ethnic minorities; sustainable livelihood development; and limit social conflicts. Choosing the first scenario – sustainable development not the most effective because this area was a - special difficult need to be considered very carefully in forest protection and local economic development. On the contrary, if choosing the third scene - Promoting economic efficiency (weighted 65%), reduces environmental efficiency and social efficiency (weights 20% and 15%, respectively) causing to reduce the forest protection efficiency. On the other hand, high economic efficiency but not equal distribution will increase social conflicts, especially between the rich and the poor, ethnic minorities with Kinh people. As a result, the sustainability of the PFES program will be seriously degraded. From the above analysis, it can be seen that the option of

Scenario	Economic		Social		Environment		Integrated effectiveness	
	score	Weight	score	Weight	score	Weight	Score	Rating
First scenario	5.63	33.33	7.51	33.33	7.5	33.33	6.88	Above average
Second scenario		25.0		25.0		50.0	7.03	Pretty good
Third scenario		65.0		15.0		20.0	6.28	Above average

Table 7.
Analysis of the integrated effectiveness of the PFES program under different scenarios.

evaluating the PFES program according to the second scenario was more feasible for the actual situation of the Ba Be district. This scenario allows the Ba Be district to sustainably protect forest resources and gradually improve local economic and social life. Focusing on forest protection while still considering the livelihoods of forest-based communities, ensuring social security and fairness.

5.3 Actual impact of the PFES program

5.3.1 Socio-economic impact

5.3.1.1 Household income

The PFES program pays forest owners, so households participating in this program will be able to increase their annual income thanks to their forest area. This can make a difference in their income compared to the group of households not participating in the PFES program (**Table 8**).

Table 8 shows that the average income and income from the forest of households participating in the PFES program are significantly higher than that of the group not participating in the program. Specifically, the average income of the group participating in the program was 2.3 million VND/year higher, and the income from the forest was 0.72 million VND/year higher than that of the households not participating in the program. Forest income of the group participating in the PFES program accounted for 6.49% of the total income of the household, while this figure was only 5.02% (1.27% lower) in the group that did not participate in the program. This shows that the PFES program has contributed to improving the average income of households participating in the program. However, this level of income is still modest.

5.3.1.2 Impact on the economic situation of households

To examine the impacts of the PFES program on people's lives, we compared some socio-economic indicators of two groups of population participating and not participating in the PFES program in Vietnam two times before and after the PFES program taken place. The results of the comparison are shown in **Table 9**. Additionally, the percentage of poor households in the group participating in the program decreased more than in the group not participating in the program. However, the percentage of

Featured		**Household participating in the PFES**	**Household nonparticipating in the PFES**	**Impact of the PFES**
Total household income (1000 VND/year)	Mean	41,105.64	38,755.50	2350.14
	SD	*50,860.60*	*45,542.49*	
Household income from the forest (1000 VND/year)	Mean	2668.31	1945.21	723.10
	SD	*12,270.38*	*6438.26*	
Ratio of Household in the ratio from the forest/Total household income (%)	6.49	5.02	1.27	

Table 8.
Comparison of total income and income from forests between two groups of households participating and not participating in the PFES program.

Feature		Participating			Nonparticipating			Impact of the PFES
		Before (X1)	After (X2)	Δ1 = (X2)–(X1)	Before (Y1)	After (Y2)	Δ2 = Y2–Y1	Δ = Δ1–Δ2
Ratio of poor household (%)	X	Households	26.50	−5.98	44.60	47.52	2.92	−8.90
	SD	*0.47*	*0.44*		*0.50*	*0.50*		
Percentage of households with savings in Bank (%)	X	12.07	14.53	2.46	2.88**	8.63**	5.75	−3.29
	SD	*0.33*	*0.35*		*0.17*	*0.28*		
Percentage of households with savings in jewelry (%)	X	3.48	5.17	1.69	3.6	5.04	1.44	0.25
	SD	*0.18*	*0.22*		*0.19*	*0.22*		
Percentage of households with debt (%)	X	46.76*	54.68*	7.92	39.66*	48.28*	8.62	−0.70
	SD	*0.50*	*0.50*		*0.49*	*0.50*		

Note: "" and"**"Statistical difference at the significance level was 0.05 and 0.01, respectively.*

Table 9.
Comparison of some socio-economic indicators between two groups of households participating and not participating in the PFES program.

households with savings in money and jewelry of the group participating in the PFES program was lower than that of the nonparticipant group. For the percentage of households with loans in both groups participating and not participating in the PFES program, there was an increasing trend; the growth rate of the participating group was lower than that of the nonparticipating group. This once again affirms that the PFES program has contributed to improving the economic lives of households participating in the program.

5.3.1.3 Impact on people's awareness of forest protection

The results of comparing the level of awareness of forest functions between the people participating and not participating in the payment for environmental services are shown in **Table 10**.

For the supply and cultural functions, there was no significant difference in awareness between the two groups of participants and nonparticipants in the PFES program. Meanwhile, the ability to recognize the regulatory functions of forests in the forest households participating in the program is always higher than in the group not participating in the program.

In general, it can be seen that the ability to recognize the functions of forests in the participants of the PFES program was much higher than in those who did not. Specifically, the participants recognized up to 9/14 forest functions higher than nonparticipants. In which 100% of the forest's regulatory functions are recognized higher by the participants than the nonparticipants. This functional group of the forest was often more difficult to identify with the people than the other function groups. This can be explained because when participating in the PFES program, people will be trained and propagated more about the functions and values of forests, especially the regulatory functional group of forests.

Functions of the forest	Participating		Nonparticipating		Impact of the PFES		
	number	Different	number	Ratio (%)	Mean	Level of significance	P-Value
Supply service							
Materials for making houses (Mainly wood)	51	43.59	63	44.37	−0.78		0.90078
Food	26	22.22	36	25.35	−3.13		0.55698
Medicine	20	17.09	15	10.56	6.53		0.13464
Seeds of plants and animals	14	11.97	15	10.56	1.41		0.72438
Firewood	65	55.56	82	58.16	−2.60		0.67617
Regulatory service							
Climate regulation	92	78.63	90	63.38	15.25	**	0.00654
Water regulation	94	80.34	108	76.06	4.28		0.40618
Protect soil and limit erosion	93	79.49	107	75.35	4.14		0.42884
Disease control	26	22.22	26	18.31	3.91		0.43931
Carbon Absorption	43	36.75	48	33.80	2.95		0.62303
Cultural services							
Beliefs/Customs	21	17.95	20	14.08	3.87		0.40304
Culture	10	8.55	13	9.15	−0.6		0.86435
Education	46	39.32	44	30.99	8.33		0.16473
Ecotourism	0	0	4	2.82	−2.82	*	0.04511

Note: "" and"**"Statistical difference at the significance level was 0.05 and 0.01, respectively.*

Table 10.
Comparison of ability to recognize forest functions between two groups of households participating and not participating in the PFES program.

5.3.2 Environmental impact

5.3.2.1 Forest exploitation activities

The results of comparing the frequency of entering the forest to collect forest products of the two groups of participants and nonparticipants in the PFES program are shown in **Table 11**.

Table 11 shows that the frequency of going to the forest of both participants and nonparticipants in the PFES program after the PFES program has taken place tends to decrease. The frequency of going to the forest of the group not participating in the PFES program was always higher than that of the participating group. Reducing the frequency of people entering the forest helps limit the exploitation of forest resources. This was demonstrated more clearly through the data on forest product exploitation of the two groups described in **Table 12**.

Table 12 showed that most of the forest product exploitation activities of people in both participating and nonparticipating groups in the payment program for forest environmental services after 2015 decreased compared to the previous time. However,

Frequency to collect forest products (Times/season)		Participating			Nonparticipating			Impact of the PFES Δ = Δ1–Δ2
		Before (X1)	After (X2)	Δ1 (X2–X1)	Before (Y1)	After (Y2)	Δ2 (Y2–Y1)	
Dry season	X	8.67	7.74	−0.93	10.4	10.21	−0.19	−0.74
	SD	*8.93*	*8.75*		*11.3*	*11.76*		
Rainy season	X	5.21*	4.46*	−0.75	5.78*	5.68*	−0.10	−0.65
	SD	*6.85*	*6.19*		*7.59*	*7.74*		

Note: (*) Statistical difference at the significance level was 0.05.

Table 11.
Comparing the frequency of collecting forest products of two groups of participants and nonparticipants in the PFES program.

Forest Products		Participating			Participating			Impact of the PFES Δ2–Δ1
		Before (X1)	After (X2)	Δ1 (X2–X1)	Before (Y1)	After (Y2)	Δ2 (Y2–Y1)	
Wood	X	56.82*	33.33*	−23.49	73.58**	39.21**	−34.37	10.88
	SD	*0.50*	*0.48*		*0.45*	*0.49*		
Firewood	X	0	0	0	64.81	64.00	−0.81	0.81
	SD	*0*	*0*		*0.48*	*0.48*		
Vegetables, bamboo shoots	X	95.7	94.62	−1.08	94.44	93.46	−0.98	−0.10
	SD	*0.2*	*0.27*		*0.23*	*0.25*		
Hunting	X	0	0	0	9.52**	6.25**	−3.27	3.27
	SD	*0*	*0*		*0.3*	*0.44*		
Honey	X	17.24	7.14	−10.1	16.67	5.26	−11.41	1.31
	SD	*0.38*	*0.26*		*0.38*	*0.23*		
Rattan	X	41.67	41.67	0	0	0	0	0
	SD	*0.20*	*0.20*		*0*	*0*		
Medicine	X	25	16.67	−8.33	25	25	0	−8.33
	SD	*0.44*	*0.38*		*0.44*	*0.44*		
Other	X	66.67	66.67	0	14.28	14.28	0	0
	SD	*0.26*	*0.26*		*0.36*	*0.36*		

Note: “” and“**“Statistical difference at the significance level was 0.05 and 0.01, respectively.*

Table 12.
The situation of people’s forest product exploitation before and after the PFES program.

whether this was an impact created by the PFES program needs to be considered by the fact that the rate of reduction in harvesting of forest products among those not participating in the program was much higher than that of the group participating in the program.

5.3.2.2 Impact on the forest management plan

The results of comparing forest protection and development plans of two groups of households participating and not participating in the payment program for forest environmental services were quite significant (**Table 13**). The participants in the PFES program had a higher tendency to keep and protect forests than the group of nonparticipants. Specifically, the group participating in the program had higher percentage of planning for forest protection, afforestation, and forest protection to receive payment than the nonparticipants in the group. In contrast, those who did not participate in the PFES program had plans such as transfer of management rights, agroforestry development and forest conversion for other purposes were higher than those participating in the program. Notably, the proportion of households that did not have a forest protection plan in the group of people participating in the PFES was quite low, only 5.98%. In contrast, the number in the group of people who did not participate in the program was nearly 2.5 times higher (13.38%).

In summary, the participants of the PFES program had better forest protection and development plans than those who did not participate in the program. When forest owners actively zoned and protecting forests, it was important for protected forest environmental services because when forest owners changed land use purposes, forest environmental services will also be lost. These cases will lose great social benefits, according to the analysis of Pagiola and Platais [29].

The results of the assessment of the IE of the PFES program in Ba Be have shown that the program has had obvious environmental effects; specifically, the program has contributed to promoting and improving forest protection and development activities. This result has also been shown in Vietnam's PFES programs in other regions such as Lam Dong, Son La, Hoa Binh and Thua Thien Hue [12, 17, 18, 20, 23]. In addition, the PFES program in Ba Be has contributed to changing people's perception of forest resources, helping people to be more aware of the value of forests. In the program, the elements of fairness and transparency have been paid attention to, especially ensuring equal access to the program for the poor and ethnic minorities. As a result, there were no major social conflicts or conflicts when implementing PFES programs [10–12]. However, the economic efficiency of the PFES program was not high because the average payment level was still low. As a result, the payment has not really helped people living in the forest to change their livelihood conditions. This was also one of the common weaknesses of most PFES programs in Vietnam [1, 5, 9, 10]. To overcome this,

Forest management plan	Participating		Nonparticipating	
	Participating	Ratio (%)	Number	Ratio (%)
Transfer of forests to others	7	5.98	9	6.34
Forest regeneration zoning	20	17.09	24	16.90
Afforestation	57	48.72	45	31.69
Development of Agroforestry	13	11.11	29	20.42
Protection	24	20.51	14	9.86
Other management plans	4	3.42	10	7.04
Nonmanagement plan	7	5.98	19	13.38

Table 13.
Comparison of forest protection plans between participants and nonparticipants in the PFES program.

it is necessary to fully exploit the environmental values of the forest, especially the carbon sequestration service of the forest. Currently, the type of carbon sequestration payment has been regulated by the Government of Vietnam in the Law on Environmental Protection (2020), but the implementation has not been carried out yet [30]. Promoting payment for carbon sequestration services will expand PFES users, which are mainly enterprises and industrial plants. From there, a large source of funding will be mobilized to contribute to raising the price paid per hectare of forest. Besides, the promotion of forest economic development, agroforestry models, planting medicinal plants under the forest canopy, etc., are also solutions that need to be promoted to contribute to raising incomes and improving livelihoods for forest-based communities.

6. Conclusion

The proposed integrated assessment method demonstrates more detail results of payment for forest environmental services in Ba Be district, Bac Kan province, Vietnam. Economic efficiency, if simply measured by the amount of money received by forest owners according to the quality of the forest they contribute, is very small and not commensurate with their efforts [5, 22]. Many researchers recognized the limitations of PFES in Vietnam such as strong state involvement, poor design and monitoring of ecosystem services, less attention on market-driven factors in PFES, and poor livelihood subsidy [5, 22, 26]. However, their evaluations were focused on individual aspects of PFES in Vietnam such as policy factors [6], enhancing forest cover and watershed [6], equality and efficiency of PFES [26], buyer's perspectives [9] or livelihood of local community [4, 12, 19–21]. But if looked at from a social perspective, the evaluation indicators have clearly shown a remarkable change in the awareness, attitude and behavior of forest owners in forest plantation and protection. In our case study, the forest owners are encouraged to participate in forest protection work, go on forest patrols and the community's awareness in forest protection work is clearly raised. This assessment approach focuses on effective exploitation of society according to local characteristics, which has been highly appreciated by researchers [19–21, 28, 29]. Social efficiency has been taken into account in other works on ethnic characteristics, religion, culture and awareness of individuals [9, 10, 26, 27] and communities [12] about the responsibility and obligation to protect forests. Meanwhile, the impacts on the environmental aspect are reflected in the fact that the payment program has protected a large area of forest and promoted forest protection activities such as managing, patrolling, and monitoring forests; reduced indiscriminate logging and deforestation; encouraged local people to protect forests, not to convert forests to other land uses as mentioned by other workers [6, 13, 14, 25].

The proposed method applies ecosystem approaches and is based on three pillars of sustainable development, i.e., economic, social and environmental development, as done by many workers [7, 28, 29]. The use of 15 diverse evaluation criteria has evaluated in detail the effectiveness of payments for forest environmental services in many respects compared with the methods used before.

However, we realize that using 15 evaluation criteria will take a lot of time, and in many cases, the number of evaluation indicators can be reduced to suit the specific conditions of each locality. In addition, our method is still focused on locality context and the upscaling is limited such as national and global dimensions [15]. However, the simplification has to ensure the evaluation of three aspects of sustainable development such as economy, society and environment, as many workers applied in the world [7, 9, 27–29].

Acknowledgements

This work was supported by DANIDA (http://drp.dfcentre.com/projectredd-forest-grab-all-times) research grant: REDD+ The forest grab of all times? 13-08KU.

Conflict of interest

The authors declare no conflict of interest.

Author details

Vien Tran Duc[1], Son Cao Truong[1*], Lam Nguyen Thanh[1], Van Dinh Thi Hai[1], Huong Le Thi Thu[1] and Thorkil Casse[2]

1 Vietnam National University of Agriculture, Hanoi, Vietnam

2 Roskilde University, Denmark

*Address all correspondence to: ctson@vnua.edu.vn

References

[1] Vietnam Forest Protection and Development Fund. Report on Implementation of Payment Policy for Forest Environment Services in 2020. HaNoi: VNFF; 2021 (in Vietnamese)

[2] Phuong PX. Speech at the summary conference on payments for environmental Services in Vietnam. In: Proceedings of the Workshop: Evaluation of the Effectiveness of Payment for Forest Environmental Services and the Participation of Local Stakeholders; November 20, 2015. Hanoi, Vietnam: Agriculture and Rural Development; 2015. pp. 26-27 (in Vietnamese)

[3] Ngai NB. Speech at the summary conference on payments for environmental Services in Vietnam. In: Proceedings of the Workshop: Evaluation of the Effectiveness of Payment for Forest Environmental Services and the Participation of Local Stakeholders; November 20, 2015. Hanoi, Vietnam: Agriculture and Rural Development; 2015. pp. 30-31 (in Vietnamese)

[4] Pham TT, Benett K, Phuong VT, Brunner J, Dung LN, Tien ND. Payments for Forest Environmental Services in Vietnam: From Policy to Practice. Occasional Paper 93. Bogor. CIFOR: Indonesia; 2013

[5] McElwee P, Huber B, Van NTH. Hybrid outcomes of payments for ecosystem services policies in Vietnam: Between theory and practice. Development and Change. 2019;**51**(1): 253-280. DOI: 10.1111/Dech.12548

[6] Suhardiman D, Wichelns D, Lestrelin G, Hoanh CT. Payments for ecosystem services in Vietnam: Market-based incentives or state control of resources? Ecosystem Services. 2013;**6**: 64-71. DOI: 10.1016/j.ecoser.2013.06.001

[7] Wunder S. Payments for environmental services: Some nuts and bolts. Occasional paper. CIFOR. Vol. 42. Indonesia: Bogor; 2005. p 23

[8] To PX, Dressler WH. Rethinking 'success': The politics of payment for forest ecosystem services in Vietnam. Land Use Policy. 2019;**81**:582-593. DOI: 10.1016/j.landusepol.2018.11.010

[9] Do HD, Vu TP, Nguyen VT, Catacutan D. Payment for forest environmental services in Vietnam: An analysis of buyers 'perspectives and willingness. Ecosystem Services. 2018; **32**:134-143. DOI: 10.1016/j.ecoser.2018.07.005

[10] Vien TD, Son CT, Dung NTT, Lam NT. A voluntary model of payment for environmental services: Lessons from Ba Be district, Bac Kan province of Vietnam. In: Shivakoti G, Leisz SJ, Thanh MV, Vien TD, editors. Redefining Diversity and Dynamics of Natural Resources Management in Asia, Volume 2: Upland Natural Resources and Social Ecological Systems in Northern Vietnam. San Diego: Elsevier; 2017. pp. 63-74. DOI: 10.1016/B978-0-12-805453-6.00005-X.ch5

[11] Ha HM, Hoan DT, Bac DV, Rohit J, Sweta P, Luan TD, et al. Tin NVT: Technical Report: Assessment of Ability and Design of Payment for Environmental Services in Bac Kan. Hanoi, Vietnam: ICRAF Viet Nam; 2017 (in Vietnamese)

[12] Duong NTB, De Groot WT. The impact of payment for forest

environmental services (PFES) on community-level forest management in Vietnam. Forest Policy and Economics. 2020;**113**:102135. DOI: 10.1016/j.forpol.2020.102135

[13] Phan THD, Brouwer R, Hoang LP, Davidson MD. Do payments for forest ecosystem services generate double dividends? An integrated impact assessment of Vietnam's PES program. PLoS One. 2018;**13**(8):e0200881. DOI: 10.1371/journal.pone.0200881

[14] Vietnam Administration of Forest. Report on payments for forest environmental services in 2018. Hanoi, Vietnam (In Vietnames): Agriculture and Rural Deverlopment; 2018

[15] Matthews RB, van Noordwijk M, Lambin E, Meyfroidt P, Gupta J, Verchot L, et al. Implementing REDD+ (reducing emissions from deforestation and degradation): Evidence on governance, evaluation and impacts from the REDD-ALERT project. Mitigation and Adaptation Strategies for Global Change. 2014;**19**:907-925. DOI: 10.1007/s11027-014-9578-z

[16] McEwin A, Nguyen MH. Review and formulation of the M&E policy decision on PFES, Technical Review Report. Greater Mekong Subregion. Core Environment Program. Vietnam; 2015

[17] Phan THD, Brouwer R, Hoang LP, Davidson MD. A comparative study of transaction costs of payments for forest ecosystem services in Vietnam. Forest Policy and Economics. 2017;**2017**(80): 141-149. DOI: 10.1016/j.forpol.2017.03.017

[18] Trædal LT, Vedeld PO, Petursson JG. Analyzing the transformations of forest PES in Vietnam: Implicationsfor REDD+. Forest Policy and Economics. 2016;**62**: 109-117. DOI: 10.1016/j.forpol.2015.11.001

[19] Loft L, Le DN, Pham TT, Yang AL, Tjajadi JS, Wong GY. Whose equity matters? National to local equity perceptions in Vietnam's payments for forest ecosystem services scheme. Ecological Economics. 2017;**135**:164-175. DOI: 10.1016/j.ecolecon.2017.01.016

[20] Hass JC, Loft L, Pham TT. How fair can incentive-based conservation get? The interdependence of distributional and contextual equity in Vietnam's payments for forest environmental services program. Ecological Economics. 2019;**160**:205-214. DOI: 10.106/j.ecolecon.2019.02.021

[21] Pham TT, Moeliono M, Brockhaus M, Le DN, Wong GY, Le TM. Local preferences and strategies for effective, efficient, and equitable distribution of PES revenues in Vietnam: Lessons for REDD+. Human Ecology. 2014;**42**:885-899. DOI: 10.1007/s10745-014-9703-3

[22] To PX, Dressler WH, Mahanty S, Pham TT, Zingerli C. The prospects for payment for ecosystem services (PES) in Vietnam: A look at three payment schemes. Human Ecology. 2012;**40**: 237-249. DOI: 10.1007/s10745-012-9480-9

[23] Tran TTH, Zeller M, Suhardiman D. Payments for ecosystem services in Hoa Binh province, Vietnam: An institutional analysis. Ecosystem Services. 2016;**22**: 83-93. DOI: 10.1016/j.ecoser.2016.10.001

[24] General Statistics Office in Vietnam. Bac Kan Statistical Yearbook 2019. Hanoi, Vietnam: Statistical Publishing House in Vietnam; 2020

[25] Vietnam Administration Forestry. Proceedings of the Conference on Evaluating the Effectiveness of Payment for Forest Environmental Services and the Participation of Local Stakeholders.

20 November 2015. Hanoi, Vietnam; 2016

[26] Pascual U, Muradian R, Rodriquez LC, Duraiappah A. Exploring the links between equity and efficiency in payments for environmental services: A conceptual approach. Ecological Economics. 2010;**69**:1237-1244. DOI: 10.1016/j.ecolecon.2009.11.004

[27] Muradian R, Corbera E, Pascual U, Kosoy N, May PH. Reconciling theory and practice: An alternative conceptual framework for understanding payments for environmental services. Ecological Economics. 2009;**69**:1202-1208. DOI: 10.106/j.ecolecon.2009.11.006

[28] Norgaard RB. Ecosystem services: From eye-opening metaphor to complexity blinder. Ecological Economics. 2009;**69**(6):1219-1227. DOI: 10.1016/j.ecolecon.2009.11.009

[29] Pagiola S, Platais G. Payments for Environmental Services: From Theory to Practice. Washington: World Bank; 2007

[30] Vietnam National Assembly. Law No. 72/2020/QH14 on Environmental Protection 2020. November 17, 2020; Hanoi, Vietnam; 2020

Chapter 6

Moving Horizon, Design Praxis through Soil Transformation: A Landscape Manifesto

Vittoria Mencarini, Luca Emanueli and Gianni Lobosco

Abstract

Moving horizon was born as a doctoral investigation that moves across research and design dimension. It explores the relationship between landscape design and soil transformation, focusing on the mutual effects and potential disciplinary developments aiming at structurally linking the two fields. Soil is one of the most complex biomaterials on Earth in continuous exchange with the terrestrial systems. The starting assumption is that the soil is a condition of inherent shifting in landscape evolution both in physical and semantic relationship. The value of soil as an element of planning and design lies in handling live and dynamic physical matter. From being 'background' for the built environment, the soil transformations become the 'foreground' both in landscape design praxis and in theoretical implications, by embedding the soil as a 'palimpsest' in reading and writing the landscape. The framework produced by this assessment has been condensed in ten propositions, collected in form of a landscape manifesto. A first application of moving horizon approach has been developed and tested in the Ravenna Climate Change Adaptation Plan (Italy), by identifying a planning procedure capable of integrating territorial adaptation measures to climate change through an approach based on understanding and transforming the soil as a fundamental material of this process.

Keywords: moving horizon approach, landscape design, soil, adaptation, planning

1. Introduction

Soil is one of the most complex biomaterials on Earth [1] in continuous exchange with the terrestrial systems that together with the pedosphere make up our planet: lithosphere, hydrosphere, atmosphere and biosphere [1].

It behaves as an open, thermodynamic system highly responsive to inputs and outputs of chemical elements and energy [2]. It is divided into 'horizons' having their own physical, chemical and biological characteristics. Soil formation, the so-called pedogenesis, is the result of long processes of interaction between the elements that compose and interfere with it. As a result, soil is defined as a non-renewable resource in reasonable time [2].

Along the pedogenesis dynamism, the environmental conditions that determine the development and soil properties are climate, lithological substrate, morphology and relief, biota, time and also human activities. This last is described as the Sixth Soil-Forming Factor[1] [3, 4].

Echoing Logan's words, we suggest that 'A soil was not a thing ... It was a web of relationships that stood in a certain state at a certain time' [5].

2. The soil as a palimpsest in reading and writing the Landscape

In western culture, the term landscape is the subject of several semantic discussions and interpretations. The erratic meanings refer to the terms which are treated by the numerous disciplines that affect the landscape and the aspects that make it up [6–14]. In the common and most widespread terminology, it refers to a portion of territory as it appears embraced by the gaze of a subject[2] [15–17]. In this establishment, it assumes a high degree of subjectivity, and hence, the landscape is perceived as a phenomenon [17].

Although they cannot give an univocal definition, the various interpretations of the term lead to the description of a place and to the interaction between the elements—anthropic and environmental—that compose and characterize it.

The sustained hypothesis is that this relationship is intrinsically linked to the soil shifting, creating ever new landscapes.[3]

This statement does not deny the approaches described above and finds support in the short essay drafted by the Austrian pedologist Peter Finke [18]. In 'Soil and Landscape' he affirms 'Soil is the part of the landscape that is less easily observed because it is below the surface. There exist however strong relations between the landscape that we see and the soil below. These relations exist because soil and landscape are affected by the same processes, and also because soils and landscape influence each other' [18]. In fact, these alterations define the spatial heterogeneity and the peculiarities. Therefore, the landscape is perceived in its diversity, even if this does not happen in a conscious way (**Figures 1–4**).

The discontinuity of edaphic factors contributes to the intriguing diversity of ecological patterns found in nature (**Figures 1–3**). Perception and spatial transformations are mutually linked and related to spatial arrangement in a symbiotic connection with soil shifting (**Figures 4** and **5**). They all combine to define the framework in which the discipline of landscape design stands and operates.

---

[1] Already at the beginning of 2000, Daniel Richter, a prominent soil scientist part of the Anthropocene Working Group, argued 'Humanity's expanding systems of food fiber, and water production are now entirely dependent on the management practiced on several billions of hectares of soil.' The Anthropocene Working Group (AWG) is an interdisciplinary research group dedicated to the study of the Anthropocene as a geological time unit supplementing the Holocene as first suggests by Paul Crutzen in 'Geology of Mankind' [4]—in which human activity shapes our planet more than nature itself.

[2] Art. 1 European Landscape Convention: "'Landscape' means an area, as perceived by people, whose character is the result of the action and interaction of natural and/or human factors" (Council of Europe, 2000).

[3] This relationship between landscape and soil transformation can also be traced backwards by following the evolutionary trajectory of the term, which ethimologically meant an action operated on a site—characterizing it—through soil manipulation. In the Latin matrix 'pays-age' the term 'pays' derives from the Latin 'pango', with the meaning of delimiting by sticking pegs. In the Germanic root, 'land-schaft' refers to 'land schaffen', with the meaning of transforming a terrain. Over time, the literal relevance has charged with cultural values, which basically denote an identifiable tract of land influenced by human activities (even if it is simply the act of viewing). As such, in this approach, landscape literally describes the state of altered land as distinct from virgin land before human influence, rather than referring to the subject matter of physical transformations operated on the ground.

Figure 1.
Soil in natural condition at 2000 mt high, Brenta Dolomite (Italy), 2020. Source: author.

Figure 2.
Soil in anthropization condition at 1500 mt high, Brenta Dolomite (Italy), 2020. Source: author.

Figure 3.
Portion of non-cultivated field in Ravenna (Italy), affected by soil salinization, 2020. Even if the visual effect can be suggestive, salinization is considered a degradation factor in terms of soil health. Source: author.

Figure 4.
Valli del Mezzano reclaimed land, Ferrara, Italy. This satellite view shows the geomorphological element (sandy ancient alluvial meander) beneath the surface, in contrast with agricultural field pattern, in relationship to different soil texture. Source: Google Earth.

By putting the soil shifting at the center of the design scene, soil becomes a matter that moves over time and space under the action of environmental flows and anthropic agents.

The re-thinking of soil shifting as a primer for landscape design praxis toward a more open-ended and dynamic conceptualization, does not only affect our understanding of landscape on a speculative way. It also calls for a revision of the very

Figure 5.
Critical coastal area (actual situation); design arrangement for dynamic shoreline stabilization. Source: author, from SECAP 2020 Ravenna Authors. SECAP Ravenna 2020.

methods and procedures, we use to plan and design the territory[4] [19–22]. From being a 'background' for the built environment, soil transformations become the 'foreground' or primary order both in landscape design praxis and in theoretical implications, by embedding the soil as a palimpsest[5] [23, 24] in reading and writing[6] [25] the landscape.

---

4 The concept of 'grounding morphology' emerges as the foreground, and the shaping praxis comes to define a common denominator between fundamental design aspects on several scales approaching territory to design. The most influential practitioners and theorists—in articulating and spreading the ideas of shaping landscape as a fundamental practice—are Charles Waldheim [19], James Corner [20] and Cristophe Girot [21, 22]. They do not directly refer to the word soil. They rather use 'terrain' [21], 'ground' [19, 20] and 'canvas' [22]. In many ways, these three concepts represent an extract of the original proposed research themes. Girot suggests to using a formal mathematical concept to think and design the landscape, by translating three-dimensional information into a two-dimensional surface (topology) [22]. For extension is reported a Girot's quote: 'Landscape is the canvas of multiple successive changes, and present-day modeling relates to this culture of change through sets of conventions and signs that eventually enable better choices on the terrain.' [22]

5 Literary a 'palimpsest' is a manuscript or piece of writing material on which later writing has been superimposed on effaced earlier writing. The term comes from the Greek 'palin psaomai' and means scraped again. This word has been borrowed in other areas to allegorically express the act of rewriting and reprogramming something. According to Paolà Viganò [23] 'The metaphor of the palimpsest alludes to the meeting/clash between different times, endless modifications and transformations.' There is great convergence on the figure of the palimpsest. Architects, urban planners, landscape designers, sociologists and naturally historians of the city all seem to agree on the usefulness of the metaphor of the territory (or land) as a palimpsest [23, 24].

6 In Ref. to James Corner suggestion in 'The Landscape Imagination' [25] "Landscape remains a profoundly imaginative project, requiring both a creative 'reading' and 'writing' of sites. [...] Here one might cite a movement from theory to practice, but it is more precise to recognize that both the writings and the designed works are in themselves projects, and they therefore share the same impulse: to project new possibilities for the field."

To make this effective, it is essential to have a systemic vision — made of visible and invisible connections — linked in an osmotic and symbiotic relationship that passes through soil envisioned as: a diaphragm, an environmental matrix, a project matter.

By proposing a critical rereading between theory and design praxis, the present investigation aims at improving the real impact of our disciplines on the topic.

3. Key to understanding, the soil as a living matter

The soil is an environmental matrix, formed by a highly variable mixture of minerals, organic matter, water, gas and microorganisms that interact with each other [2–4].

Richter [26] describes the soil as: 'the biomantle of unconsolidated material that makes life possible on planet Earth'. According to the researcher, soil is the hidden layer supporting our daily life. It is a great and extensive connective tissue, through which environmental networks spread and allow us to live our daily life as we imagine it today. The natural and the built environment are anchored to the ground through very complex relationships. The surface layer and the subsoil exchange matter, energy and information, in a sort of osmotic relation [27].

Soil-forming processes include atmospheric deposition of water, dust and solutes, mineral weathering, organic decomposition, pedoturbation, plant rooting, redox reactions, fire effects, chemical leaching and erosion. The combination of all these agents contributes to produce soil organic matter, organo-mineral complexes, secondary minerals, aggregates, clay skins, complex surface areas, soil pans and pore networks [26]. Many substances are stored, filtered and transformed in the soil including water, nutrients and carbon. Soil also provides a habitat for soil biota, and the preservation of its biodiversity is essential for maintaining processes and functions—like nutrient cycling, decomposition and bioturbation—thereby for maintaining a flow of ecosystem services[7] [1, 28, 29].

In this regard, in ecology, soil is considered the central processing unit of the Earth's environment [30].[8]

With humanity being nowadays the Earth's primary geomorphic agent, the quality of human life and the earth's environment have never been more related to soil management than it does today[9] [19, 27, 28, 33].

7 Some ecosystem services [29] provided by soils [1, 28] include producing adequate quantities of nutritious and safe food, feed, fiber and other biomass for industries; storing and purifying water, regulating flows, recharging aquifers and reducing the impact of droughts and floods, thereby helping adaptation to climate change; capturing carbon from the atmosphere and reducing emission of greenhouse gases from soils, thereby contributing to climate mitigation; nutrient cycling supporting crop productivity and reducing contamination; preserving and protecting biodiversity by preserving habitats both above and within the soil; supporting the quality of our landscapes and greening of our towns and cities.

8 On the institutional level, the definition of the soil is not univocal [31, 32]. In the following pages we will talk about soil, meaning the thin porous and biologically active medium that represents 'the top layer of the earth's crust, formed by mineral particles, organic matter, water, air and living organisms. It is the interface between earth, air and water and hosts most of the biosphere.' [32], that can sustain the life of plants, characterized by its own flora and fauna and by a particular water economy.

9 The importance of soil protection is now recognized in international policy programs—such as AGENDA 2030, (SDGs ONU, 2015) or international scientific report, such as the Special Report on Climate Change and Land drafted by IPCC [19], the Report of the Mission Board for Soil health and food [24] drawn up by the EU [20] and FAO's report [33].

The President of the European Society for Soil Conservation, José Luis Rubio, thus clarifies the importance of soil in relation to major global challenges, echoing that 'Soil is a crucial link between global environmental problems such as climate change, water management and biodiversity loss' [34].

The new challenge facing soil science is how to create a policy to address its health[10] embracing the whole system instead of single soil properties or processes [1, 31]. As first conclusion, the value of soil as an element of planning and design [21, 22][11] lies in handling live and dynamic physical matter.

Soil is the vibrant matter that we interpret and draw up. Soil is alive and in continuous exchange. On very distant time horizons the soil itself compose and recompose its history and so ours.

4. The moving horizons approach

Starting from the proved correspondence between the soil transformation and landscape evolution, the approach named moving horizons has been traced for

- Increasing awareness, by exceeding human-sight sensing boundary and involving new spatiality across over-layered depths;
- Addressing the design workflow, in manipulating and transferring matter for performative grounds;
- Orientating the attitude in managing complexity, through a non-deterministic approach encompassing new parameters across the time-framed process.

The moving horizon approach implicitly criticizes traditional landscape practice's seemingly uncritical reproduction of stereotypical 'aestheticized' images.[12] It is not a question of rejecting or abandoning a formal and compositional language, but rather of encouraging a view that favors investigation and observation of reality in its different stratifications offered by embedding the soil as a palimpsest in 'reading' and 'writing' the landscape (**Figures 6–8**) [25].

The proposed approach is not a mere conceptual overcoming in a speculative sphere. It is rather presented as the attempt to concretely express the linkage between fixity and mutability features, capable of transcending the idea of still image. The horizon here is the line of the visible, a recognizable layer of soil and a time-framed process.

---

[10] The soil health is considered as the most important, functional characteristic of any soil ecosystem service. The soil unhealth expresses its degradation.

[11] As evidenced by Girot on one hand 'This lack of understanding about terrain is quite typical of our modern age and has been detrimental to landscape in general, where it is always assumed that a site can be made flat to assume a program' [22]. On the other hand, Girot continues 'Understanding territorial continuity physically helps to better identify qualitative priorities in a landscape' [22].

[12] Over time the landscape appreciation has evolved. As we have seen through several examples from Corner [20, 36, 37], Belanger [38], Sjimons [39] and many others, contemporary landscape design approach is moving away from the ancient, controlled and Arcadian image, and it is embracing this new process framework of design.

Figure 6.
Ravenna pedological units, used at the basis for understanding territorial asset and geo-pedological continuity. Source: Emilia Romagna GIS open source, author re-elaboration.

Figure 7.
Analysis vocation, reference pattern synthesis in south coast area, used as reference for landscape evolution. Source: SECAP Ravenna 2020.

Figure 8.
Ravenna geomorphological units and isophreatic, used at the basis for understanding territorial underground asset and geomorphological continuity. Source: Emilia Romagna GIS open source, author re-elaboration.

The thesis methodology can be described as deductive process headed to set a model based on research by design. In this regard, research stand as 'development of new knowledge' and design as a 'counterintuitive thinking' [35].

The aim is to assist designers, scholars, and professionals involved in territorial transformations, as well as decision-makers, by elaborating and visualizing prospective landscape shifting on several scales.

5. Approaching planning and design scale

The mapping and visualization of data in design culture has changed both in relationship with the advancement of technology [19]—in bringing about the possibility of greater proximity between the real and its representation—and in the way of building landscape idea. The trajectory of representation—of concept and context—has moved from the material and physical description of the ground toward the depiction of unseen and often immaterial fields, forces and flows.

Moving horizons is an advance for mapping, manipulating, and designing with geospatial gaze, with the goal of transcending the flat[13] [19, 21, 22], static map into live documents that expand the representation of time and space—in order to better address the dynamic conditions for landscape project. The attempt is to develop a method capable of building a coherent relationship between planning and design scale, according to soil transformations.

The value of soil as spatial planning matrix lies in situating the parts in relation to the whole, by laying out the physical and spatial relationships at the dimension of a territory (mainly hydrogeological components both on surface both underground). The value of soil as design element lies in handling the physical dynamic matter, by preparing the ground across highly contextualized actions in terms of soil shape, coverage and composition.

Therefore, the interpretation of soil as a palimpsest[14] [30] requires a critical comparison between: (1) the pre-existing structural and perceptual hydrogeological arrangement to identify the valuable components and the main issues; (2) the current planning framework according to their systemic inclusion; (3) a diachronic and synchronic analysis of the territorial transformations according to plan predictions [40], to define management, requalification and valorization criteria starting from the critical points; (4) understanding about paleo-climates, biota, geomorphology, changes in geologic substrates and soil residence times; (5) incorporate ecological dynamicity, connecting biological, hydrological and pedological processes.

6. A first application: Ravenna Climate Change Adaptation Plan

A first application of this approach has been developed and tested in the Ravenna Climate Change Adaptation Plan [41, 42] (**Figures 5** and **6**), by identifying a planning procedure capable of integrating territorial adaptation measures to climate change through an approach based on soil's understanding and processing as fundamentals.

The whole research project for Ravenna assumes that climate change projections can only be described in probabilistic terms and over long-time horizons[15] [43–48].

Extreme events linked to climate change sometimes evolve at a speed that is difficult to manage with the current tools of planning. This may require anticipating the complexity of uncertainty by imagining the future through scenarios (**Figures 9–11**), relied on the comparative analysis of exploratory meta-projects stage. In such perspective, the two main attitudes explored deal with alternative perspectives on the soil management and transformation.

[13] According to Richter [30]: 'Understanding soils as polygenetic palimpsests requires much more understanding about paleo-climates, biota, geomorphology, changes in geologic substrates, and soil residence e times. While we can read the basics of many soils, we are far from understanding soil as an archive, and must realize that at some level the soil may always remain at least a bit shrouded in mystery.'

[14] For global sea level rise forecasts, reference data shall be based on studies from the Fifth IPCC Assessment Report [43] with time reference to 2100. These forecasts have been translated at a regional scale by ENEA [44], which estimated how many and which areas will be below sea level, and which are at risk of sea ingression [45–47].

[15] For climate data, Climate Projection Data Sheets 2021–2050 have been produced for homogeneous areas in the Emilia Romagna Region as part of the Regional Strategy for Mitigation and Adaptation to Climate Change, together with the ARPAE Climate Observatory and ART-ER [48].

Figure 9.
SCENARIO TRANSFER 2050. Aerial view for Landscape evolution in Ravenna Climate Change Adaptation Plan 2020. Authors. SECAP Ravenna 2020.

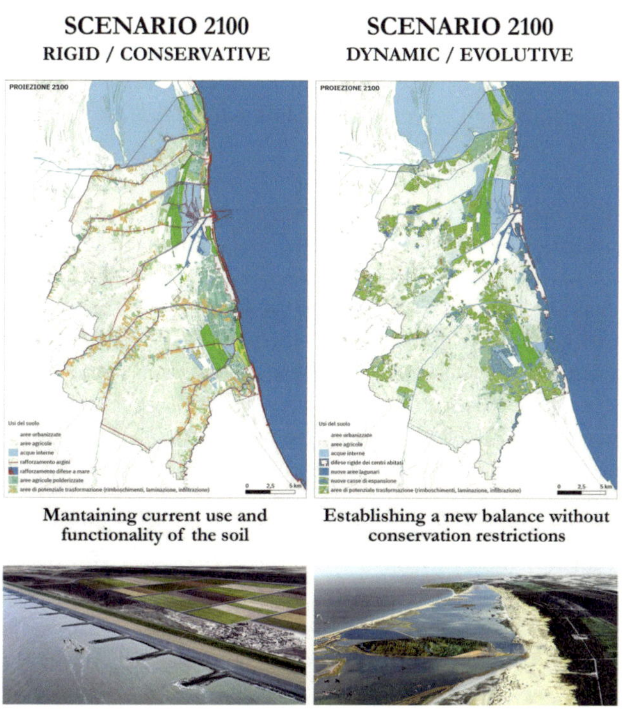

Figure 10.
Scenario's Reference: Preserving land use or accommodating geomorphological characteristics? Representation of the two phases of the adaptation strategy and the long-term projections summarized in the 'rigid' and 'soft' scenarios at 2100 (south coast area). Source: SECAP Ravenna 2020.

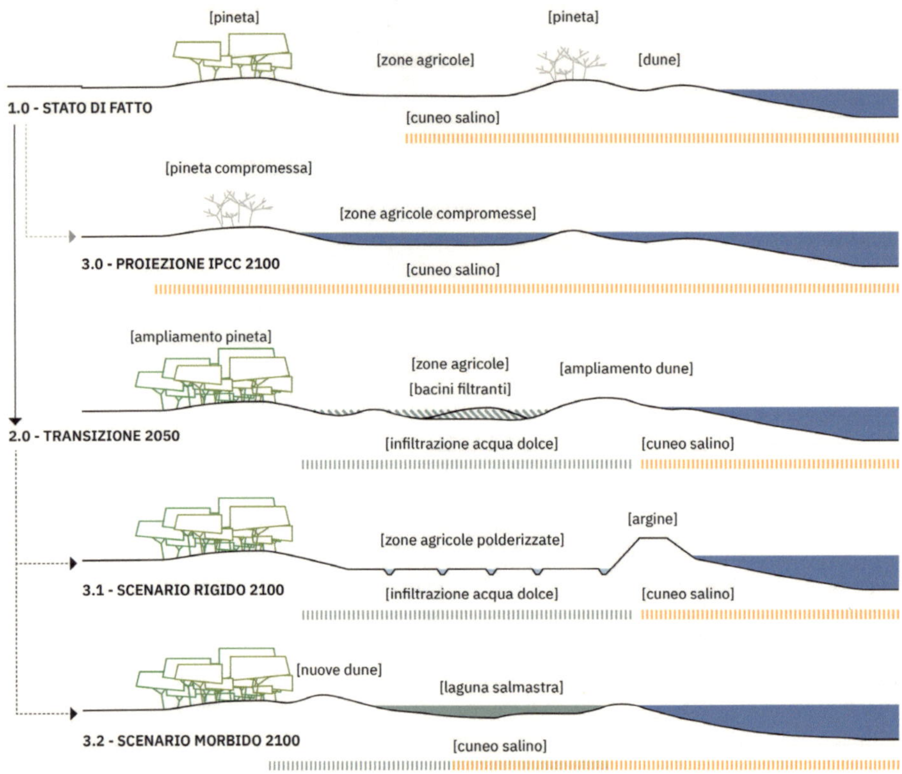

Figure 11.
Scenarios comparison through schematic section in south coastal area for landscape evolution in Ravenna Climate Change Adaptation Plan 2020. Authors. SECAP Ravenna 2020.

In a future Rigid Scenario, the priority of defending inhabited and productive areas aimed at maintaining soil use and functionality. Instead, the dynamic one landscape transformations addressed to establish a new balance between human and environmental systems, by assuming geomorphology as a referential state for soil-forming. The resultant synthesis—scenario transfer (**Figures 5**, **9**, **12** and **13**)—allows to represent in a more direct and better communicable way to the outside the consequences and the presuppositions of some actions on the territory.

The synthesis between these two long-run perspectives—both plausible in terms of scenario thinking [49]—results in an intermediate strategy, to be developed in the next few years, open to alternative futures.

The soil is strategically transformed into levels of essential infrastructures for an organic vision of the territory, capable of evolving in the space–time relationship. Thus, it acquires a new role following the international focus of adaptation to global challenges.

This step brings out the interdependence between spatial, anthropogenic, environmental and ecosystem aspects of the context, and how from these relationships arises the complexity of the city-territory system to which it refers, by considering soil as a primer in territorial arrangement. By analyzing this information through the cartographic study of biophysical and geospatial systems (geomorphology, topography, soil composition, etc.) (**Figures 6–8**), they have been reworked in the maps presented in the research and synthesized in some GIS cartographies through mapping overlay process.

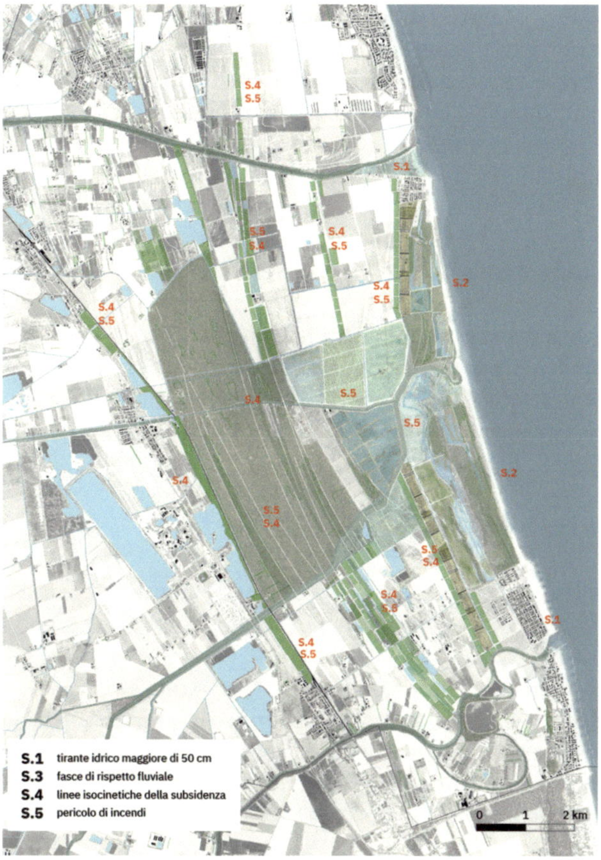

Figure 12.
Scenario transfer 2050, South coastal area focus. Cartographic landscape evolution in Ravenna Climate Change Adaptation Plan 2020, supported by the geomorphological reshape and soil coverage. Authors. SECAP Ravenna 2020.

Figure 13.
Scenario transfer 2050, South coastal area focus. Aerial view for landscape evolution in Ravenna Climate Change Adaptation Plan 2020, supported by the geomorphological reshape and soil coverage. Authors. SECAP Ravenna 2020.

The evidence of this process lies in the identification of the transformation bands suitable to host interventions to increase resilient infrastructures and naturalness in those zones of friction between risks exposure, soil vocation and pressures, pointed out in the reference pattern outlined in the analytical phase (**Figures** 7 and **12**).

The related actions, as well as the overall approach, can be summarized in the propositions presented in the next paragraph in the form of a landscape manifesto.

7. A landscape manifesto

The strategy we have utilized in outlining the manifesto is the result of an effort to describe, in a simplified and understandable way, the soil as an emerging component of landscape complexity toward design praxis. Each statement is also inspired by the critical reading of transdisciplinary literature of prominent authors that are reported for each related point of the manifesto.

7.1 Screening the landscape imagery

Screening the landscape imagery since the landscape is not a passive scene anymore but is in fact an active working system connected to the human habitat, which it also supports [12, 13, 18, 21, 50–52].

The territorial structure is subject to a constant evolution, and so the aspect we perceive. Its components of fixity or dynamism are related to the vision and sharing of values that redefine the relationships between the parts in a logic of necessity. Visions that change in time along with the conformation that the territory are involved in an ongoing adaptation process that passes through the soil.

7.2 Crossing layer

Crossing layer refers to sharing information among manifold depths [52–56].

Landscape evolution does not proceed with regular continuity but is presented as a series of steps in height, age, value and size. The ability to driving decisions passes through the comprehension, codification and contextualization of those signs, signals and related meaning. Therefore, the model implies a series of steps that should bring to outline compressed and decompressed information that crosses the ground depths.

7.3 Crossing time

Crossing time refers to a diachronic and synchronic analysis of the territorial transformations according to plan predictions [57, 58].

In dynamic systems, we can only study and predict some behaviors of this process, but the real consequence can only be forecasted. The predictability is sensitive to initial conditions, and beyond a certain time it can no longer be predictable. Complexity of a system is not an internal characteristic, and it can only be analyzed and represented across time horizons.

7.4 Crossing scale

Because landscapes themselves are spatially heterogeneous entities, their structure, function and dynamics are scale dependent [20, 37, 59].

Scale generally refers to the spatial–temporal dimensions in which organisms, patterns or processes are recognizable. A worthwhile perspective can represent these different scales not as a nested hierarchy, but assuming the concept of multiscale. In this concept the global scale is not placed above the local one, but rather each scale is present and operates at the same time.

7.5 Building geography

We should interpret design as a geographic agent that is still focused on the physical configuration of human occupation of the ground [38, 57, 60].

The proposed approach foresees to first understand how natural processes and peculiarities, coupled with mankind activities, have contributed to mutually building geography, in terms of shaping territory and landscape, as the effects between these two forces, although reflexive to the spatially transcendent systems of flows and processes. Landscape design presupposes a reliable level of awareness in managing the aforementioned agents and a certain care about the consequences of the transformation impressed in a specific site by anthropic activities.

7.6 Grounding metabolism

Grounding metabolism suggests the need for a more explicit and systematic exploration of the geographical imprint of metabolic processes [60–63].

It interprets urban metabolism as an inherently geographic condition, investigating the possibility for a redefinition of the design context in a manner that can grasp both the fluidity of metabolic processes and their geographical engraving on the earth and soil, reshaping landscape. It builds upon an understanding of a contemporary design context that is not merely being upscaled but is in constant circulation through the weaving together of a multiplicity of variegated geographies.

7.7 Resetting spatiality

Every spatial arrangement is the product of structural information [12, 64–66].

Information has been considered as a basic property of the universe like energy and matter. Information refers to order, structure and organization. Moving materials and debris from one place to another for maintaining the status of human habitat means reshaping topography and creating new processes that lead to the creation of new topological and ecological patterns.

7.8 Shaping action

Design is envisioned as a series of actions that intentionally induce spatial alterations with the aim of putting in place a clear form of evolution [20, 22, 68].

The project is intended as a precise and sophisticated tool able to synthesize agents and complexities generating an alteration of place, and which the place itself will be able to metabolize through time and space. One has not to look for an appreciable formal composition in a still image, but rather has to seek the connections and relationships between the elements that make up a landscape, of visible and invisible components. Soil is the physical dynamic matter influencing these transformations.

7.9 From fragment to framework

Starting from the resolution of local issues through environmental specificities, soil is proposed as catalyst element involved in situating the parts in relation with the whole. The spatial configuration of contemporary territories is pervaded by the figure of the fragment and the dispersion. Reframing the soil as a palimpsest provides to detect the matrix of structural transformations approaching territorial scale to neighborhood unit. Thus, the fragments become framework components for a structure of connections, strategically transformed into levels of essential infrastructures as a qualification for an organic vision of the territory, capable of evolving in the space–time relationship by defining a direction of change [20, 21, 37, 69].

7.10 Processing possible reality

Processing possible reality affords the greater proximity to what exists and what is yet to come. In replacing natural dynamism and features, landscape design praxis should be addressed to take care of the impact of moving materials and energy flows and to analyze the design effects through several assessment scenarios. Simulating a field of possibilities offers the greatest closeness to the manifestation and manipulation of the ground itself, making the landscape present and vivid, as it exists and as it could be [19, 49].

8. Conclusions

As main conclusion, the study of literary sources combined with the study of concrete practical examples constitutes the basis for elaborating on the research objective and research questions toward an argued theory, which is not based on rigid consistency but on correspondences. The result is not the proof of a theorem but the discovery of an unexpected point of view.

The landscape design tries to interpret the contemporary needs in updating and adapting the territories to new challenges. The aim is to drive these values into the future by increasing the level of compatibility between the evolution of the human habitat and the maintenance of nature's regeneration times toward a novel esthetic.

The research offers a comprehensive and detailed overview on the topic without finalizing the debate on it. The lack of a specific bibliography and the high interdisciplinarity of the topic—landscape and soil—leads to this effort of creating a new approach, able to bring innovative contributions. For a matter of time and possibilities, the argument cannot be completed or ended but can be highly implemented both in speculative terms and in landscape design praxis.

Moving from theoretical frameworks to operational approaches is, however, still a challenge, for a number of issues, and one has to be aware that there are also difficulties for designers who want to conduct research by design. From an operative point of view, it can be deployed on more case studies in combination with parametric programs, and the interpolation of soil data could bring to design implementation and more effective and realistic forecasting in territorial transformation. Otherwise, the soil data and information basis are often not adequate—or it is at insufficient resolution, or it is contradictive—and the simulation tools that can be used to test the design hypotheses are not always as much reliable as needed.

Even if the recognition of the multifunctionality of soil was already present in the definition of soil quality, the difficulty of finding indicators able to describe this complexity remains a critical issue. Since soil data and simulation tools are constantly developed and their reliability is continually improved, their value for design hypothesis testing within research by design continuously increases.

The framework is flexible, in defining indicators and in calculating them. It can be used at different spatial scales and is capable to integrate new knowledge when available. In this view this framework opens new avenues for more research by design in the academic field of landscape architecture and environmental design in the future.

Nevertheless, for further implementation, William Bryant Logan work 'Dirt, the ecstatic skin of the Earth' [5] remains a good inspiration for those who are approaching to the topic: "We spend our lives hurrying away from the real, as though it were deadly to us. 'It must be up there somewhere on the horizon,' we think. And all the time it is in the soil, right beneath our feet."

Acknowledgements

The work presented is an excerpt from the PhD's thesis work of Vittoria Mencarini. The work concerning the SECAP of Ravenna represents only an application of the methodology elaborated during the development of the thesis. All the authors took part in this work as well as Lorenzo Tinti and Beatrice Magagnoli, from University of Ferrara (Italy). This work would not have been possible without the help, guidance and support provided by many individuals I have had the pleasure of getting acquainted with over the course of the thesis. In particular we would like to extend my gratitude to the following people for their contribution in transferring the results of my research into effective impacts: Dott.ssa Luana Gasparini, responsible of Educational Environment Office in the Municipality of Ravenna; Dott.ssa Laura Prometti, geologist, management staff CBR (Consorzio di Bonifica della Romagna); Dott. Massimiliano Costa, biologist, Director of 'Delta del Po' Park; Dott. Paolo Mannini, agronomist, General Director of CER (Canale Emiliano Romagnolo); Dott. Simone D'Acunto, biologist, Director of CESTHA (Centro Sperimentale per la Tutela degli Habitat); Dott. Luciano Vogli, enviromental scientist, researcher at CIRI EA (Interdepartmental Centre for Industrial Research on Energy and Environment) University of Bologna.

Since July 2021, Vittoria Mencarini has been working at the Municipality of Ravenna, as designer and building site director in Naturalistic Area office. She is also in charge to the SECAP dissemination and implementation. This work allows her to carry on applied research on the topic and to transfer the result of PhD thesis into reality.

Conflict of interest

The authors declare no conflict of interest.

Author details

Vittoria Mencarini*, Luca Emanueli and Gianni Lobosco
University of Ferrara, Ferrara, Italy

*Address all correspondence to: vittoria.mencarini@unife.it

References

[1] Adhikari K, Hartemink AE. Linking soil to ecosystem services - A global review. Geoderma. 2016;**262**:101-111

[2] Markewitz D, Richter DD. Understanding Soil Changes, Soil Sustainability over Millennia, Centuries, and Decades. 2007th ed. Cambridge: Cambridge University Press; 2001

[3] Richter DD. humanity's transformation of earth's soil: Pedology's New Frontier. Soil Science. 2007;**112**(12):957-067

[4] Paul J. Crutzen publish year: 2002 geology of mankind. Nature. 2002;**415**(6867):23. DOI: 10.1038/415023a

[5] Logan WB. The Ecstatic Skin of the Earth. Reprint ed. New York, USA: W W Norton & Co Inc.; 2017

[6] Antrop M. Geography and landscape science. In: Klijn JA, Vos W, editors. From Landscape Ecology to Landscape Science. Wageningen: Kluwer Academic; 2000. pp. 9-35

[7] Antrop M, Van Eetvelde V. Territory and/or scenery: Concepts and prospects of Western landscape research. In: Mueller L, Eulenstein F, editors. Current Trends in Landscape Research. Cham, Switzerland: Springer; 2019. pp. 3-39

[8] Gibelli, G. (2008). Paesaggio e Paesaggi: tante definizioni per una parola sola. In C. Teofili, & R. Clarino, Riconquistare il Paesaggio. La Convenzione Europea del Paesaggio e la conservazione della Biodiversità in Italia (pp. 108-123). Roma: WWF Italia ONG ONLUS, Ministero dell'Istruzione, dell'Università e della Ricerca.

[9] Zagari F. Questo è paesaggio. 48 definizioni. Roma: Mancosu Editore; 2006

[10] Forman RT, Godron M. Landscape Ecology. Hoboken: John Wiley and Sons; 1986

[11] Naveh Z, Lieberman AS. Landscape Ecology, Theory and Application. New York: Springer-Verlag; 1990. DOI: 10.1007/978-1-4757-4082-0

[12] Farina A. The landscape as a semiotic interface between organisms and resources. Biosemiotics. 2008;**1**:75-83

[13] Farina A. Ecology, Cognition and Landscape. Dordrecht: Springer; 2010

[14] Farinelli F. Geografia. Un'introduzione ai modelli del mondo. Milano: Einaudi; 2003

[15] Council of Europe. European Landscape Convention. Florence: European Commission; 2000

[16] Assunto R. Il paesaggio e l'estetica. Palermo: Novecento; 1994

[17] Jakob M. Il paesaggio. Bologna: Il Mulino; 2009

[18] Finke, P. (2016). Soil and Landscape. In: S. Northcliff (A cura di), Task Force: Soil Matters - Solutions Under Foot (p. 8-10). Reiskirchen, Germany: Catena Verlag.

[19] Waldheim C, Desmini J. Cartographic Grounds: Projecting the Landscape Imaginary. New York: Princeton Architectural Press; 2016

[20] Corner J. Terra fluxus. In: Waldheim C, editor. The Landscape Urbanism Reader. New York: Princetown Architectural Press. 2006

[21] Girot C. Immanent Landscape. Vol. 36. Cambridge, MA: Harvard Design Magazine; 2013. pp. 6-16

[22] Girot C. The elegance of topology. In: Girot C, editor. Landscript 3. Topology. Topical Thought on the Contemporary Landscape. Berlin: Jovis; 2013. pp. 79-115

[23] Viganò P. Palimpsest metaphor: Figures and spaces of the contemporary project. Urban Planning. 2020;**5**(2):167-171

[24] Secchi B. Progetto di suolo. Casabella. 1986;**520**:19-24

[25] Corner J, Bick Hirsch A. The Landscape Imagination, Collected essays of James Corner 1990-2010. New York: Princeton Architectural Press; 2011

[26] Richter DD. The changing model of soil - Revisited. Soil Science of America Journal. 2012;**76**:766-778

[27] IPCC Intergovernmental Panel on Climate Change. Climate Change and Land. In: IPCC Intergovernmental Panel on Climate Change. Geneve: IPCC Press; 2019

[28] Commission, E. Caring for Soil is Caring for Life, Mission Board for Soil health and food. Brussels: European Commission; 2020

[29] MEA Millennium Ecosystem Assessment. Ecosystems and human well-being: Current state and trends findings of the condition and trends. In: Working Group Millennium Ecosystem Assessment. Washington: Island Press; 2005

[30] Richter D, Bacon A, Brecheisen Z, Mobley M. Soil in the Anthropocene. Environmental. Science. 2015;**25**

[31] FAO Food and Agriculture Organization. World Reference Base for Soil Resources. International Soil Classification System for Naming Soils. Rome: FAO; 2014

[32] ISPRA Istituto Superiore per la Ricerca e la Protezione Ambientale. L'italia perde terreno. Il consumo di suolo e il degrado del territorio. Rome: ISPRA; 2011

[33] FAO, & ITPS. Status of the World's Soil Resources. Rome: FAO; 2015

[34] Rubio. Soil, the forgotten resource [Internet]. 2010. Available from: Soil — The forgotten resource — European Environment Agency (europa.eu)

[35] Roggema R. Research by design: Proposition for a methodological approach. Urban Science. 2017;**1**(1):1-19

[36] Corner J. Recovering Landscape. New York: Princeton Architectural Press; 1999

[37] Corner J, MacLean A. Taking Measure Across the American Landscape. London: Yale University Press; 1996

[38] Belanger P. Landscape as Infrastructure. London: Routledge; 2016

[39] Sijmons D, Hugtenburg J, Feddes F, Van Hoorn A. Landscape and Energy: Designing Transition. Rotterdam: Nai Uitgevers Publisher; 2014

[40] Abbruzzese L, Mencarini V. Moving into Peri-urban Mosaics. Building Resilient Relationships Along the Margins: The Green System Plan of Ravenna for a New Liveability in Refraiming Urban Resilience Implementation. Barcellona: Published: 17 December 2018 by MDPI in IFoU 2018: Reframing Urban Resilience Implementation: Aligning Sustainability and Resilience session Urban Design and Management: Infrastructures and Services. DOI: 10.3390/IFOU2018-05957

[41] Comune di Ravenna. PAESC: Piano d'Ezione per l'Energia Sostenibile e il Clima. Adattamento. 2022. Available

from: https://www.comune.ra.it/aree-tematiche/ambiente-e-animali/ambiente-e-territorio/strumenti-di-gestione-ambientale/paes-piano-dazione-per-lenergia-sostenibile/

[42] Lobosco G, Mencarini V. "Landscape and climate change. A resilient strategy for the adaption plan of the Ravenna area in Italy", in the international review Convergencias, Journal of Research and Arts Education, edited by Escola Superior de Artes Aplicadas (Portugal) – published on the 30 of November 2020. 2020

[43] IPCC Intergovernmental Panel on Climate Change. Ocean and Cryosphere in a Changing Climate. Geneve: IPCC Press; 2019

[44] ENEA Agenzia nazionale per le nuove tecnologie, l'energia e lo sviluppo economico sostenibile. ENEA Eventi Cambiamenti climatici e variazioni del livello del Mar Mediterraneo. Roma: Edizioni ENEA; 2018

[45] Perini L, Calabrese L, Luciani P. Rischi costieri da mareggiata in Emilia Romagna e analisi scenari futuri. In: Oral Presentation at 1st National Workshop on Climate Change and Sea Level Rise in the Mediterranean Sea, 5th–6th July 2018, Regione Emilia Romagna. Roma: Servizio geologico sismico e dei suoli; 2018

[46] Antonioli F, Anzidei M, Amorosi A, Lo Presti V, Mastronuzzi G, Deiana G, et al. Sea-level rise and potential drowning of the Italian coastal plains: Flooding risk scenarios for 2100. Quaternary Science Reviews. 2017;**158**:29-43

[47] Presti VL. Risalita relativa del livello del mare, proiezioni sulla vulnerabilità ed erosione. Mappe con scenari di rischio allagamento previsto al 2100. In: Oral Presentation at 1st National Workshop on Climate Change and Sea Level Rise in the Mediterranean Sea, 5th–6th July 2018. Rome; 2018

[48] ARPAE. Proiezioni climatiche in Emilia-Romagna. 2020. Available from: https://www.arpae.it/it/temi-ambientali/clima/previsioni-e-proiezioni/proiezioni-climatiche

[49] Di Giulio R, Emanueli L, Lobosco G. Scenarios' evaluation by design, un approccio per scenari al tema della resilienza. Techne. 2018;**15**:92-100

[50] Doherty G, Waldheim C. Is Landscape...? Essay on the Identity of Landscape. New York: Routledge; 2016

[51] Laureano P. The Water Atlas, Traditional Knowledge to Combat Desertification. Torino: Bollati Boringhieri; 2001

[52] Panzini F. Progettare la Natura. Bologna: Zanichelli; 2005

[53] McHarg I. Design with Nature. Garden City, N.Y: American Museum of Natural History [by] the Natural History Press; 1969

[54] Corboz A. The Land as a Palimpsest. Diogenes. 1983;**31**(121):12-34

[55] Gustavson K. Is landscape... philosophy? In: Doherty G, Waldheim C, editors. Is Landscape...? Essay on the Identity of Landscape. New York: Routledge; 2016

[56] Belanger P. Altitudes of urbanization. In: Sterling R, Bobylev N, editors. Urban Underground Space: A growing imperative, perspective and current research in planning and design for underground space use -Tunnelling and Underground Space Technology. Pierre Bélanger, Altitudes of urbanization, Tunnelling and Underground Space Technology. Elsevier. 2016;**55**:5-7.

ISSN 0886-7798. DOI: 10.1016/j.tust.2015.09.011. Available from: https://www.sciencedirect.com/science/article/pii/S0886779815300134

[57] Laureano P. La Piramide Rovesciata, il Modello dell'Oasi per il Pianeta Terra. Torino: Bollati Boringhieri; 2013

[58] Capra F. The Web of Life: A New Understanding of Living Systems. New York: Anchor Books; 1996

[59] Farina A. Principles and Methods in Landscape Ecology. 2nd ed. Dordrecht: Springer; 1998

[60] Ibanez D, Katsikis N. Grounding metabolism. In: Ibanez D, Katsikis N, editors. New Geographies - Grounding Metabolism. Vol. 06. Cambridge MA: Harvard University Press; 2014. pp. 2-9

[61] Farinelli F. L'invenzione della Terra. Palermo: Sellerio Editore; 2007

[62] Odum HT. Environment, Power and Society. New York: Wiley-Interscience; 1971

[63] Izard TG. Regenerative Empathy: Complex Assemblages in a Shared Environment. Cambridge: Harvard University; 2019

[64] Hobbs RJ, Arico S, Aronson J, Baron J, Bridgewater P, Cramer V, et al. Novel Ecosystems: Theoretical and management aspects of the new ecological world order. Global Ecology and Biogeography. 2006;**15**:1-7

[65] Ellis EC. Ecologies of the anthropocene: Global upscaling of social-ecological infrastructures. Katsikis DI, A cura di. New Geographies - Grounding Metabolism. 2014);Vol. 06. pp. 20-27

[66] Clement G. Piccola pedagogia dell'erba. Riflessioni sul giardino planetario. Jones L., A cura di. Roma: Derive Approdi. 2015

[67] Naveh Z. The Total Human Ecosystem: Integrating Ecology and economics. Bioscience. 2000;**50**(4):357-361

[68] Lister NM, Reed C. Ecology and design: Parallel genealogies. Places Journal. 17 Feb 2023. DOI: 10.22269/140414

[69] Forman RT. Ecology and Planning Beyond the City. Cambridge: Cambridge University Press; 2008

Chapter 7

Perspectives and Application of Land Use Management Strategies to Address Mangrove Ecosystem Degradation in Guyana: A Case Study of Mon Repos

Linda Johnson-Bhola

Abstract

Destruction and threats to coastal mangrove ecosystems have been a perennial problem for policy-makers in Guyana. The problem is due in part to the erosion cycles, spontaneous infrastructure development and environmental degradation. To address these multiple issues, the National Mangrove Project Office employed several different strategies, including public awareness programmes. Despite the efforts, the issues continue to plague the country. The aim of this paper was to illustrate the efficacy of zoning and regionalization for combating the problems associated with mangrove ecosystem degradation at Mon Repos, East Coast Demerara. A survey of the literature and analysis of selected documents were done and ArcGIS Pro and remote sensing were applied to the case study. The results showed that while efforts could undoubtedly have a positive impact on mangroves at Mon Repos in terms of sustaining ecosystem services, facilitating livelihood opportunities and addressing the waste management issue, the effectiveness of such actions is likely to be impeded by the lack of real-time data. To adequately address these issues, the collection and use of more accurate and up-to-date scientific from the application of Geographic Information System and Remote Sensing and implementation of a multiple-use conservation zoning plan are among the strategies recommended for implementation.

Keywords: mangrove ecosystem, degradation, land use management strategies, geographic information system, remote sensing

1. Introduction

Land use has long sustained human societies, but its ecological consequences have been diverse and sometimes opposing, both degrading and enriching soils and affecting and shaping habitats [1, 2]. In the first half of the twentieth century, attempts to understand land use regulation and management and concomitant changes were restricted to the application of theories and models that emphasized the allocation of land for complementary purposes. For instance, the theories and models associated with urban and rural land use, such as those postulated by Harris & Ullman, Hoyt, Burgess and Von Thunen [3] focused on arranging land uses around and radiating outwards from the Central Business District (CBD). However, these theories and models have been limited in scope and application, especially in terms of some of the very restrictive assumptions under which they were constructed. Each theory allocated certain land uses in proximity to industries, adjacent to low-income areas and promoted spatial and social segregation. Land use management generally refers to the implementation of any measure that regulates the use or a change in the form or function of land to achieve stated objectives. However, in circumstances where there is a failure to satisfactorily address a range of social, urban and community, and environmental issues conflicts emerge among various groups and degradation to the natural physical environment and ecosystems results [3, 4].

Briassoulis [1] noted that it is important to reconcile and integrate three epistemological approaches to determine land use and change. These are: (i) inductive approach—to observe and describe to understand; (ii) deductive approach—to model to understand; and (iii) dialectic approach—to integrate to understand. These traditions were first proffered by the Brundtland Commission Report of 1987 [5]. Further emphasis has been placed at the time when there was almost universal concern about global environmental change resulting in a significant number of research and policy initiatives worldwide, especially after the Rio Summit in 1992 [6]. Policy issues, for examples, have emerged from research initiatives undertaken by the FAO, the European Environment Agency (EEA) as well as the United Nations which focused on the Conventions on Climate Change (UNFCCC), Desertification (UNCCD), and Biological Diversity (UNCBD). Land use changes in various physiographic and administrative regions, including coastal areas, soon became recognized as a significant component of the global environmental system.

Over the past few decades, the management of land use, including coastal ecosystems became a popular talking point among planners and policy-makers and concerted efforts have since been made to integrate geospatial models and the use of technologies to have a deeper insight into the issues surrounding land use change and better understanding of the various management strategies to employ for addressing land use [7–9]. Land use now focuses on incorporating the models and technologies for both extensive and intensive land management initiatives. The use of Geographic Information System (GIS) and Remote Sensing (RS) in land use management has therefore reshaped global patterns of biodiversity, ecosystems, and landscapes planning and management [2, 10].

The degree of efficiency of such practice has resulted in some instances of orderly arrangement of land uses, protection of the natural environment and ecosystems, reduction in pollution and promotion of good health and well-being of various populations worldwide [9, 11, 12]. It does not mean that the practice is without shortcomings also, especially in the absence of stringent regulatory frameworks and prudent fiscal management systems. This has been recognized by the many issues with the land selection process, resulting in conflicts among various land and resource users [12]. According to the Canadian Institute of Planners [13] and Pelling [14], failure to effectively regulate land use leads to deterioration of physical, economic, social, and environmental conditions. These conditions, in turn, affect ecosystems and the services they provide.

In Guyana, some practices associated with land use do not often address key elements of ecosystems management [15, 16]. Planning decisions for managing the fragile coastal ecosystems, for instance, have been very limited because of the lack of or insufficient accurate and up-to-date scientific data on several interconnected elements including land use, biodiversity, and coastal dynamics (tidal movements, ocean currents and sediment cycles) and anthropogenic activities. These phenomena are now strongly influenced by climate variability and climate change and population growth rate demand for land, especially among the poorer sections of society.

A fundamental starting point for confronting coastal land use and ecosystems management issues is to understand how the dynamics of land use planning interact with urban and rural systems and resource users in the ever-changing coastal environment. This can only be understood and appreciated with the aid of some geospatial applications and the requisite technical skills to interpret the data. Too often decision-makers and planners in the country view land use management as a transient phenomenon and do not appreciate its value for sustainable coastal ecosystems management. For this reason, development activities have been expanding and accelerating in areas for which no land use plan exists, mangroves are destroyed to facilitate industrial and other developments and livelihood activities, and indiscriminate disposal of domestic and industrial effluent in mangrove areas is widespread [17–19]. The absence of land use plans is a recipe for incompatible land use because development is done in a haphazard manner, failing to incorporate key socioeconomic, physical, and environmental factors in the decision-making process [7, 15]. Such actions are also oblivious to legal and institutional systems, some of which are outdated and in urgent need of review.

The main objective of this paper is to illustrate the efficacy of integrating two sets of geospatial technologies (GIS and Remote Sensing) in zoning and regionalization as land use management strategies to address the issue of mangrove ecosystem degradation at Mon Repos, Guyana. The study draws attention to the need for the use of GIS and remote sensing to develop a comprehensive understanding of and appreciation for the complexity of land use and mangrove ecosystems management at the study area and how these interact with the dynamics of coastal processes and human intervention. It presents a conceptual framework of land use management and mangrove ecosystems sustainability and analyses the challenges for the effective management of the ecosystem. Finally, the study provides a variety of perspectives, proposed strategies, and lessons to support the transferability of knowledge and experiences to similar coastal ecosystems in Guyana.

2. Methodological approach

2.1 Research design and approach

The research and design approach was conducted through an in-depth analysis of selected documents related to land use and mangrove conservation and management. These include publications on the UN Conventions and Annual Reports from the Mangrove Restoration Project under the National Agricultural Research and Extension Institute (NAREI), Guyana. Further, literature surveys on scholarly research undertaken on coastal land use, land use management strategies, mangrove ecosystem conservation, coastal environmental issues and geospatial applications were reviewed, and ArcGIS Pro and remote sensing were applied to illustrate how they can be used for the subject matter. The case study area was selected based on four criteria outlined below in the section on '*Land use management strategies for addressing*

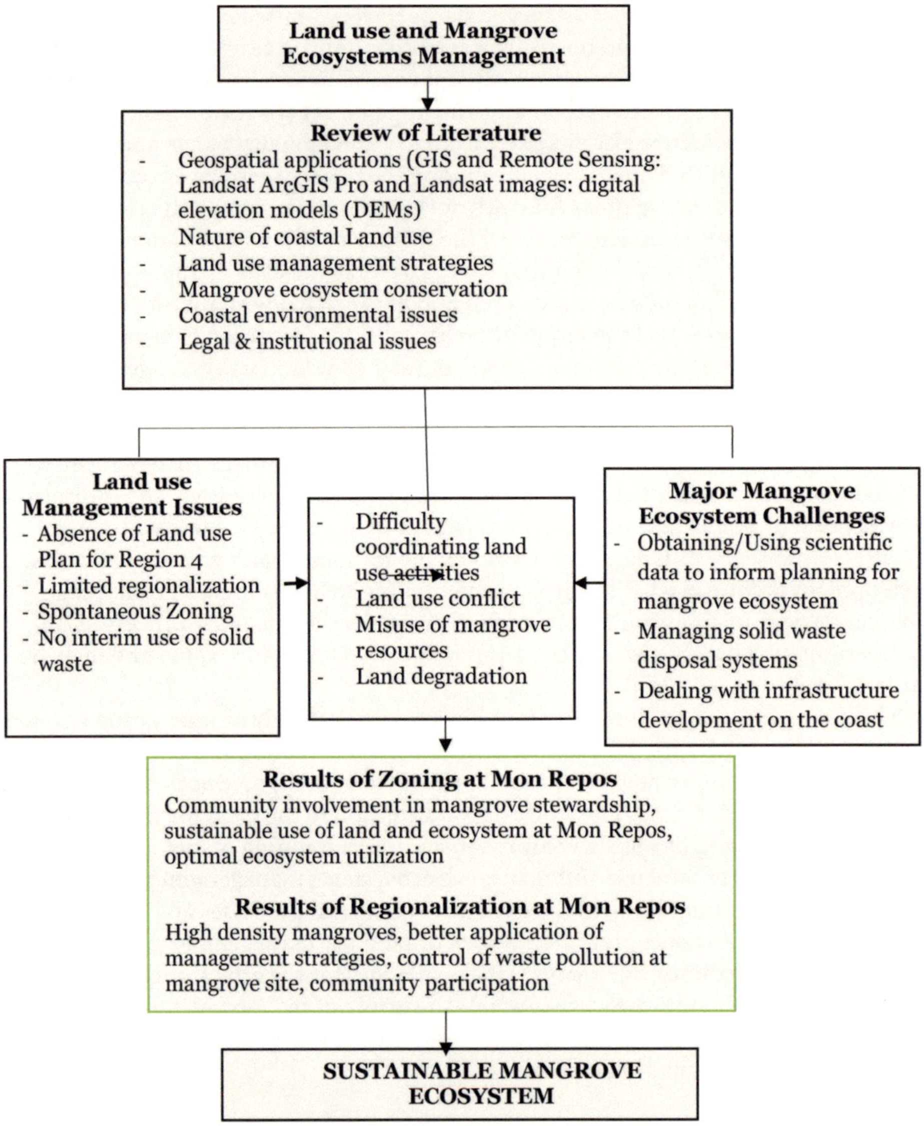

Figure 1.
Conceptual framework for land use and mangrove management. Data compiled by the author.

mangrove ecosystem degradation at Mon Repos'. The conceptual framework in **Figure 1** outlines the main concepts and various issues associated with land use and mangrove ecosystems management.

2.2 Application of geographic information system and remote sensing for zoning and regionalization

Despite the relatively huge body of literature on the use of various applications for spatial and biological diversity studies in general, few have provided overviews on the current state of play about the use of the applications to study coastal environments and to identify potential avenues for further research [10]. The myriad of environmental issues facing coastal ecosystems today, ranging from pollution, erosion and sedimentation, and sea level rise to biodiversity loss have a spatial dimension and as such surmounting them without the aid of geospatial technologies (e.g., GIS and RS) and information technology (IT) has proven to be very challenging [20–22]. This holds true in the context of mangrove ecosystems.

The rapid development and use of such technologies have led to a better understanding of some geophysical and ecological systems that were once difficult to map, track and monitor [23]. It is the geospatial information (GI) system connected to computer science that created the digital product for managing the physical environment in any part of the world. In fact, there is a very strong connection between geospatial technology and information and communication systems. Prior to their existence, data access and data application scales were limited also. While some researchers explained that Geomatics fields such as GIS and RS can be facilitated by information and communication technologies (ICT) tools for database management, data sharing, networking, computer graphics and visualization, some other authors posited that the technologies and ICT are inseparable [2, 10, 24].

The emerging applications that integrate the two groups of tools are based on wireless network of geo-sensors that detect, monitor, and track environmental phenomena and processes [10]. One aspect that matters to scientists, planners and environmental managers is the application of various geospatial technologies and interpretation and communication of the outputs to enhance knowledge about the biophysical environment for current and future use [25, 26].

Many studies conducted to date have used GIS and RS-based techniques to track vegetation and ecosystems change temporally, automate the process of waste planning and management, and make predictions about their future [22, 23]. These are three of the many possible uses of the technologies in this context [27]. In contrast, there has been much less research concerned with using GIS and RS to simulate mangrove geographical distribution and change based on landscape classifications, ecosystem degradation by natural and anthropogenic means, mangrove ecosystem dynamics in a changing coastal environment, and ecological risk assessment for the adaptation of different mangrove species to a changing environmental condition [28, 29].

There are even fewer studies that focused on modeling periods of favorable environmental conditions for mangroves such as estimating the rates of forest fragmentation and the overall health of mangroves, validating ecological theories, classifying vegetation types based on the underlying geology using GIS, and delimiting units/areas into sub-regions for better management [2]. These are made possible due to the capability of GIS, which is enhanced by various software, such as Arc GIS, GRASS GIS, gvSIG, ILWIS, JUMP GIS, uDIG, Capaware, FalconView, TerraView, and Geosoft, and modern GIS digitization which is the most common method for collecting and analyzing the data.

2.3 Zoning

Zoning is the process whereby compatible land uses and related activities are aggregated and regulated, and the character of an area/community is preserved. It deals with the demarcation of areas into small units for the purpose of different land uses. Several criteria such as topography, soils, climate, and vegetation can be used to subdivide a large area into zones. For zoning, satellite data obtained through RS are used to demarcate suitable mangrove areas and monitor and manage the vegetation. For instance, the Forest Survey of India (FSI) used Linear Imaging Self Scanning

Sensor (LISS-III) and PAN in their study of mangroves. The LISS-III technology is an optical sensor that works in four spectral bands (green, red, near infrared and short-wave infrared) and covers a 141 km wide swath with a resolution of 23v meters in all spectral bands. Landsat TM images were used to locate and measure the accreted mudflat areas along Cox's Bazar coast of Bangladesh and then land suitability classification was done considering the important spatial criteria for zoning the area and managing mangrove plantation. Other cases include the coasts of Indonesia, Iran, Brazil, Mexico, Thailand, and Malaysia where mangroves exist in significant proportions and are under constant research and monitoring [30, 31]. RS-based satellite techniques such as IRS LISS II and LISS III, LANDSAT TM consist of the modern and advanced databases which are boosting the application of mangrove management strategies in a virtuous manner [32, 33].

2.4 Regionalization

Regionalization in the context of this study refers to the practice of delineating regions into smaller units for administrative purposes and the application of management strategies at a smaller scale [34]. Having borders is not a requirement for the units to be demarcated. Each unit consists of certain criteria of its own and has its own characteristics that differentiate it from other units. Regionalization also allows for demarcating areas/zones into units based on parameters such as soil classification types, elevation, vulnerability to floods and potential for developmental activities, among others [35, 36]. Separating an area into units has its advantages, such as facilitating better management and fostering local community and household involvement in coastal resources management as custodians and stewards, but it also has disadvantages since it could result in the units having similar, overlapping representations, and coinciding with administrative/political boundaries.

2.5 Land use and mangrove ecosystems management in coastal Guyana

Land use and coastal ecosystems management in the country is impacted by the lack of zoning and planning control mechanisms visible in the choice of location for development activities. Evidently, limited use of geospatial technology and poorly guided planning decisions regarding land use are major factors contributing to the difficulties experienced in protecting many coastal ecosystems in the country. Urban expansion has also brought about many environmental problems not only in urban locales, but also in surrounding rural areas. These include illegal disposal of waste and land degradation [37–39]. Further, coastal mangrove management is complicated by the issue of land ownership in many areas. Private land ownership creates problems for policy implementation as owners of the land often do not comply with regulations and demand compensation from the authorities before complying with rules and regulations for land use.

In an attempt to address the issues locally, the Guyana Mangrove Restoration Project (GMRP) has embarked on an impressive drive over the last decade to protect and where necessary rehabilitate and restore mangroves in various sections of the coast, in addition to seeking the collaboration of private landowners. The goal is to promote mangroves for coastal protection and to facilitate livelihood initiatives by using ecosystems-based approaches [40, 41]. From 2010, the GMRP laid out plans for the establishment of sustainable mangrove ecosystems. Between 2012 and 2019, several mangrove sites have been brought under the control of the Project

Office [40, 42]. In many instances, however, the activities have been constrained by inadequate technological resources and a paucity of staff capable of utilizing geospatial technologies and techniques for scientific data collection and analysis.

While tremendous efforts have been made, both public and private sector agencies, such as Sea & River Defense Department (S&RDD) of the Ministry of Public Works and Conservation International Guyana Inc. (CI) respectively, and local communities to intensify mangrove ecosystems management activities, not all of the activities have been well-sustained [39, 40]. The result is that the targets set for mangrove ecosystems management have not been fully materialized and some of the challenges persist today [38, 43, 44]. The Guyana Forestry Commission, which has the legal mandate for mangroves, has begun to utilize geospatial technologies to aid forest management in the country. If geospatial technologies are not utilized in a highly efficient manner in land use and ecosystems management, coastal mangroves will continue to be exposed to various risks and vulnerabilities, such as land degradation and sea level rise [17, 45].

3. Land use management strategies for addressing mangrove ecosystem degradation at Mon Repos

The focus of this section of the study is to examine the ways in which the application of zoning and regionalization can contribute the sustainability of the mangrove ecosystem at Mon Repos, Guyana.

3.1 Location and site selection criteria

The study area, Mon Repos, is located on the 1,803,312 ha Coastal Plain which is a narrow strip of land adjacent the Atlantic Ocean or on the north-eastern coast of Guyana, South America and in the Demerara-Mahaica Administrative Region/Region 4 (**Figure 2**). Its Geographical coordinates are 6.8064° N Latitude and 58.0523° W Longitude, and it is found approximately 17 km from the capital city of Georgetown. Mon Repos is bounded to the west and east by the villages of Triumph and Goed Hope respectively and to the north by the Atlantic Ocean. It extends for about 5 km inland (southward) from the coast.

The study area is part of the coast which experiences wave height above 3.5 m only about 2% of the time when unusually high spring tides occur; 2 m from December to June and 1–1.5 m from July to November. Wave energy is therefore considerably reduced on the coast because of the continental shelf that stretches for an average distance of 140 km. Similar to other areas along the coast, Mon Repos is influenced by tropical climatic conditions with two wet (May–August and December–January) and two dry seasons (February–April and September–November) experienced annually. Annual rainfall averages 2200 millimeters (mm) with an average of 200 coastal rain days annually. Humidity is high all year round, and there is a narrow range of temperature (26–28°C) [37].

The northeast trade winds affect the area with an average wind speed of 12.2 kilometers per hour (kph). The coast accommodates unique ecological niches and habitats for a variety of marine and terrestrial animals, and it is at risk of inundation due to sea level rise. Its level of vulnerability increases following projections of sea level rise for the country of as much as 0.88 m by the end of the century [37]. Increases in storm surges of about 5 m are expected to affect more than 22,000 hectares of the

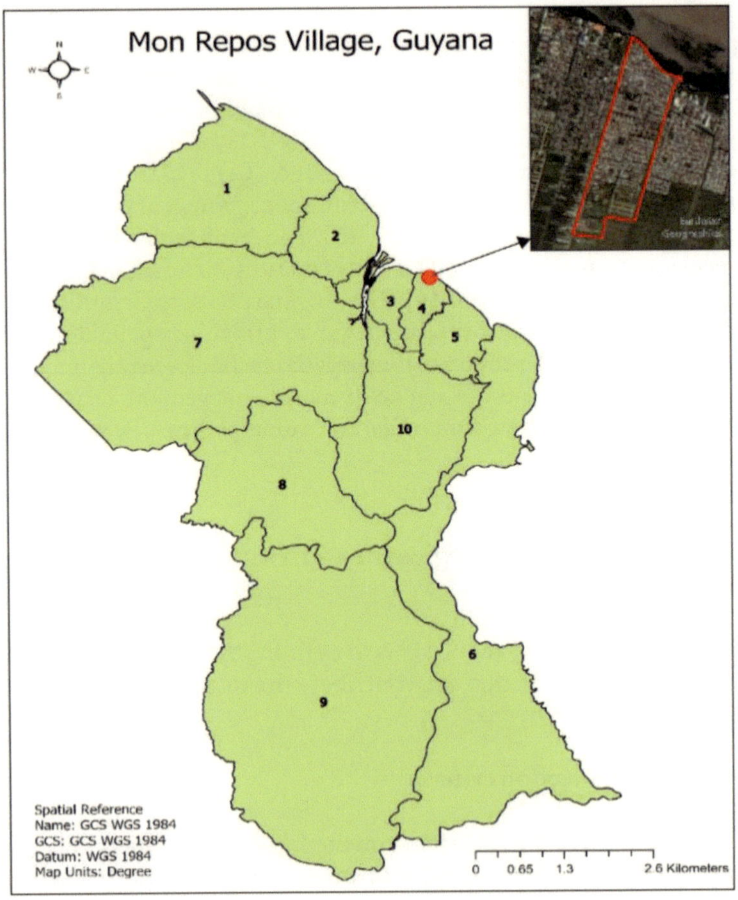

Figure 2.
Location of the study area, Mon Repos. Source: Compiled by the Author.

coastal zone, leading to further inundation and erosion [37, 17]. Mangroves function as natural breakwaters along the coast and represent an important natural sea defense for Guyana [46, 47].

Soils found there originated from different types of parent materials, but they are predominantly impervious clays and pegasse soils (fluvio-marine deposits) which become inundated during high tides. Despite the presence of an elaborate drainage network and mechanical drainage facilities, the area floods from heavy and continuous rainfall. The area is protected by a portion of the 69 km of masonry sea walls and the 78 km of sand banks which exist along the coast, and several hectares of mangroves as well. No marked change in land use has been identified over the past decade, except the expansion of residential and light commercial zones and mangrove proliferation naturally (**Figure 3a** and **b**).

Four criteria were used in the selection of the study site for data collection. These are:

i. Ecological consideration: the need to identify a site where mangroves have colonized naturally and profusely so that research on the conditions could be considered for replicability; and

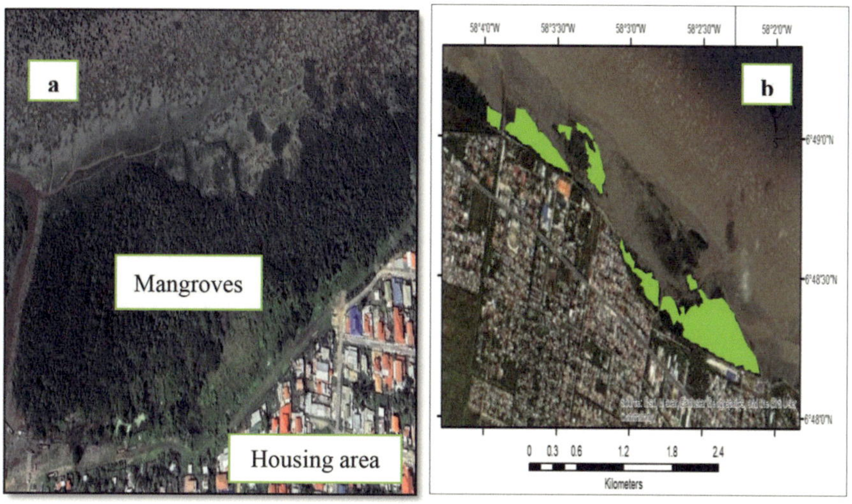

Figure 3.
(a and b) Main Land uses identified at the study area. Note: Google Earth Images, June 2023. Source: Compiled by the Author.

ii. Environmental condition: the need to identify a polluted mangrove site for the issue of waste management to be addressed.

iii. Accessibility of site: the proximity of the study area to the main transport route allowed for relative ease of visits to the site.

iv. Proximity of mangrove study area to densely populated area: this creates potential for land use conflict and presents a scenario that occurs almost throughout the coastal Regions of 2, 3, 4, 5 and 6, thus allowing for the development of a model that could be widely replicated in Guyana

3.2 Data collection, procedure and process

Landsat TM image was used to locate and measure the mangrove area at Mon Repos in 2013 and 2022, then land use classifications were identified considering important spatial criteria for better planning and scientific management of the mangrove ecosystem. Mangrove cover and land-use maps were created using ArcGIS Pro and Landsat images. Landsat imagery covering the study area was downloaded from the USGS Earth Explorer and ancillary data were gathered from additional datasets such as digital elevation models (DEMs) and existing land-use maps. Radiometric calibration was done to the downloaded Landsat images to convert digital numbers to reflectance values using appropriate band-specific calibration coefficients with Landsat 8 OLI/TIRS Sensor: Band 4 (Red): Calibration coefficient = 2.0000; Band 5 (Near-Infrared): Calibration coefficient = 1.2500; Landsat 7 ETM+ Sensor: Band 3 (Red): Calibration coefficient = 2.0000 and Band 4 (Near-Infrared): Calibration coefficient = 1.2500. Correction was also done to remove atmospheric effects.

For mangrove mapping, Supervised Image Classification techniques were applied to the preprocessed Landsat images in ArcGIS Pro. This involved assigning different land cover classes to the pixels based on their spectral characteristics. An accuracy assessment of the matrix was done to validate the accuracy of the classified image by comparing a representative sample of classified pixels with ground truth data.

The mangrove cover map and ancillary data on existing land use were used to create a comprehensive land-use map for the two years. This involved digitizing and classifying different land-use types. To validate the land-use map, images (pictures) of the area were used as reference.

3.3 Zoning, regionalization and Mangrove ecosystem degradation at Mon Repos

Attempts have been made in the past to allocate specific sections of the community to specific uses. Over the years, Mon Repos has benefited from basic infrastructure upgrading, facilitating a thriving market, commercial banks, super marts, and small businesses. The surrounding land uses recognized from the mapping exercise are residential, commercial and infrastructure (roads and seawalls). These social and economic units are in proximity to the mangroves as shown in **Figure 3**. Population growth in the community has led to encroachment on and removal of mangroves especially along the south-western section of the mangrove areas. It is well-established that any adverse land use in proximity to mangroves could lead to their destruction thereby affecting the ecosystem as well as the integrity of the coastline in that location.

The study revealed that approximately 53.0 hectares of apparently healthy mangroves existed at Mon Repos as of June 2023. This figure represents 11 times the number of hectares of mangroves when compared to 4.7 hectares in 2013 (**Figure 4**). This is a relatively significant amount of mangrove cover, given the size of the community. The significant difference in changes in mangroves between the two years highlight the relevance of more detailed and local studies to understand the processes

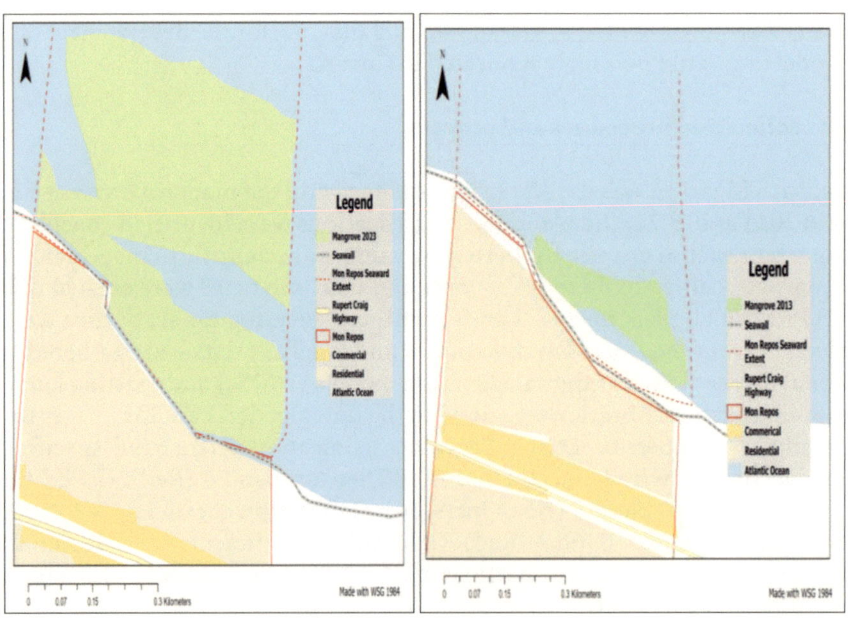

Figure 4.
Mangrove Coverage in 2023 and 2013 . Note. Images created from ArcGIS Pro. Landsat images, digital elevation models (DEMs) and existing land-use maps. Source: Compiled by the Author.

leading to the proliferation of the vegetation despite encroachment and removal of the vegetation in some sections.

The risk of conflicts at the community level, particularly because of the population encroachment on the south-western periphery of the mangrove site and potential mangrove conservation efforts, can be addressed by establishing functional zones in which zoning control mechanisms are applied for optimal coastal land and ecosystem utilization. In zoning this area, two aspects ought to be considered. These are the quantity to be assigned for different land-use activities and how to allocate different amounts of land use in the space available (spatial allocation). This can be achieved by using a framework of land-use suitability evaluation and a cell-based approach to allocate residential, commercial, infrastructure and wetland (mangrove) land uses in land-use spatial zones (LUSZ) or functional zones at Mon Repos. In this case, land suitability maps become necessary to guide all land use decisions. If this is avoided, the result could be viewed as a spatial optimization problem.

While the study area has fostered mangrove colonization over the years, contiguity and compatibility of land-uses appeared to be an issue. For instance, huge volumes of solid waste (both biodegradable and non-biodegraded) were observed in the mangrove stands (**Figure 5**). Here the applications of GIS and RS are relevant and suitable decision-support tools for monitoring of the mangrove site. This is likely to solve the spatial optimization problem at the study area and prevent degradation of the ecosystem there. The study showed that RS with a high spatial resolution can assist with the (a) acquisition of information at relatively small spatial scales such as Mon Repos and (b) production of repeated measurements for the site.

Regionalization was performed based on land-use in and around the study site and its potential (recreational, tourism) and ecological service (forest utilization, material production, faunal habitats) interpreted from the Landsat images. These were analyzed in accordance with the integrity of the ecosystem status quo. As it

Figure 5
Mangroves and Domestic and Industrial Effluents at the Study Site, May 2023. Note: Picture was obtained from the National Mangrove Restoration Project, NAREI, Guyana.

relates to proximity, the mangrove ecosystem was found to be surrounded by three natural functional units, which are marine ecosystem, offshore tidal flat, and estuary/ocean waters.

It appeared that the mangrove ecosystem has not been under the control of sub-region/Neighborhood Democratic Council (NDC) or the Mangrove Project Unit at NAREI. This could have been one reason for encroachment of the site, destruction of the mangroves and solid waste disposal issue. Having the site under sub-regional control could result in a high-density mangrove stand, better application of management strategies, control of waste pollution, and encourage community participation. A caveat though is that while having mangroves under sub-regional protection is an idealistic approach, it could be counter intuitive since the lack of updated zoning regulations and standards and enforcement of outdated ones could result in governance issues and conflicts over mangrove ecosystem use. There are other factors that need to be considered too. These include limited coordinated effort among relevant agencies to maximize benefits from the application of regionalization, limited technical skills to collect and analyze scientific data using GIS and RS technologies.

3.4 Main challenges associated with the effective management of the Mangrove ecosystem at Mon Repos

Despite the proliferation of mangroves at some sections of the study site, there are several key challenges confronting the effective management of the mangroves. Among them are the following:

i. *Obtaining more accurate, up-to-date, and scientific data such as anthropogenic activities, tidal movement, and erosion and accretion, on the mangroves at the site*—research revealed that there is lack of level data on the mangrove ecosystem at Mon Repos has proven to be a hindrance to sound planning and decision-making.

ii. *Conducting research to determine whether there is compatibility between the designated use of the mangrove site and the national policies and plans for the study area*—huge sums of money are expended to revegetate and protect coastal mangroves while activities, such as dumping of solid waste, that are detrimental to the mangrove rehabilitation sites are allowed to occur.

iii. *Determining alternative sites for solid waste management activities that are incompatible with mangrove ecosystem management*—policies must be clearly identified and defined with suitable legal and institutional framework for enforcement to allow for cost-effective investment in coastal mangrove ecosystem management.

iv. *Reforming the regulatory and policy frameworks to address solid waste management and pollution*–Solid Waste Management as a deliberate policy has been largely limited to the municipalities, but the Local Authorities, which fall under the Neighborhood Democratic Councils (NDCs) are responsible for domestic waste collection and disposal. While the Mon Repos/La Reconnaissance NDC has been able to improve the garbage collection system over the past years, with assistance from the Environmental Protection Agency (EPA), the extent to which it can address the pollution issue is restricted in part by the loopholes in the regulations and absence of a policy framework and limited financial resources.

v. *Changing the non-compliance culture*—penalties for non-compliance are limited and, in some cases, non-existent, leading to continuous disregard for the impact of the solid waste on the mangrove ecosystem.

vi. *Promoting public awareness among local stakeholders*—while numerous interventions with respect to education and awareness in the Mon Repos community, careless use of the coastal mangrove ecosystem has been a perennial problem. More robust education and awareness programmes must be considered in harmony with the legal and institutional framework.

These challenges threaten the integrity and resilience of the mangrove ecosystem and if they remain unattended will in the long-run lead to degradation and destruction of the mangrove ecosystem and other related consequences, such as intrusion

Strategies needed to overcome the main challenges	Cost for addressing the challenges	Beneficiaries
Collect and analyze scientific data supported by GIS a RS technologies to conduct in-depth study of mangroves at Mon Repos	Conducting training of local stakeholders engaging personnel with GIS and RS skills to support local agencies through training	Government agencies, such as NAREI and the local authorities as they would save from reduced expenditure on soil and crop damage from floods from the sea
Undertake research to determine whether there is a need for expansion of the mangrove site, identify appropriate land use/s, and establish whether there is compatibility between the designated use of the mangrove site and the national policies and plans for the study area	Establishing and strengthening collaborative arrangements with various agencies to support mangrove restoration and expansion	Guyana, residents of Mon Repos, volunteer organizations Planning agencies such as CH&PA, Guyana Lands and Surveys Commission (GLSC)
Reform and strengthen the regulatory and policy frameworks to address pollution and solid waste management in local authority areas	Hiring technical personnel to prepare and up-date regulatory and policy framework (Legal skills)	Government agencies. FEES students and staff, Workshop participants, NAREI, Local community
Prepare a multiple use conservation zoning plan for Mon Repos to preserve the multiple ecosystem services that the mangroves could provide for the community	Organizing meetings, workshops, and community seminars to mobilize for local participation	Mon Repos and Region 4 communities
Change the non-compliance culture	Virtual and face-to-face training sessions, TV programmes, print and distribute informational material	Residents of Mon Repos community, Government agencies
Promoting public awareness among local stakeholders	Assisting local stakeholders in identifying and developing and managing alternative solid waste site; organize community groups to overseen protection of site	Local and Regional Authorities

Table 1.
Proposed strategies to address the challenges of the Mon Repos mangrove ecosystem.

of saline water and soil degradation and damage to crops and other near shore developments from flooding.

4. Conclusions

Mangrove ecosystem protection and management has been a problematic and difficult undertaking across Guyana for several decades. Apart from the natural processes associated with ocean currents and tidal changes that compound the issues, there are a range of social, economic, and environmental areas of concerns that are also involved. Many of the local coastal communities continue to degrade the coastal environment and destroy mangrove forests with impunity. Overall, the problem does not appear to point to a single solution. In a sense, lack of collaboration among the stakeholder groups seems germane to the problem.

This study focused on the community of Mon Repos as a case study of the nature, context, and possible directions in which the authorities and local community members need to go if meaningful actions are to be taken to deal with mangrove ecosystem management. One of the key areas identified in the study is the application of GIS and Remote Sensing technologies to undertake real-time scientific data for zoning and managing the site and monitoring the mangrove ecosystem. However, the study alludes to the fact the technology while it exists in some of the key agencies in Guyana, there is no coordinated effort to maximize benefits from its use. There is the problem of limited technical skills and financing and fragmentation to enable proper coordination and maximization of efforts to address the problem. There is still a long way to go before real progress can be made to manage the site effectively.

Finally, several actions/strategies have been proposed in the paper to address the issues that confront mangrove ecosystem management at the study area of Mon Repos. These include collecting more accurate, up-to-date, and reliable scientific data supported by GIS a RS technologies to conduct in-depth study of mangroves at Mon Repos and preparing a multiple use conservation zoning plan to preserve the multiple ecosystem services that the mangroves could provide for the community. Some of these suggestions are not only applicable to the study area but also several other mangrove sites along the coast. Reference has been made to Regions 2, 3, 4, 5, and 6. While specific timelines and costings have not been provided in the paper, **Table 1** provides some guidance on the line of thought that could give an insight into policy direction to address this difficult issue. Greater inter-agency collaboration seems to be one of the actions that need to be undertaken urgently.

Conflict of interest

The author declares no conflict of interest.

Thanks

Gratitude is extended to Ms. Kim Chan and Mr. Muzzammil Mohabir for the support rendered.

Author details

Linda Johnson-Bhola
Department of Geography, University of Guyana, Georgetown, Guyana

*Address all correspondence to: inda.bhola@uog.edu.gy

References

[1] Briassoulis H. Analysis of Land Use Change: Theoretical and Modeling Approaches. 2nd ed. Morgantown: WVU Research Repository; 2020

[2] Wang Y, Mitchell BR, Nugranad-Marzilli J, Bonynge G, Zhou Y, Shriver G. Remote sensing of land-cover change and landscape context of the National Parks: A case study of the northeast temperate network. Remote Sensing of Environment. 2009;**113**:1453-1461

[3] Dieleman F, Wegener M. Compact ciity and urban sprawl. Built Environment (1978-). Vol. 30. No. 4. Washington DC: The National Academies of Sciences, Engineering, and Medicine; 2004. pp. 308-323. Available from: http://www.jstor.org/stable/24026084

[4] World Bank. Principles for a Code of Conduct for the Management and Sustainable Use of Mangrove Ecosystems. United Kingdom, Center Aarhus: ISME; 2004

[5] United Nations. Report of the World Commission on Environment and Development. 1987. Available from: https://digitallibrary.un.org/record/139811

[6] United Nations. United Nations Conference on Environment and Development. 1992. Available from: https://www.un.org/en/conferences/environment/rio1992

[7] Dasgupta R, Shaw R. Participatory Mangrove Management in a Changing Climate. Tokyo: Springer; 2017. DOI: 10.1007/978-4-431-56481-2

[8] Damastuti E, de Groot R. Participatory ecosystem service mapping to enhance community-based mangrove rehabilitation and management in Demak, Indonesia. Regional Environmental Change. 2018;**19**:65-78. DOI: 10.1007/s10113-018-1378-7

[9] Narayan S, Beck MW, Reguero BG, Losada IJ, van Wesenbeeck B, Pontee N. The effectiveness, costs and coastal protection benefits of natural and nature-based defences. PLoS One. 2016;**11**(5):e0154735

[10] Mondal P, Trzaska S, Sherbinin A. De. Landsat-Derived Estimates of Mangrove Extents in the Sierra Leone Coastal Landscape Complex. New York: Columbia University; 2018. DOI: 10.3390/s18010012

[11] Goodbody I, Thomas-Hope EM, editors. Natural Resource Management for Sustainable Development in the Caribbean. Jamaica: Canoe Press; 2002

[12] Proffitt CE, Devlin DJ. Long-term growth and succession in restored and natural mangrove forests in southwestern Florida. Wetland Ecological Management. 2005;**13**:531-551. DOI: 10.1007/s11273-004-2411-9

[13] Canadian Institute of Planners. Plan Canada | CIP — Canadian Institute of Planners. Canada: Canadian Institute of Planners; 2007. Available from: https://www.cip-icu.ca/Resources/Plan-Canada

[14] Pelling M. The Vulnerability of Cities: Natural Disasters and Social Resilience. London: Earthscan; 2003

[15] Guyana Lands and Surveys Commission. Guyana National Land Use Plan. Guyana: Guyana Lands and Surveys Commission; 2013. Available

from: http://goinvest.gov.gy/wp-content/uploads/GuyanaNLUP.pdf

[16] Johnson-Bhola L. Setting the Foundations for Zero Net Loss of the Mangroves That Underpin Human Well-Being in the North Brazil Shelf LME: Systematization and Descriptive Analysis of Policies and Regulations That Affect the Conservation and Sustainable Use of Mangrove Ecosystems in Guyana. Report by Conservation International and L. Johnson-Bhola. 2019. Available from: https://nbslmegef.wordpress.com/

[17] Anthony EJ, Gratiot N. Coastal engineering and large-scale mangrove destruction in Guyana, South America: Averting an environmental catastrophe in the making. Ecological Engineering. 2012;**47**:268-273. DOI: 10.1016/j.ecoleng.2012.07.005

[18] Bovell O. The code of practice for mangrove harvesting. Guyana Mangrove Restoration Project & European Union. 2011. Available from: https://www.gcca.eu/sites/default/files/catherine.paul/code_of_practice_for_mangrove_harvesting_2011.pdf

[19] FAO. Mangrove Forest Management Guidelines. Guyana, Rome: FAO Forestry Paper No. 1119; 1994

[20] Hussain M, Butt AR, Uzma F, Ahmed R, Irshad S, Rehman A, et al. A comprehensive review of climate change impacts, adaptation, and mitigation on environmental and natural calamities in Pakistan. Environmental Monitoring and Assessment. 2020;**192**:48. DOI: 10.1007/s10661-019-7956-4

[21] United Nations Climate Change Secretariat. Opportunities and Options for Integrating Climate Change Adaptation with the Sustainable Development Goals and the Sendai Framework for Disaster Risk Reduction 2015-2030. 2017. Available from: https://unfccc.int/sites/default/files/resource/techpaper_adaptation.pdf

[22] Aizpuru M, Achard F, Blasco F. Global assessment of Cover Change of the Mangrove forest using Satellite imagery at medium to high resolution. In: EEC research project n° 15017-1999-05 FIED ISP FR, Brussels, Ispra: Joint Research Center; 2000

[23] Son NT, Chen CF, Chang NB, Chen CR, Chang LY, Thanh BX. Mangrove mapping and change detection in Ca Mau peninsula, Vietnam, using landsat data and object-based image analysis. IEEE Journal of Selected Topics in Applied Earth Observations and Remote Sensing. 2015;**8**(2):503-510

[24] Sui D, Goodchild M. The convergence of GIS and social media: Challenges for GIScience. International Journal of Geographical Information Science. 2011;**25**(11):1737-1748

[25] Zemba AA, Yusuf MB. Implications of land use and land cover dynamics on arable lands in Jalingo region, Nigeria: Remote sensing and GIS approach. Adamawa State University Journal of Scientific Research. 2012;**2**(2):62-69

[26] Park T, Lee WK, Woo SY, Yoo S, Kwak DA, Stiti B, et al. Assessment of land-cover change using GIS and remotely-sensed data: A case study in Ain Snoussi area of northern Tunisia. Forest Science and Technology. 2011;**7**(2):75-81

[27] Oyedotun T, Burningham H. The need for data integration to address the challenges of climate change on the Guyana coast. Geography and Sustainability. 2021;**2**(4):288-297

[28] Lacambra C, McLover A, Moller I, Spalding M, Spencer T. Mangroves, Tropical Cyclones, and Coastal Hazard

Risk Reduction. United Kingdom: Elsevier; 2015

[29] Lewis R. Ecological engineering for successful management and restoration of mangrove forests. Ecological Engineering. 2005;**24**(4):403-418. DOI: 10.1016/j.ecoleng.2004.10.003

[30] Gopal B. Mangroves are wetlands, not forests: Some implications for their management. In: Faridah-Hanum I, Latiff A, Hakeem KR, Ozturk M, editors. Mangrove Ecosystems of Asia. New York: Springer; 2014. pp. 439-453. DOI: 10.1007/978-1-4614-8582-7_20

[31] Agraz-Hernández CM, García-Zaragoza C, Iriarte-Vivar S, Flores- Verdugo FJ, Moreno-Casasola P. Forest structure, productivity and species phenology of mangroves in the La Mancha lagoon in the Atlantic coast of Mexico. Wetlands Ecology and Management. 2011;**19**:273-293

[32] Zekeng JC, Sebego R, Mphinyane WN, Mpalo M, Nayak D, Fobane JL, et al. Land use and land cover changes in Doume Communal Forest in eastern Cameroon: Implications for conservation and sustainable management. Modeling Earth Systems and Environment. 2019;**5**:1801-1814

[33] Samanta K, Hazra S. Landuse/landcover change study of Jharkhali Island Sundarbans, West Bengal using remote sensing and GIS. International Journal of Geomatics and Geosciences. 2012;**3**(2):299-306

[34] Domínguez-Domínguez M, Zavala-Cruz J, Rincón-Ramírez JA, Martínez-Zurimendi P. Management strategies for the conservation, restoration and utilization of mangroves in southeastern Mexico. Wetlands. 2019;**39**:907-919

[35] Lei JS, Yin W, Zhu D. Research on ecological function regionalization based on the ecological service function-take Shenzhen River and Xinzhou River Estuarine Wetland for example. Advanced Materials Research. 2015;**1073**:1171-1177

[36] Mishra M. Geomorphic regionalization of coastal zone using geospatial technology. International Journal of Environment and Geoinformatics. 2016;**3**(2):11-23

[37] Government of Guyana. Report on the State of Guyana's Coastal Landscape – A Rapid Assessment. Guyana: Department of Environment, Ministry of the Presidency; 2018

[38] Environmental Protection Agency. State of the Environment Report. Guyana: United Nations Development Project; 2016. Available from: https://www.epaguyana.org/epa/epa-reports1/summary/18-epa-reports/280-state-of-the-environment-report

[39] Guyana Forestry Commission. Integrated Coastal Zone Management (ICZM)-EPA. Guyana: Environmental Protection Agency; 2001

[40] Moseley K. Increasing Coastal Resilience and Social Development Opportunities. Guyana: Guyana Mangrove Restoration Project (GMRP); 2020. Available from: https://panorama.solutions/en/solution/increasing-coastal-resilience-and-social-development-opportunities-guyana-mangrove

[41] Sharples C. Going Under: Mangrove Restoration in Low-lying Guyana a Vital Need, Say Experts. 2017. Available from: https://news.mongabay.com/2017/07/going-under-mangrove-restoration-in-low-lying-guyana-a-vital-need-say-experts/

[42] NAREI. The National Mangrove Management Action Plan (NMMAP) for 2010 to 2012. Guyana: NAREI; 2010

[43] Government of Guyana. Guyana's National Action Plan (NAP) to combat land degradation, Guyana. 2019. Available from: https://faolex.fao.org/docs/pdf/guy199297.pdf

[44] Johnson-Bhola L, Oyedotun TDT. Coastal defence roles of mangroves on the Amazon-influenced coast of Guyana, South America: A review of intervention project of an eroding coastline. In: The Zone. Dubai: Spring Edition; 2018. pp. 12-14

[45] Bholanath P, Dewnath N, Singh J. Developing Monitoring, Reporting and Verification System for REDD+ in Guyana. Guyana: Guyana Forestry Commission; 2013

[46] World Wildlife Fund. Biodev2030 Guyana [210701273_1] Final Report 09/03/2022. 2022. Available from: https://www.biodev2030.org/wp-content/uploads/2022/04/Guyana-national-biodiversity-threat-assessment-EN.pdf

[47] Environmental Protection Agency. Guyana National Biodiversity Strategy and Action Plan 2012-2020. Guyana: Environmental Protection Agency; 2014

Chapter 8

Soil Evolution after Riparian Buffer Installation

Michael Aide and Indi Braden

Abstract

Riparian buffers are engineered landscapes designed to protect fresh-water resources and to promote esthetics, soil and habitat health, reduce flooding, and provide economic benefits. An emerging attribute of riparian buffers is the preservation and accumulation of soil organic carbon. This review discusses riparian buffers to support and protect ecosystem services, the potential to sequester carbon, and the presentation of a case study to demonstrate soil fertility enhancement and soil organic matter accumulation. The riparian buffer involved in this study was in east-central Missouri and the stand age was approximately 18 years. Within the riparian buffer, soil organic matter averaged 3.4%, whereas in the adjacent production field soil organic matter averaged 1.7%, showing that the riparian buffer significantly supported soil carbon capture and preservation. Similarly, ammonium and sulfate concentrations were significantly greater in the riparian buffer. Habitat and soil water quality are important outcomes.

Keywords: carbon sequestration, riparian buffer strips, water quality, nutrient capture, soil organic matter

1. Introduction

Riparian buffer strips, also called riparian buffers, are vegetated engineered landscapes typically along waterways and are designed to provide ecosystem services, potentially including: (i) shade that moderates stream water temperatures, (ii) runoff sediment capture zones, (iii) nutrient retention to preserve water quality, (iv) streambank stabilization, (v) wildlife and fish habitat, (vi) esthetic urban green belts, (vii) improved soil health, and (viii) soil organic carbon sequestration [1–4]. Design criteria to improve or protect water quality, support habitat, encourage erosion abatement, which consider the influences of climate, hydrology, vegetation, topographic and geologic factors. Many nations have design specifications for publicly supported riparian buffers [3–6]. The design criteria generally involves: (i) a minimum total buffer width, (ii) typically installing a three-zone buffer system (stream side zone, middle zone, and outer zone), (iii) establishing of native vegetative communities, (iv) expansion and contraction of the riparian buffer to accommodate steep slopes, wetlands and other naturally occurring features, (v) buffer crossings, (vi) storm water runoff, and (vii) buffer land use flexibility. The United States Department of Agriculture minimum buffer width is typically 30.5 meters (100 feet);

IntechOpen

however, considerable variance exists with buffers ranging from 6 to 61 meters (20 to 200 ft) [7]. Three-zone buffer systems protect the physical and ecological integrity of the stream (stream side zone), provide appropriate distance between the stream and the upland or agricultural field to optimize desired benefits (middle zone), and an additional setback, typically grasses, to provide additional benefits (outer zone). Typically, the middle zone is usually vegetated with trees and shrubs, with climate and other exceptions supporting alternative native species. Feld et al. [8] asserted that riparian design configurations (width, length, zonation, density) influence ecological services, including riparian biology, nutrient flux, and sediment capture; however, the riparian designs vary in effectiveness across different landscapes.

The objectives of this manuscript are: (i) to review recent investigations involving riparian buffers and their ecosystem service provisions, (ii) to document the carbon sequestration potential of riparian buffers, and (iii) to provide evidence of soil health benefits from a riparian buffer along William Creek in east-central Missouri.

2. Riparian influences on nutrient and sediment transport

A major water quality benefit of well-designed riparian buffers involves nutrient and sediment capture. Craig et al. [9] proposed that small streams that receive nitrogen-bearing runoff during moderate rainfall events offer significant opportunities for water quality improvement. Wu et al. [10] documented that riparian buffers reduce non-point source pollution in streams and other freshwater resources. Riparian buffers filter sediment and nutrients, limit pesticide leakage, protect from floods, provide habitat and improve biodiversity, minimize erosion, and provide habitat connectivity. Cole et al. [1] observed that wooded riparian buffers are generally less effective than grass riparian buffers in capturing nutrient-bearing sediments.

Omidvar et al. [11] performed a global meta-analysis which proposed that the total soil nitrogen content increased after riparian establishment. In general, the total nitrogen increases were in the order of forested buffers more than shrublands buffers and least for grassland buffers. In Australia, Neilen et al. [12] compared catchment nitrogen and phosphorus capture by riparian vegetation. These authors reported that phosphorus leaching losses were smaller in wooded riparian zones than grasslands. During high rainfall events, nitrogen leaching losses were smaller from grassland riparian zones; however, under low rainfall events the comparative nitrogen loss rates attributed to leaching were complex, with influencing factors: (i) soil type, (ii) soil C and N stocks, and (iii) soil microbial activity. In the United Kingdom, Dlamini et al. [13] compared carbon dioxide flux from woodland and grass riparian buffers with adjacent non-buffer land areas. Woodland riparian buffers presented the largest CO_2 emissions, whereas the grass riparian buffers exhibited the smallest CO_2 emissions.

In Missouri, primarily on claypan soils, Udawatta et al. [14] noted that land management options that maintain appropriate vegetative covers inhibit phosphorus losses. Udawatta et al. [15] investigated nonpoint-source pollution reduction and demonstrated that agroforestry and grass buffers limited water runoff, sediment transport and total nitrogen and phosphorus flux. Riparian buffers were particularly effective as a grazing land management practice. In Australia, Gageler et al. [16] compared existing riparian rainforests, pastures, and reforestation land parcels to estimate soil properties. In their study, reforestation plantings improved soil bulk densities and infiltration rates, suggesting that soil structures were improved.

3. Soil carbon sequestration in riparian buffers

Riparian buffer installation is an important land management option to support soil carbon sequestration. In Ontario, Canada, Vijayakumar et al. [17] compared carbon stocks of riparian buffers and associated agriculture fields. Soil organic carbon concentrations of mature riparian buffers averaged 193 Mg C ha^{-1}, whereas the associated agricultural fields exhibited soil organic carbon concentrations of 88 Mg C ha^{-1}. Riparian buffers having deciduous vegetation had greater soil organic carbon concentrations than riparian buffers with coniferous vegetation.

In Quebec, Canada, Fortier et al. [18] compared riparian buffers having (i) hybrid poplar (*Populus deltoides* and *Populus nigra*), (ii) natural woodlands, and (iii) herbaceous species. Considering the soil organic carbon concentrations to a depth of 0.6 meters, the hybrid poplar riparian buffer carbon concentrations ranged from 9 to 27 t C ha^{-1}, (ii) natural woodlands ranged from 8.8 to 74 t C ha^{-1}, and (iii) the herbaceous species ranged from 0.6 to 1.3 t C ha^{-1}. In the natural woodlots the fine root mass correlated with the soil organic carbon. In southern Ontario, Canada, Ofosu et al. [19] recorded that a 103-year-old coniferous stand exhibited 358 Mg C ha^{-1} and a 94-year-old deciduous stand exhibited 311 Mg C ha^{-1}. Rehabilitated buffers accumulated carbon at a rate of 4.7 Mg C ha^{-1} $yr.^{-1}$, whereas as a natural forest accumulated carbon at a rate of 3.1 Mg C ha^{-1} $yr.^{-1}$. Dybata et al. [20] performed a meta-analysis of carbon sequestration in riparian forests. Their data analysis demonstrated the potential for rapid initial carbon sequestration, with carbon stocks ultimately ranging from 68 to 158 Mg C ha^{-1}.

Across the lower reaches of the Yellow River in China, Hou et al. [21] studied changes in the carbon stocks across reclaimed soil chronosequences. In the upper 20 cm soil, soil organic carbon accumulated at an average rate of 2.7 Mg C ha^{-1} $yr.^{-1}$, whereas the average soil inorganic carbon accumulation rate was 5.5 Mg C ha^{-1} $yr.^{-1}$. In California, Matzek et al. [22] observed revegetation projects across 42 streambank sites. Soil organic carbon accumulation averaged 0.87 Mg C ha^{-1} $yr.^{-1}$ for floodplains and 1.17 Mg C ha^{-1} $yr.^{-1}$ for more elevated landforms. Soil carbon persistence was supported by increased C:N ratio and smaller fulvic acid contents.

4. Soil carbon preservation

Initially, soil scientists attributed soil carbon preservation to the decomposition of particulate soil organic matter to humus, with the ever-increasing abundance of recalcitrant soil organic materials. Emerging soil concepts now strongly include studies indicating that particulate organic matter inclusion in soil structures and organic material adsorption on phyllosilicates and oxyhydroxides are major factors supporting soil organic matter preservation [23–29]. Currently debate is concentrating on the soil's formation of macro-aggregates and micro-aggregates and how these soil structures influence how soil carbon species are preserved and their residence time [23–29]. Schmidt et al. [26] reiterated that multiple influences determine soil organic matter accumulation and persistence, including: (i) root type and root biomass, (ii) physical separation of particulate organic matter from microbial activity, (iii) deep soil carbon is associated with very long turnover rates, (iv) permafrost thawing and the emission of greenhouse gases, and (v) microbial metabolic activities and community structures. Thus, all soil processes that support soil structure development and maintenance are likely to support soil carbon sequestration.

5. Design criteria considerations

The design structure of a riparian buffer involves estimating the appropriate size, shape, and vegetation composition to address multiple objectives at a particular location. The location provides information concerning climate, stream characteristics, watershed water delivery, native vegetation inventory, and other factors [7]. Initial considerations must assess which resource issues are particularly important to the design process. Seven key resource considerations include: (i) water quality, (ii) biodiversity, (iii) fertile and productive soils, (iv) economic opportunities, (v) protection and safety, (vi) esthetics and visual appearance, and (vii) recreation potential. The landowner, in consultation with a professional soil engineer, must establish the problems and opportunities, then determine site-specific objectives. Within this context, a resource inventory is conducted and evaluated to complete the riparian buffer design [7].

In our case, we selected water quality as the most important resource consideration. Our objective was to reduce nitrate transport because of overland flow and shallow groundwater flux towards Williams Creek. Our defined buffer functions were: (i) slow water runoff by optimizing soil infiltration, (ii) trap nitrate from both overland and subsurface flow because of enhanced infiltration and plant uptake, and (iii) reduce soil surface and bank erosion. In this project, published design guidelines selected for water quality are partitioned as: (i) location and arrangement, (ii) size and pollutant type (nitrate), (iii) native vegetation, (iv) management, and (v) incorporation of additional guidelines that may benefit water quality [7].

For water quality, the category of size and pollutant type contains the following guidelines germane to reducing nitrate pollution: (i) variable buffer width correlation with runoff volume, (ii) effective buffer area ratio by considering upslope runoff area to the riparian area, (iii) slope and soil type adjustments, (iv) buffer sediment capturing requirements based on sediment particle size distribution, (v) nitrogen soil capture because of leaching, and (vi) presence of shallow groundwater. Criteria for the seven resource issues are expertly detailed [7].

6. Case study: the influence of riparian buffer on the evolution of soil properties

6.1 Design of the riparian buffer and climate considerations

The riparian buffer in Cape Girardeau County, Missouri, resides along William Creek for approximately 630 meters (2070 ft). Williams Creek is a third order stream that experiences flooding annually. The riparian buffer is 23 meters (75 ft) in depth and is composed of native deciduous trees, shrubs with herbaceous understories. Additionally, 8 meters (25 ft) if interior buffer is composed of warm season grasses. The stand age is approximately 18 years. The adjacent agriculture field typically has a corn (Zea mays) – soybean (Glycine max) rotation.

The mean annual temperature is approximately 13°C (56°F), and mean annual precipitation is approximately 1.12 mm (44 inches). Rainfall is typically greater from March to May; however, Gulf of Mexico weather events may provide heavy rain events from June to October. The growing season is approximately 210 days.

6.2 Methodology

Five surface soil samples were obtained in the riparian buffer and five surface soil samples were obtained from the production field, but adjacent to the riparian buffer. All sampled surface samples were from the Wilbur soil series. Measured soil properties included: (i) pH in water, (ii) soil organic matter by loss on ignition, (iii) sulfate by 2 M KCl extraction, (iv) ammonium and nitrate extraction, and (v) phosphorus by the Bray-1 extraction. These laboratory tests were performed by the University Missouri Soil Test Laboratory using routine protocols. The soil profile morphology was performed by USDA with subsequent analysis in the USDA soil characterization laboratory.

6.3 The soil of the riparian buffer

The Wilbur series (Coarse-silty, mixed, superactive, mesic Fluvaquentic Eutrudepts) consists of very deep, moderately well-drained soils that formed in silty alluvium. The mean annual temperature is about 13°C and mean annual precipitation is about 1.1 m. The typical horizon sequence is Ap (Ochric)–Bw (Cambic) – Cg. The soil series generally has redoximorphic features from 0.43 to 2 m.

The sampled pedon of the Wilbur series was in a land-graded floodplain of Williams Creek in Cape Girardeau County and cultivated to a corn (*Zea mays*) – soybean (*Glycine max*) rotation. The pedon exhibited the typical Ochric – Cambic – Cg horizon sequence. All soil horizons were silt loam. Munsell soil colors are 10YR4/3 (brown) to 10YR 4/4 (dark yellowish brown) from the Ap through the Bw horizons. The Cg horizons have 10YR5/3 (grayish brown) to 10YR5/1 (gray) and 10YR4/1 (dark gray) Munsell colors, suggesting gleyed soil conditions. The Ap and Bw horizons have weak, fine to medium, granular structures, whereas the deeper soil horizons have weak, fine to medium, subangular blocky structures.

The pH is neutral in the surface horizons and acidic to very strongly acidic in the subsurface horizons (**Table 1**). The soil organic matter content was 1.2% in the Ap horizon and 0.7 in the A horizon. The Cambic horizon's soil organic matter contents ranged from 0.6 to 0.3%, whereas the Cg horizons were 0.1%. Exchangeable calcium in the dominant exchangeable cation and the cation exchange capacity is medium in the Ochric and Cambic horizons and low in the Cg horizons. Interestingly, exchangeable sodium is more evident in the Cg horizons.

Horizon	**Depth (cm)**	**pH**	**SOM %**	**Ca**	**Mg**	**K**	**Na**	**Total Acidity**	**CEC**
							cmol charge kg^{-1}		
Ap	13	6.9	1.2	12.2	1.2	0.3	0.1	5.7	17.2
A	25	6.9	0.7	11.9	1.2	0.5	0.1	3.6	16.6
Bw1	41	6.5	0.6	9.7	1.2	0.1	0.1	3.8	14.1
Bw2	56	5.8	0.5	7.6	0.8	0.1	0.1	5.3	13.3
Bw3	74	5.3	0.3	4.8	0.8	0.1	0.1	5.2	11.0
Cg1	89	4.7	0.1	1.9	0.4	0.1	0.1	4.1	5.7
Cg2	104	4.8	0.1	3.3	1.2	0.1	0.2	4.6	8.8
Cg3	152	5.5	0.1	5.6	2.4	0.1	0.3	3.1	10.8

Horizon	Depth (cm)	pH	SOM %	Ca	Mg	K	Na	Total Acidity	CEC
Cg4	183	5.8	0.1	5.2	2.5	0.1	0.3	3.0	10.4
Cg5	203	5.9	0.1	5.4	2.4	0.1	0.3	3.0	10.5

pH in water, SOM is soil organic matter by loss on ignition. Exchangeable cations by ammonium acetate (pH 7) extraction, total acidity by BaCl2-thriethanolamine (cmol charge/kg), CEC is cation exchange capacity by ammonium acetate saturation (cmol charge/kg).

Table 1.
Chemical properties for a pedon of the Wilbur series.

6.4 Soil changes attributed to the installation of the riparian buffer

Soil pH was slightly more acidic in the riparian buffer, but the difference was not significant. Similarly, nitrate-N and phosphorus concentrations were not significantly different. Conversely, soil organic matter contents, sulfate-S, and ammonium-N concentrations were significantly different. Soils in the riparian buffer had greater soil organic matter contents, averaging 3.4%, whereas the production field exhibited an average soil organic matter content of 1.7%. (**Table 2**). Similarly, sulfate-S and ammonium-N concentrations were greater in the riparian buffer (**Table 2**). The riparian buffer's greater soil organic matter content was generally attributed to both detritus (particulate soil organic matter) and humus. The riparian forest vegetation created a living root web permeating the A horizon, that most likely reduced soil erosion, strengthened the soil structure, improved infiltration, and contributed to the soil organic matter accumulation. Greater sulfate-S and ammonium-N accumulations were likely attributed to greater mineralization rates.

Riparian buffers are natural-solutions, permitting soil processes to operate without human imposed stresses. Outside of the riparian buffer, subsurface and primary tillage is required because the silt loam soils exhibit compaction because of weak soil structures. However, tillage generally degrades soil structure, exposing soil organic matter to microbial activity. Establishment of the riparian buffer supported greater organic matter incorporation in the soil, a consequence likely attributable

	pH water	SOM %	SO_4-S ppm	NO_3-N ppm	NH_4-N ppm	P ppm
Inside the Riparian Buffer (5 sites)						
Mean	5.7	3.4	2.96	0.94	4.8	34.4
CV	0.11	0.13	0.10	0.72	0.18	0.19
CI	0.82	0.57	0.37	0.85	1.06	8.17
Adjacent to the Riparian Buffer (5 sites)						
Mean	6.2	1.7	2.14	2.04	2.6	39.2
CV	0.09	0.06	0.03	0.40	0.11	0.05
CI	0.07	0.14	0.07	1.01	0.34	2.2
T-test	0.20	0.0008	0.003	0.05	0.003	0.18

Note: CV is coefficient variation, CI is the confidence interval at p = 0.5. SOM is soil organic matter, P is Bray-1 phosphorus. T-test and other statistical analysis performed using Excel.

Table 2.
Selected surface properties in and adjacent to the riparian buffer.

to maintenance of the soil structures and a greater net primary production. The presence of rooting activity supports the formation of micro- and macro-aggregates that act to preserved the soil organic matter. O'Brien and Jastrow [30] isolated (i) non-aggregated material, (ii) free microaggregates, (iii) macroaggregates and (iii) microaggregates-within-macroaggregates to investigate how soil organic matter contents recover in plant community restorations. Microaggregates isolated from within macroaggregates contributed the greatest quantities of C and N to whole soil; however, the soil organic matter pools may recover over various time scales. Thus, restoration will succeed, but the time spans may be lengthy.

7. Conclusion

The presented literature conclusively demonstrates that the riparian buffer design criteria is predicated on which resource considerations are the most vital to address. The design criteria will vary if habitat improvement is integral to the purpose of the riparian buffer or water quality is the primary issue. Additionally, design criteria must consider the soil functionality, climate, existing and future land management, vegetation selection, and other factors.

Long-term outcomes from expertly designed riparian buffers are predicated on the selected resource considerations. However, emerging interest in riparian buffers to accumulate soil carbon and its long-term preservation are increasingly recognized as an integral design consideration. Additionally, riparian buffers are expected to sustain natural resources from increasing intense weather caused by climate change.

The study area is a riparian buffer established along Williams Creek in Cape Girardeau County, Missouri. The mixed deciduous stand increased the soil organic matter content compared to the adjacent agriculture field, a consequence attributed to increased soil carbon additions because of a greater net primary production. Sulfate and ammonium were similarly greater in the riparian buffer, a feature attributed to increased rates of mineralization. This project reflects outcomes predicted by the literature cited.

Author details

Michael Aide* and Indi Braden
Department of Agriculture, Southeast Missouri State University, USA

*Address all correspondence to: mtaide@semo.edu

References

[1] Cole LJ, Stockan J, Helliwell R. Managing riparian buffer strips to optimize ecosystem services: A review. Agriculture, Ecosystems and Environment. 2020;**296**(17):106891. DOI: 10.1016/j.agee.2020.106891

[2] Stutter MI, Chardon WJ, Kronvang B. Riparian buffer strips as a multifunctional management tool in agricultural landscapes: Introduction. Journal of Environmental Quality. 2012;**41**(2):297-303. DOI: 10.2134/jeq2011.0439

[3] Udawatta R, Gold M, Walter WD, McCoy R, Schultz RC. Establishing and Managing Riparian Forest Buffers. USA: University Missouri Extension; 2022 Available from: https://extension.missouri.edu/publications/af1009

[4] Singh R, Tiwari AK, Singh GS. Managing riparian zones for river health improvement: An integrated approach. Landscape and Ecological Engineering. 2021;**17**:195-223

[5] Mayer PM, Reynolds SK, McCutchen MD, Canfield TJ. Riparian Buffer Width, Vegetative Cover, and Nitrogen Removal Effectiveness: A Review of Current Science and Regulations. EPA/600/R-05/118. Cincinnati, OH: U.S. Environmental Protection Agency; 2006

[6] Buffler S. Riparian Buffer Design Guidelines for Water Quality and Wildlife Habitat Functions on Agricultural Landscapes in the Intermountain West: Appendix C. General Technical Reports RMRS-GTR-203. Fort Collins, CO: U.S. Department of Agriculture, Forest Service, Rocky Mountain Research Station; 2008. 59 p

[7] Bentrup G. Conservation Buffers: Design Guidelines for Buffers, Corridors, and Greenways. General Technical Reports SRS-109. Asheville, NC: Department of Agriculture, Forest Service, Southern Research Station; 2008. 110 p

[8] Feld CK, Fernandes MR, Ferreira MT, Hering D, Ormerod SJ, Venohr M, et al. Evaluating riparian solutions to multiple stressor problems in river ecosystems - a conceptual study. Water Research. 2018;**139**:381-394. DOI: 10.1016/j.watres.2018.04.014

[9] Craig LS, Palmer MA, Richardson DC, Filoso S, Bernhardt ES, Bledsoe BP, et al. Stream restoration strategies for reducing river nitrogen loads. Frontiers in Ecology and the Environment. 2008;**6**:529-538. DOI: doi.org/10.1890/070080

[10] Wu S, Amjad BM, Qurat-Ul-Ain R, Abdur R, Yucong G, Lei C. Application of riparian buffer zone in agricultural non-point source pollution control—A review. Frontiers in Sustainable Food Systems. 2023;7:985870. Available from: https://www.frontiersin.org/articles/10.3389/fsufs.2023.985870. DOI: 10.3389/fsufs.2023.985870

[11] Omidvar N, Xu Z, Nguyen TTN, Selehin B, Ogbourne S, Ford R, et al. A global meta-analysis shows soil nitrogen pool increases after revegetation of riparian zones. Journal of Soils and Sediments. 2021;**21**:665-677. DOI: 10.1007/s11368-020-02864-0

[12] Neilen AD, Chen CR, Parker BM, Faggotter SJ, Burford MA. Differences in nitrate and phosphorus export between wooded and grassed riparian zones from farmland to receiving waterways under varying rainfall conditions. Science of

the Total Environment. 2017;**598**:188-197. DOI: 10.1016/j.scitotenv.2017.04.075

[13] Dlamini J, Tesfamariam EH, Dunn R, Hood J, Hawkins JM, Blackwell MSA, et al. Soil carbon dioxide (CO_2) fluxes in permanent upslope pasture and downslope riparian buffers with varying vegetation. Journal of Plant Nutrition and Soil Science. 2023;**186**:406-416. DOI: 10.1002/jpln.202100292

[14] Udawatta RP, Motavalli PP, Garrett HE. Phosphorus loss and runoff characteristics in three adjacent agricultural watersheds with claypan soils. Journal of Environmental Quality. 2004;**33**:1709-1719

[15] Udawatta RP, Garrett HE, Kallenbach RL. Agroforestry buffers for non-point source pollution reductions from agricultural watersheds. Journal of Environmental Quality. 2011;**40**:800-806. DOI: 10.2134/jeq2010.0168

[16] Gageler R, Bonner M, Kirchhof G, Amos M, Robinson N, Schmidt S, et al. Early response of soil properties and function to riparian rainforest restoration. PLoS One. 2014;**9**(8):e104198. DOI: 10.1371/journal.pone.0104198

[17] Vijayakumar S, Bazrgar AB, Coleman B, Gordon A, Voroney P, Thevathasan N. Carbon stocks in riparian buffer systems at sites differing in soil texture, vegetation type and age compared to adjacent agricultural fields in southern Ontario, Canada. Agriculture, Ecosystems & Environment. 2020;**304**:107149. DOI: 10.1016/j.agee.2020.107149

[18] Fortier J, Truax B, Gagnon D, Lambert F. Root biomass and soil carbon distribution in hybrid poplar riparian buffers, herbaceous riparian buffers and natural riparian woodlots on farmland. Springerplus. 2013;**17**(2):539. DOI: 10.1186/2193-1801-2-539

[19] Ofosu E, Bazrgar A, Coleman B, Deen B, Gordon A, Voroney P, et al. Soil organic carbon enhancement in diverse temperate riparian buffer systems in comparison with adjacent agricultural soils. Agroforestry Systems. 2022;**96**:623-636. DOI: 10.1007/s10457-021-00691-x

[20] Dybala KE, Matzek V, Gardali T, Seavy NE. Carbon sequestration in riparian forests: A global synthesis and meta-analysis. Global Change Biology. 2018;**25**:57-67. DOI: 10.1111/gcb.14475

[21] Hou C, Li Y, Huang Y, Zhu H, Ma J, Yu F, et al. Reclamation substantially increases soil organic and inorganic carbon stock in riparian floodplains. Journal of Soils and Sediments. 2021;**21**:957-966. DOI: 10.1007/s11368-020-02836-4

[22] Matzek V, Lewis D, O'Geen A, Lennox M, Hogan SD, Freirer ST, et al. Increases in soil and woody biomass carbon stocks as a result of rangeland riparian restoration. Carbon Balance and Management. 2020;**15**:16. DOI: 10.1186/s13021-020-00150-7

[23] Schrumpf M, Kaiser K, Guggenberger G, Persson T, Kogel-Knabner I, Schulze ED. Storage and stability of organic carbon in soils as related to depth, occlusion within aggregates, and attachment to minerals. Biogeosciences. 2013;**10**:1675-1691. DOI: 10.5194/bg-10-1675-2013

[24] Schweizer S, Mueller C, Höschen C, Ivanov P, Kögel-Knabner I. The role of clay content and mineral surface area for soil organic carbon storage in an arable toposequence. Biogeochemistry.

2021;**156**:401-420. DOI: 10.1007/s10533-021-00850-3

[25] Liu D, Li S, Zhu W, Wang Y, Zhang S, Fang Y. Storage and stability of soil organic carbon in two temperate forests in Northeastern China. Land. 2023;**12**(5):1019. DOI: 10.3390/land12051019

[26] Schmidt MW, Torn MS, Abiven S, Dittmar S, Guggenberger G, Janssen IA, et al. Persistence of soil organic matter as an ecosystem property. Nature. 2011;**478**(7367):49-56. DOI: 10.1038/nature10386

[27] Verchot LV, Dutaur L, Shepherd KD, Albrecht A. Organic matter stabilization in soil aggregates: Understanding the biogeochemical mechanisms that determine the fate of carbon inputs in soils. Geoderma. 2011;**161**:182-193. DOI: 10.1016/j.geoderma.2010.12.017

[28] Kumar R, Rawat KS, Singh J, Singh A, Rai A. Soil aggregation dynamics and carbon sequestration. Journal of Applied and Natural Science. 2013;**5**(1):250-267. DOI: 10.31018/jans.v5i1.314

[29] Witzgall K, Vidal A, Schubert DI, Hoschen C, Schweizer SA, Buegger F, et al. Particulate organic matter as a functional soil component for persistent soil organic carbon. Nature Communications. 2021;**12**:4115. DOI: 10.1038/s41467-021-24192-8

[30] O'Brien SL, Jastrow JD. Physical and chemical protection in hierarchical soil aggregates regulates soil carbon and nitrogen recovery in restored perennial grasslands. Soil Biology and Biochemistry. 2013;**61**:1-13. DOI: 10.1016/j.soilbio.2013.01.031

Chapter 9

Threats and Sustainability of Brazil Nut (*Bertholletia excelsa* Bonpl.) Pre-Industrialization in the Amazon Region

Diego Oliveira Brandão, Julia Arieira and Carlos Afonso Nobre

Abstract

Brazil nut (*Bertholletia excelsa*) is an important species in the Amazon, but the relationships between seed production and climate change are still poorly understood. Seed production data were obtained for the entire Brazilian Amazon, while data on precipitation, relative humidity, vapor pressure deficit, and temperature (mean and maximum) were collected to test their relationship with seed production in the Baixo Amazonas. Annual seed production in the Baixo Amazonas varied between 2156 and 10,235 tons per year from 1990 to 2021, with an average of 5192 tons per year. Linear regression analyses did not identify significant relationships between seed production and climatic variables during the same year ($p > 0.05$). However, significant relationships were found between the volume of seeds in the base year and climatic variables from 1 year before seed collection ($p < 0.05$), except for total precipitation ($p = 0.15$). Temperature was the main climatic variable affecting Brazil nut production, indicating that each 1°C increase in temperature is associated with an average decrease in seed volume ranging from 2595 to 2673 tons. Temperature measures explain between 38% and 42% of the variability in seed volume in the Baixo Amazonas. Therefore, it is crucial to mitigate global warming, invest in technological processes to add value to the remaining seeds, and adopt *B. excelsa* varieties more adapted to climate change.

Keywords: Brazilian Amazon, climate change, climatic variability, El Niño, industrialization, non-timber forest product, relative humidity, temperature, vapor pressure deficit

1. Introduction

Brazil nut (*Bertholletia excelsa* Bonpl.) holds a key role in socio-bioeconomies [1, 2] providing vital economic inputs to local, national, and global markets during different seasons and bringing benefits to tens of thousands of small-scale producers [3] who live under a diversified economic portfolio [4]. It is also a source of food consumed in various forms, including fresh, roasted, or pressed for milk-like extract [5] within the Amazon, and outside (e.g., USA, China). Brazil is one of the leading producers of Brazil nut harvesting 33,406 metric tons in 2021 [6]. *B. excelsa* is a monotypic genus of Lecythidaceae, a pantropical botanic family. These trees can reach heights of up to 60 meters and diameters of 5 meters, often occupying upland moist forest (non-flooded) and transitional zones between Amazon forests and Cerrado savannas, with some trees reaching up to 1000 years old [1, 5].

Human influences have contributed to shaping the geographic distribution and abundance of Brazil nuts in the Amazon, following the movement of Indigenous peoples across the Amazon for thousands of years by mean of area expansion and shifting cultivation activities [5, 7, 8]. Today the Brazil Nut is one of the 20 super-dominant trees of the Amazon contributing beyond food security to the carbon cycle of the forest [9, 10]. The economy of the Brazil Nut in the Amazon is a forest-based extractive activity [6]. Brazil Nut trees form biodiverse forests gathered and traded by traditional communities, including extractivists, Indigenous groups, and African descendents (quilombola) [11–13]. This dynamic collaboration yields most of the Brazil nuts, creating a dual impact of income generation and biodiversity conservation [13, 14], impacting positively local people's livelihoods [15]. Brazil nut management may account for >40% of the annual extractivist family income [12].

The flowering phase is most pronounced during the driest months corresponding to the period of longer photoperiods. The mutualistic interactions between Brazil nut and their pollinators have significant implications for fruit production [16]. Fruiting occurs during the early rainy season (e.g., SON). The maturation process that lasts about 14 months indicates that the environmental conditions and biological interactions that occurred in the previous year can impact Brazil nut productivity in the following year [17]. Research conducted by Maués in 2002 revealed that precipitation, temperature, relative humidity, and photoperiod play a role in shaping the phenology of *B. excelsa* [17]. Pastana et al. showed that in a forest-savanna transition in the eastern Brazilian Amazon, the 2015/2016 El Niño phenomenon, when temperatures of the ocean increased more than 2°C during the dry season, fruit production decreased by up to 97% in 2017 [18]. The temporal variability in Brazil nut productivity influenced by climate oscillations pose major social and economic impacts on such forest-based extractivist communities in the Amazon, in some cases increasing by a quarter the prices of nut production unit (from USD 10 in 2016 to USD 38 in 2017) [18].

While Brazil nuts have gained significant economic importance in terms of both form and production volume, deforestation and climate changes are major threats to forest resilience impacting mainly large trees, subjected to drier and warmer climate, such as the Brazil nut tree [19, 20]. However, because the reproductive success of Brazil nut is intrinsically linked to the interaction of climatic conditions, pollination dynamics and human activities, the limits of resilience to the increasing changes in forest climate are not fully understood. Recent study, for instance, indicates that climate change could impact positively *B. excelsa* but only when seedlings are irrigated pointing to the fact that water restriction in the dry season in the Amazon is a key limiting factor [21].

To observe how seed productivity of Brazil nut varies across time and assess the potential impact of climate on its productivity, we compared temporal patterns of nut production between 1990 and 2021 in the Brazilian Amazon and in different socioecological Amazon sub-regions. To assess the influence of the climate variability on seed productivity we took the mesoregion Baixo Amazonas, one of the regions of the Amazon with the highest historical productivity and socioeconomic importance for the Brazil nut national market. Understanding the influence of climate variability in productivity provides an indicator of ecosystem stability and resilience, guiding sustainability of forest management systems [12].

2. Material and methods

2.1 Study area

The Amazon Forest is located in South America (**Figure 1A**). The forest region covers 6.3 million square kilometers, spanning Brazil, Bolivia, Colombia, Ecuador, French Guiana, Guyana, Peru, Suriname, and Venezuela. The human population in the region is estimated at 38 million inhabitants [26], with indications of 6 million

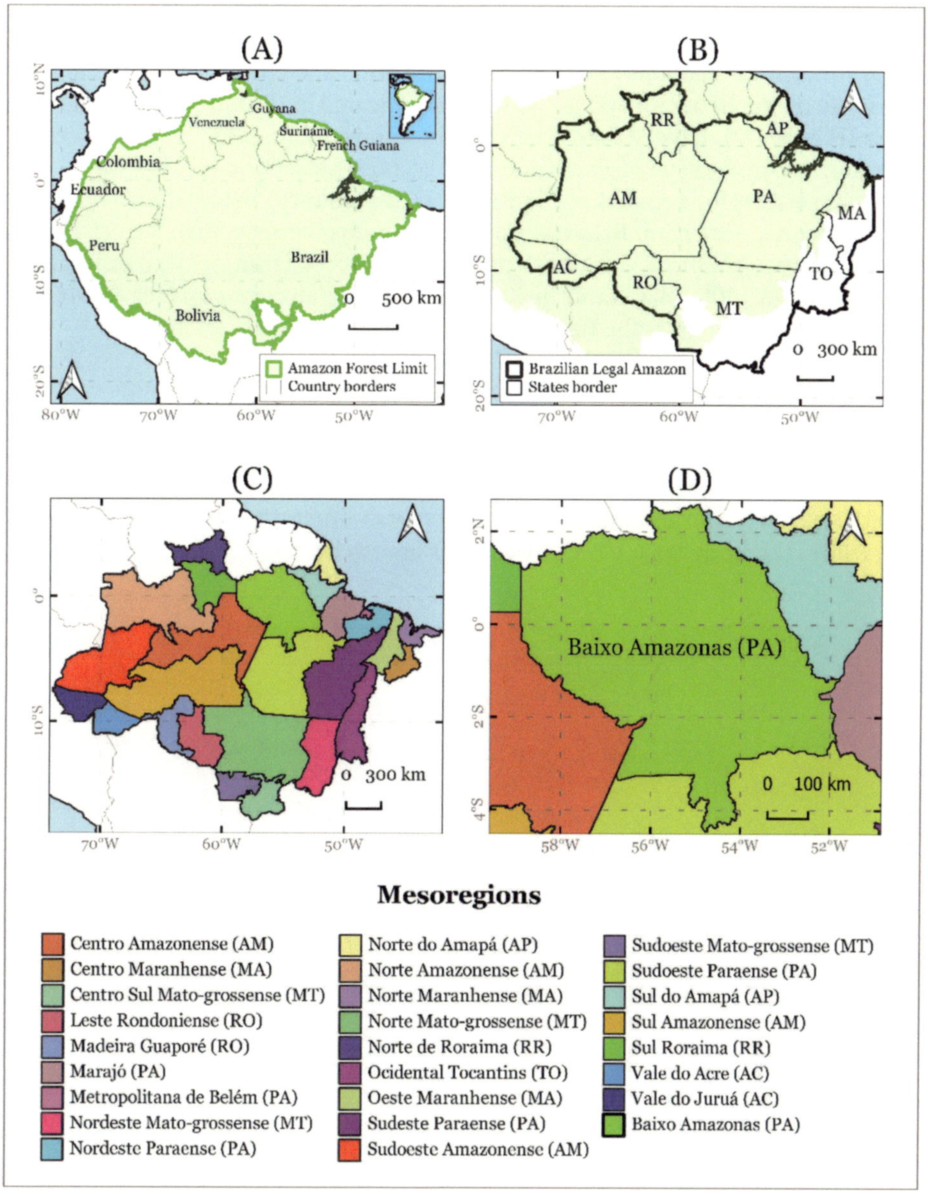

Figure 1.
Study area. Data source: INPE [22], QGIS [23], IBGE [24, 25].

people directly dependent on the forest for subsistence in the Brazilian Amazon [27]. The study area is located in Brazil (**Figure 1B**), occupying approximately 4.2 million square kilometers [24].

The study area was subdivided into mesoregions, which were analyzed in terms of Brazil nut production volume (**Figure 1C**). As defined by Brazilian Institute of Geography and Statistics [25], a mesoregion is a geographical delineation within a Federal Unit, shaped by the dimensions of social processes as a determining factor, natural conditions as a conditioning factor, and the network of communication and places as elements of spatial articulation. These dimensions collectively confer a regional identity to the mesoregion, a construction over time by the local society. In total, the study area consisted of 26 mesoregions, which together covered a total area of 4.7 million square kilometers (**Figure 1C**).

The study of interactions between seed production and climatic variables focuses specifically on the Baixo Amazonas mesoregion, located in the northwest of the state of Pará (**Figure 1D**). Baixo Amazonas is the most important mesoregion for Brazil nut production in the state of Pará's non-timber forest extraction [6]. The Baixo Amazonas mesoregion consists of 13 municipalities (county) that make up the territory: Alenquer, Almeirim, Belterra, Curuá, Mojuí dos Campos, Faro, Juruti, Monte Alegre, Óbidos, Oriximiná, Prainha, Santarém, and Terra Santa, with an estimated population of 785,000 inhabitants in 2022 [28]. The region covers an area of 340,000 square kilometers, roughly the size of Germany (357,000 square kilometers).

2.2 Brazil nut production data

The information regarding Brazil nut seed (**Figure 2**) production was obtained from sources at the Brazilian Institute of Geography and Statistics [6]. IBGE conducts annual data collection through the administration of questionnaires in each municipality within the study area. IBGE gathers this information by consulting agricultural

Figure 2.
Seeds of Bertholletia excelsa *(Brazil nut). Photo source: Diego Oliveira Brandão.*

and livestock establishments, industries, companies, government agencies, and other organizations involved in Brazil nut extraction, using the reference year as the survey's base. The dissemination of data is carried out through the IBGE Automated Recovery System (SIDRA), under the Production of Vegetable Extraction and Forestry (PEVS) survey, Table 289, and is accessible openly and online. The information regarding the quantity of Brazil nut seed production is expressed in tons. The data used covers the period from 1990 to 2021 and was collected for all mesoregions within the study area (**Figure 1C**).

2.3 Climatic variable data

Monthly climate data for precipitation, relative humidity, and temperature (average and maximum) were obtained from the Meteorological Database (BDMEP) of the National Institute of Meteorology of Brazil [29] to represent the climatic variations in the Baixo Amazonas mesoregion. These climate data originated from meteorological station 82,178, located in the municipality of Óbidos, Pará, Brazil, in the Baixo Amazonas mesoregion. This station is at an altitude of 54.7 meters, latitude −1.905° S, and longitude −55.52° W, and operated from January 1927 until July 2021, currently being closed. The data covered the period from 1989 to 2020 and were requested on July 24 and August 28, 2023.

The monthly climate data was transformed into annual climate data using the arithmetic mean. This calculation was done by summing the monthly values and dividing the result by 12 (the number of months in a year). However, in some cases, monthly climate data for certain variables were not available from the BDMEP. To fill in these missing data, the monthly arithmetic mean for the period from 1989 to 2020 was used. However, it's important to mention that the maximum and average temperature data for the years 2019 and 2020 were also unavailable, and it wasn't possible to fill them with the arithmetic mean. The missing data represented 4% of precipitation data, 2% of relative humidity data, and 2% of temperature data (average and maximum).

Finally, annual climate data for Vapor Pressure Deficit (VPD) was obtained. However, INMET did not provide VPD data at the Óbidos station [29]. Therefore, the VPD calculator [30] from the College of Agriculture and Life Science at the University of Arizona was used to obtain annual climate data for VPD from annual climate data for relative humidity and average temperature obtained at the Óbidos station. VPD data is a climatic variable used to assess plant water stress [31]. MS-Excel software was used to process the climate data.

2.4 Data analyses

Analyses of variations in Brazil nut production were conducted for the Brazilian Amazon and the 26 mesoregions studied between 1990 and 2021 and are presented graphically. These results were also presented with statistics including minimum, maximum, arithmetic mean, and standard deviation. All the graphical figures presented were created by the authors using the software MS-Excel, R, and QGIS.

The Baixo Amazonas mesoregion (PA) was selected as the case study to assess the impact of climatic variables on the temporal fluctuations in Brazil nut production. This region, besides being one of the largest Brazil nut producers in the Amazon, also provides long-term time series of climatic data. Therefore, simple linear regression analyses were conducted to investigate the relationship between Brazil nut production and each of the five climatic variables.

The regression analyses were conducted using the climatic data from the same year in which the Brazil nut production data were recorded (referred to as the 'base year'). Additionally, climatic data from 1 year before seed collection were correlated with the seed production observations in the base year. This allowed for the assessment of potential delays in the response of Brazil nut production to annual climatic variations. Before conducting these analyses, the Shapiro-Wilk test was performed to check the normality of the seed production data, including residual analysis.

The values of intercept, slope coefficient, adjusted R-squared, and p-value estimated by the models were presented in the figure depicting the relationship between seed production and climatic variables. The intercept and slope coefficient represent the model's fitting parameters. The R-squared value and p-value indicate the explanatory power of the model and its significance. Hypothesis testing and model construction were conducted using the statistical software R, version 4.3.1 [32].

3. Results

3.1 Annual Brazil nut production in the Brazilian Amazon

Brazil nut seed production in the Brazilian Amazon between 1990 and 2021 exhibited significant variations (**Figure 3**). Annual production ranged from a minimum of 21,468 tons (1996) to a maximum of 50,521 tons (1990). The years with relatively lower production were 1992, 1993, 1996, 1997, 1998, 1999, 2003, and 2017, representing the lower 25% of the data when production was below 27,008 tons. On the other

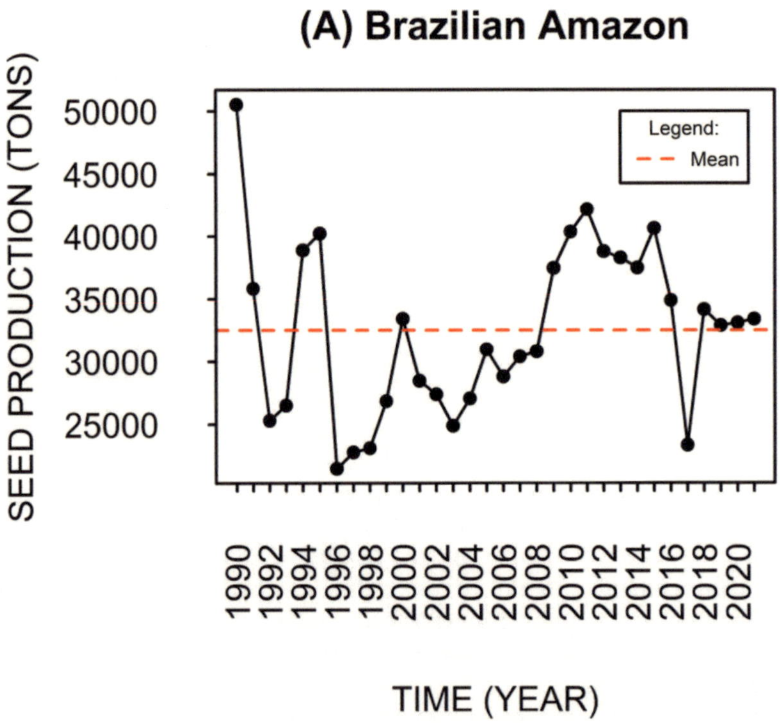

Figure 3.
Quantity of seeds produced in the Brazilian Amazon between 1990 and 2021. Data source: IBGE [6].

hand, the years with higher production were 1990, 1994, 2010, 2011, 2012, 2013, and 2015, representing the upper 75% of the data when production exceeded 37,701 tons. The average annual production was 32,525 tons, with a dispersion around this average indicated by a standard deviation of 6844 tons.

The average seed production in the 26 studied mesoregions showed significant variability (**Figure 4**). Out of these mesoregions, a total of 18 had seed production during the analyzed period (**Table 1**). On the other hand, eight mesoregions did not record any seed production during the study period. Among these, six were located in the states of Maranhão (Norte Maranhense, Oeste Maranhense, and Centro Maranhense) and Mato Grosso (Centro Sul Mato-grossense, Nordeste Mato-grossense, and Sudoeste Mato-grossense). The other two mesoregions that did not have seed production were Vale do Juruá (AC) and Norte do Amapá (AP). These results highlight significant differences in seed production among the mesoregions during the study period (**Figure 4**; **Table 1**).

Regarding the most productive mesoregions, five stood out in terms of average seed production volume (**Figure 5**): Vale do Acre (AC), Sul Amazonense (AM), Baixo Amazonas (AM), Centro Amazonense (AM), and Madeira Guaporé (RO). These five mesoregions are within the upper 75% of the average data (3rd quartile) and are located along a diagonal that extends from the northeast to the southwest of the Brazilian Amazon.

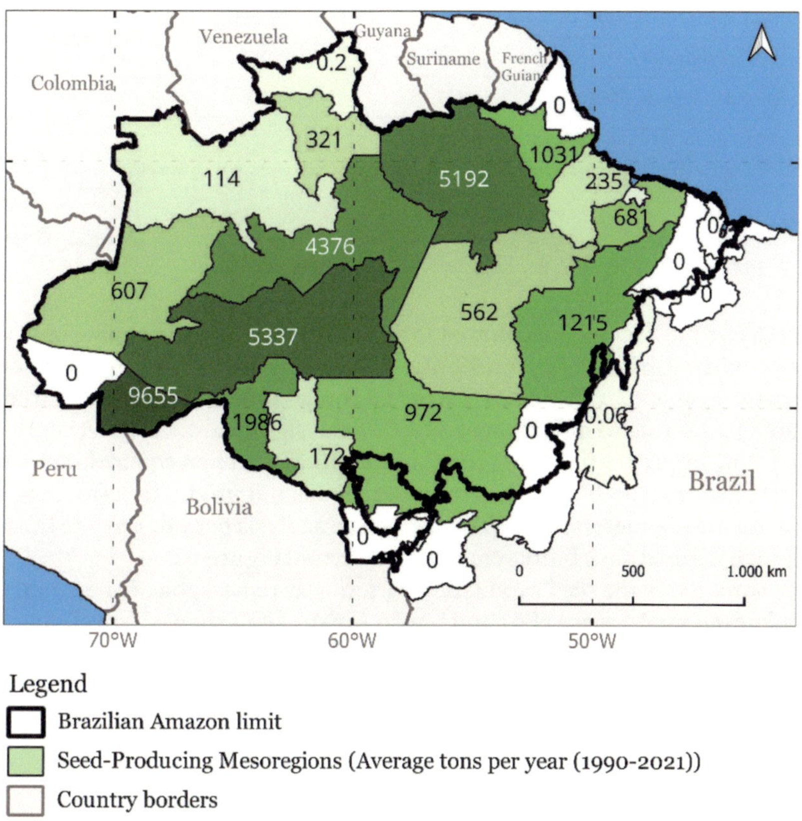

Figure 4.
The average Brazil nut production in the Brazilian Amazon mesoregions from 1990 to 2021. Data source: IBGE [6].

Mesoregion (State)	Minimum (year)	Maximum (year)	Mean	Standard deviation
Vale do Acre (AC)	3378 (1997)	17,497 (1990)	9665	3623
Sul Amazonense (AM)	87 (1992)	10,378 (1994)	5337	1834
Baixo Amazonas (PA)	2156 (1999)	10,235 (1990)	5192	1781
Centro Amazonense (AM)	101 (1992)	10,049 (2009)	4376	2630
Madeira Guaporé (RO)	364 (1997)	6424 (2000)	1986	1378
Sudeste Paraense (PA)	582 (2021)	2872 (1991)	1215	563
Sul do Amapá (AP)	390 (2009)	2250 (1990)	1031	610
Norte Mato-grossense (MT)	230 (1997)	2234 (2011)	972	730
Nordeste Paraense (PA)	434 (1996)	1237 (2016)	681	248
Sudoeste Amazonense (AM)	2 (1993)	1033 (2010)	607	316
Sudoeste Paraense (PA)	126 (2017)	2118 (1990)	562	435
Sul de Roraima (RR)	0 (1992–1997)	2230 (2018)	321	658
Marajó (PA)	137 (1990)	335 (2015)	235	56
Leste Rondoniense (RO)	31 (2002)	581 (1998)	172	151
Norte Amazonense (AM)	0 (1991)	358 (2014)	114	123
Metropolitana de Belém (PA)	4 (1994–1995)	121 (2015)	57	40
Norte de Roraima (RR)	0 (*)	6 (2017)	0.2	1
Ocidental de Tocantins (TO)	0 (*)	2 (2017)	0.06	0.36

**Every year except for 2017.*
Data source: IBGE [6].

Table 1.
Statistics for the quantity (in tonnes) of Brazil nut seeds produced between 1990 and 2021 in the 18 mesoregions of the Brazilian Amazon.

These five mesoregions accounted for 73.6% to 85.7% of the annual seed volume in the Brazilian Amazon between 1990 and 2021 (**Figure 5, Table 1**). On average, these mesoregions contributed 81.2% of the annual production, with a variation indicated by a standard deviation of 3.5%. This is significant, considering that these five mesoregions cover only 29% (equivalent to 1.354 million square kilometers) of the total study area or 33% of the area where Brazil nut production (totaling 4.070 million square kilometers) occurred during the analysis period. Despite the high production, annual variability remains significant (**Figure 6**).

The variation in the seed production pattern was remarkable. For example, mesoregions like Sudeste Paraense (PA) and Sul do Amapá (AP) showed a declining trend in production, whereas Norte Mato-grossense, Sul de Roraima (RR), and Marajó (PA) exhibited a growing trend (**Figure 7**). This variation in seed production highlights the need for more in-depth research to understand the nuances behind these fluctuations.

3.2 Climatic trends observed at the Óbidos Station in the Baixo Amazonas

The data precipitation and temperature data provided an understanding of the monthly climatic conditions at the Óbidos station (**Figure 8**). The highest amounts of

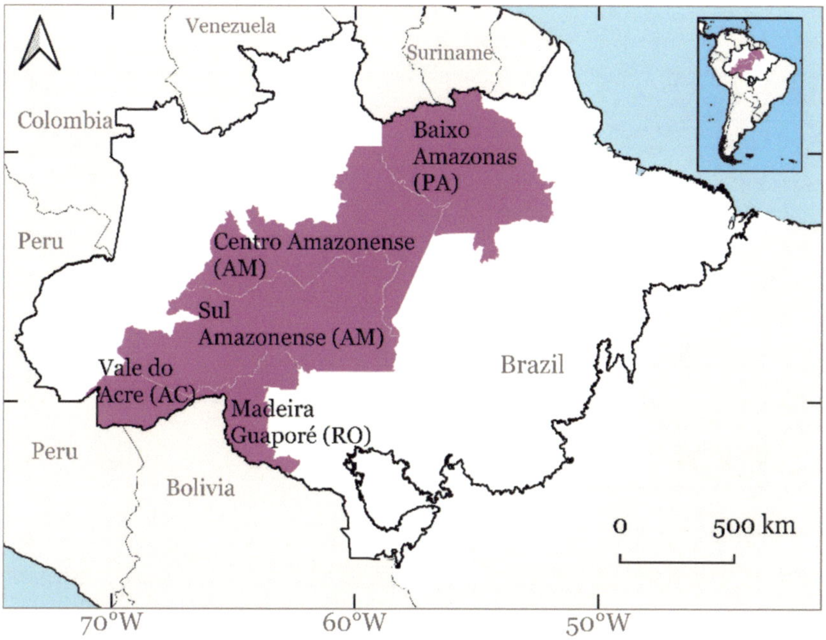

Figure 5.
Major Brazil nut producing mesoregions. Data source: IBGE [6].

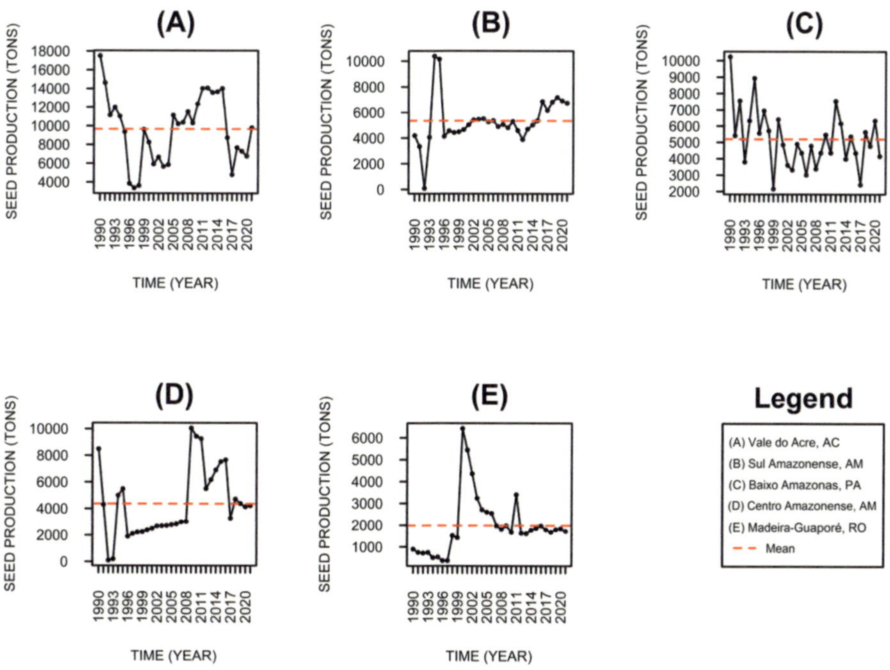

Figure 6.
Representation of the annual variation in Brazil nut seed production in the five most productive mesoregions between 1990 and 2021: (A) Vale do Acre, AC. (B) Sul Amazonense, AM. (C) Baixo Amazonas, PA. (D) CentroAmazonense, AM. (E) Madeira-Guaporé, RO. Data source: IBGE [6]. The dotted red line represents the arithmetic mean of seed production during the study period

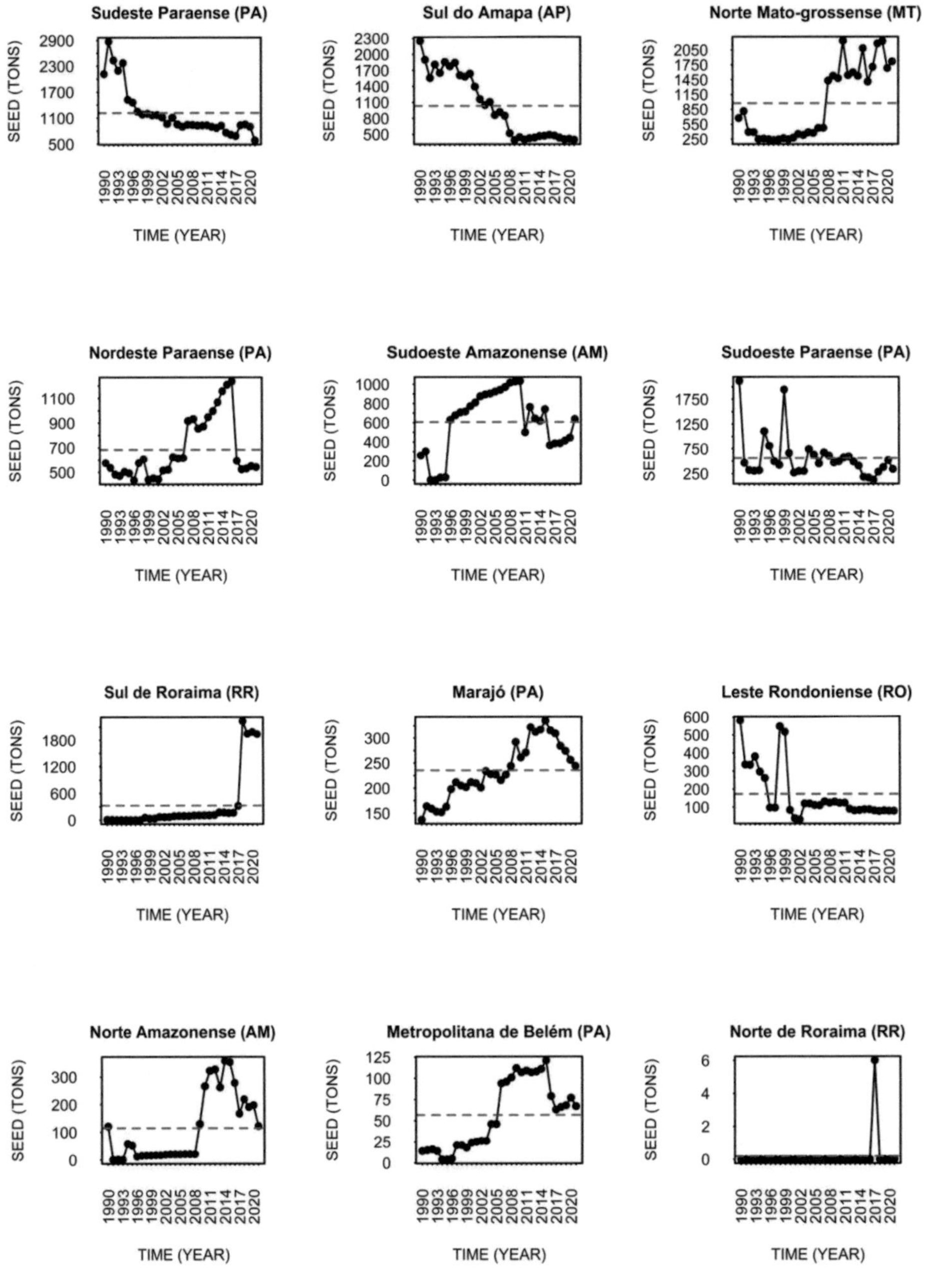

Figure 7.
The mesoregions of the Brazilian Amazon with an average Brazil nut production ranging from 0.2 to 1215 tons per year between 1990 and 2021. Data source: IBGE [6]. The dotted red line represents the arithmetic mean of seed production during the study period.

rainfall occurred during the austral summer, from December to February, extending into the autumn months of March to May. On the other hand, the driest months, from June to October, coincided with average and maximum temperatures, especially during the transition from the dry season to the wet season in October. In fact, temperatures were lower in February and March and higher in October.

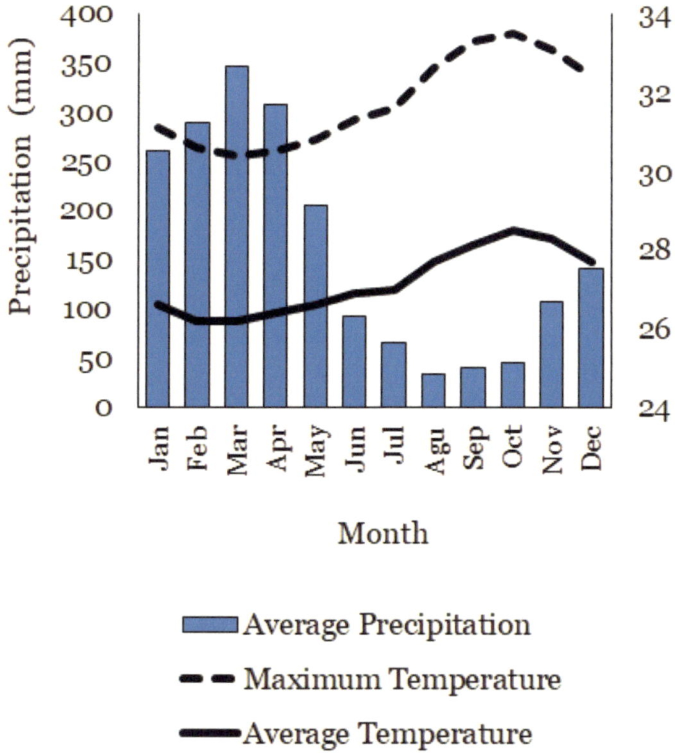

Figure 8.
Climatological normal at the Óbidos station in the Baixo Amazonas mesoregion (PA) during the period from 1989 to 2020. Data source: INMET [29].

The observed data also provided an overview of the average annual climatic conditions and their variability (standard deviation) between 1989 and 2020 (**Figure 9**). The average precipitation was 1943 millimeters (± 314 mm), with the lowest volume of 1209 mm in 1992 and the peak of 2624 mm in 2008. The average relative humidity was 82.8% (± 1.75%), with the lowest record of 80.2% in 2017 and the highest of 86.7% in 1992. The annual average VPD was 0.62 kilopascals (± 0.08 kPa), ranging from 0.47 in 1994 to 0.74 in 2016. In turn, the average and maximum temperatures were observed at 27.15°C (± 0.43°C) and 31.73°C (± 0.47°C), respectively. These temperatures recorded their lowest values in 1990, at 26.34°C and 30.66°C, respectively. On the other hand, the highest values were recorded in 2016 and 1998 at 27.83°C and 32.33°C, respectively.

It was possible to visually observe some trends in the climatic data over the analyzed period (**Figure 9**). While there is no trend in total precipitation, the VPD showed an increasing trend, reflecting the rise in average temperatures and the decrease in relative humidity over the years. Average and maximum temperatures also increased during the study period. **Figure 9** provides a more detailed visual representation of the climatic data collected at the meteorological station located in Óbidos.

It's important to note that many of the climatic variables are correlated (**Figure 10**). As VPD and average and maximum temperatures increase, relative humidity tends to decrease. On the other hand, no significant linear relationships were observed between temperature and total precipitation, as well as between relative humidity and total precipitation.

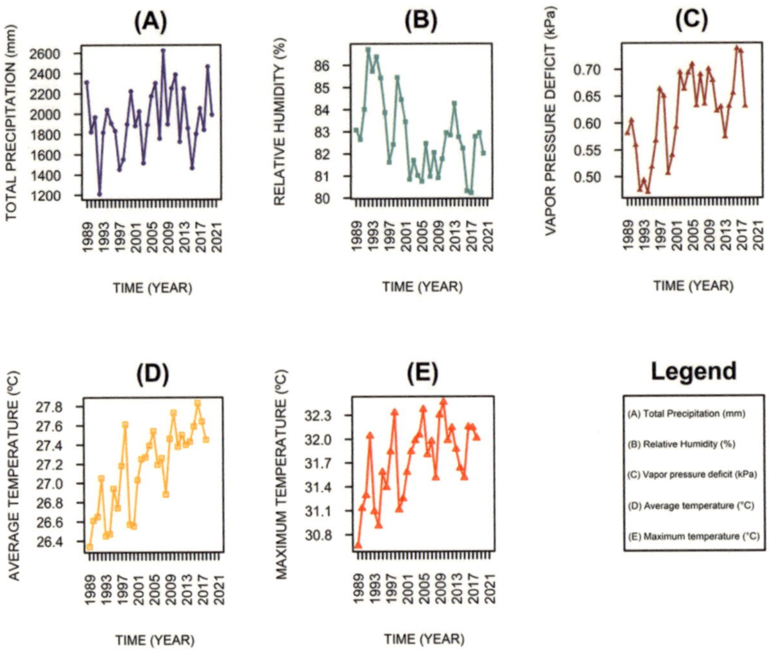

Figure 9.
Climatic variability in the Baixo Amazonas mesoregion between 1989 and 2021: (A) Total precipitation. (B) Relative humidity. (C) Vapor pressure deficit. (D) Average temperature. (E) Maximum temperature. Data source: INMET [29], University of Arizona [30].

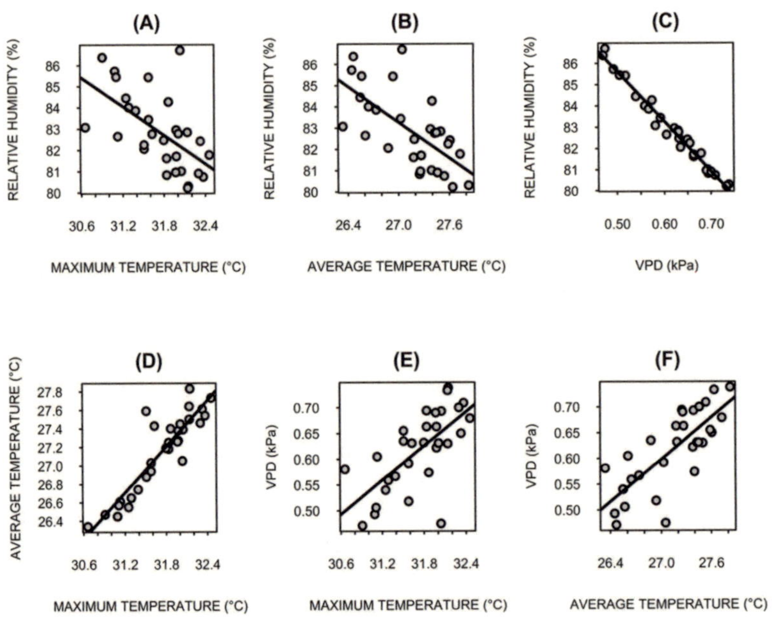

Figure 10.
Significant relationships between climatic variables in the Baixo Amazonas between 1989 and 2020: (A) Relative humidity and maximum temperature. (B) Relative humidity and average temperature. (C) Relative humidity and vapor pressure deficit. (D) Average temperature and maximum temperature. (E) Vapor pressure deficit and maximum temperature. (F) Vapor pressure deficit and average temperature. Data source: INMET [29], University of Arizona [30].

3.3 Relationships between seed production and climatic variables in the Baixo Amazonas

Brazil nut seed production in the Baixo Amazonas (PA) varied over the period from 1990 to 2021. The lowest value was recorded in 1993, with 3797 tons, while the peak occurred in 1990, with 10,235 tons (**Table 1**). Despite the annual fluctuations, the data analysis did not reveal a significant relationship between seed production and climatic conditions during the fruit collection year. This suggests that climatic variations did not have a direct and linear influence on seed production in the same year.

On the other hand, there are significant relationships between variations in seed production from the base year and climatic variables from 1 year before seed

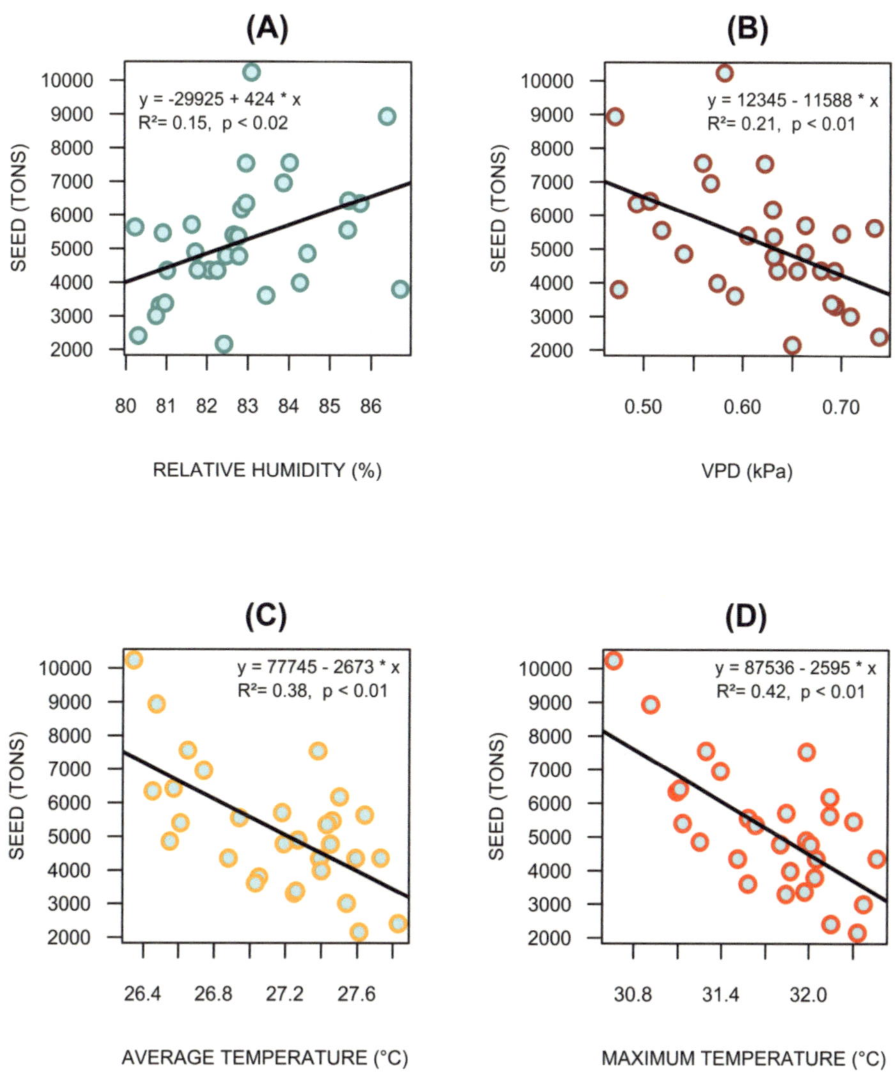

Figure 11.
Representation of the linear regression models between seed production and climatic variables in the Baixo Amazonas: (A) Seed and relative humidity. (B) Seed and vapor pressure deficit. (C) Seed and average temperature. (D) Seed and maximum temperature. Only significant relations are presented ($p<0.05$). Data source: IBGE [6], INMET [29], University of Arizona [30].

collection, indicating significant associations between the climatic conditions of the preceding year and nut production in the base year. Although there is no linear relationship with total precipitation, the other climatic variables exert an influence on seed production. While relative humidity has a positive influence, VPD and temperature have a negative influence on seed production (**Figure 11**).

Regarding relative humidity, the results of the linear regression estimated a slope coefficient of 424. This indicates that a 1% increase in relative humidity is associated with an increase of 424 tons of seeds. The model suggests that approximately 15% of the variability in seed volume was explained by relative humidity.

Regarding VPD, the results of the linear regression estimated a slope coefficient of −11.588. This indicates that a 0.1 unit increase in the VPDt variable is associated with a decrease of 1.158 tons of seeds. The model suggests that approximately 21% of the variability in seed volume was explained by the VPD.

The results of the linear regression analysis showed slope coefficients of −2673 and − 2595 for the average temperature and maximum temperature variables, respectively. This implies that a 1°C increase in temperature is associated with an average decrease in seed volume ranging from 2595 to 2673 tons. Temperature measures explain between 38–42% of the variability in seed volume. This indicated that average and maximum temperatures played an important role in explaining variations in seed volume in the Baixo Amazonas (PA).

To sum up, as temperatures rise (1°C increase), it leads to an increase in VPD (0.14 increase), which in turn contributes to a decrease in seed production at order of 1622 tons. This relationship highlights the sensitivity of seed production to climatic factors, particularly temperature and VPD, which can have a substantial impact on harvesting outcomes.

4. Discussion

4.1 Variability of Brazil nut production in the Brazilian Amazon

The analysis of seed production in the Brazilian Amazon from 1990 to 2021 revealed significant variability, a result that has also been observed in other mesoregions within the study area. For example, in the Vale do Acre (AC), areas located approximately 30 km apart showed differences of more than three times in the number of fruits during the period from 2010 to 2019 [33]. In the Sul de Roraima mesoregion, a difference of 52 times was observed between the year of highest production and the year of lowest production during the period from 2006 to 2012 [34]. Regarding fruit production per tree, the observed variation ranged from 12 to 216 [34]. Therefore, the variability identified in this study is consistent with the variability found at the population and tree levels of *B. excelsa*.

The contrast in seed production in the studied area can be explained by variations in soil chemistry. The availability of phosphorus has been associated with higher Brazil nut fruit production [33] as it improves physiological characteristics of trees such as electron transport and gas exchange and increases nutrient efficiency, including nitrogen, potassium, calcium, and magnesium [35]. In fact, phosphorus availability in the Amazon is higher near the Andes [36], where the Vale do Acre (AC) mesoregion is located, characterized in this study with the highest average annual seed production (**Figure 2**). Furthermore, a relatively higher total phosphorus content in the drainage basins of the Solimões, Juruá, Purus, and Amazon rivers [37] can explain the location of the five most productive mesoregions for Brazil nut, as shown in the results of this study (**Figure 2**). This suggests that the area with the highest seed production, extending diagonally from southwest to northeast of the Brazilian Amazon (**Figure 3**), is associated with regions with greater phosphorus availability.

Deforestation may potentially explain a part of the variation in seed production in the study area. In fact, the negative relationship between increasing deforestation and Brazil nut seed production has been observed since the 1950s in the mesoregions of Tocantins, Maranhão, and Pará [38–40]. Previous studies have examined deforestation rates and Brazil nut seed production and found significant and negative relationships across the entire Brazilian Amazon [41]. In this context, the reduction in seed production is a direct result of the loss of Brazil nut trees, but it is also related to the effects of fragmentation, forest fires, loss of pollinators, and climate change attributed to deforestation [42]. This indicates that seed production tends to decrease as deforestation proceeds in the studied mesoregions.

Ecological interactions have also been associated with variability in fruit production. CARDOSO et al. [43] found that canopy size and the proximity between trees are significantly related to fruit production, with higher production for trees with larger canopies and trees that are closer to each other, which was attributed to greater pollination efficiency. Several studies suggest a negative relationship between the activities of Brazil nut pollinators (*Eulaema mocsaryi* and *Xylocopa frontalis*) and the presence of smoke from wildfires and an increase in environmental temperature [44, 45]. This indicates that in more fragmented forests, such as in the mesoregions of North Maranhão (MA), West Maranhão (MA), Central Maranhão (MA), Central South Mato Grosso (MT), Northeast Mato Grosso (MT), Southwest Mato Grosso (MT), and Western Tocantins (TO), the lower seed quantity could be related to a reduction in pollinator efficiency.

4.2 Influence of climate variation on Brazil nut production in the Baixo Amazonas

The analyzed data did not reveal a significant relationship between climatic variables and the volume of Brazil nuts in the Baixo Amazonas when considering data from the same year. This underscores the complexity of the fruiting process and highlights the importance of not only considering the climatic conditions of the base year in seed production in the Amazon. In fact, according to Maués [17], the process between anthesis and fruit dispersal spans 14 months. Therefore, the lack of a significant relationship between the analyzed climatic variables and the volume of Brazil nuts when considering data from the same year may be related to the reproductive development cycle of *B. excelsa*.

On the other hand, significant relationships were found between the volume of Brazil nuts from the base year and climatic variables from 1 year before seed collection, except for total precipitation. In fact, previous studies did not identify significant changes in precipitation in the Baixo Amazonas when analyzing the period from 1973 to 2013 [46]. In the Central Amazonian mesoregion, in the municipality of Tefé, fruiting between 2013 and 2018 was not correlated with precipitation [47], corroborating the results of the present study. However, seed production in other mesoregions may be influenced by precipitation. This was evident in the Sul do Amapá mesoregion, where an association was observed between low precipitation and reduced production [18], and in the Sul Amazonense (AM) mesoregion, where a relationship was noted between excessive precipitation and Brazil nut tree mortality [48], potentially reducing fruit production.

Air relative humidity had a positive effect on the volume of Brazil nut production. This possibly occurred because, under conditions of high air relative humidity, stomatal pores tend to remain open, favoring the assimilation of carbon dioxide (CO_2) by Brazil nut trees. The assimilation of CO_2 is essential for photosynthesis, which is the process by which plants convert CO_2 and sunlight into glucose and other sugars [49]. These substances are essential for fruit development, and it is possible to argue that air relative humidity can positively influence the production of Brazil nut fruits in the Baixo Amazonas mesoregion.

However, relative humidity in the Baixo Amazonas showed a decrease between 1989 and 2020 (**Figure 9** A). Lower air relative humidity in a pasture area in the Baixo Amazonas was also significantly related to lower fruit production when compared to fruit production in a forest fragment [43]. Although higher relative humidity creates favorable conditions for fruit production [31], it is important to note that other climatic variables, such as VPD and temperature, are significantly related to relative humidity (**Figure 10**). In fact, air relative humidity has been decreasing as VPD and average and maximum temperatures are increasing. This trend raises concerns about Brazil nut fruit production in the study area.

The increase in VPD has effects on the growth and reproductive development of plants. Although studies are limited, scientific literature indicates that an increase in VPD reduces the number of flowers and may cause changes in fruit composition, resulting in significant reductions in productivity [31]. Furthermore, reduced photosynthesis, changes in gas exchange (stomatal conductance), alterations in architecture, changes in hormonal production, and increased transpiration rate are other biophysical and biochemical changes associated with increased VPD [31, 50]. This corroborates with the results of the present study, which showed a reduction in seed volume preceded by years with higher VPD.

The increase in global temperature has intensified atmospheric demand for evaporation [51] and has led to an exponential increase in VPD in the atmosphere [52]. In the Amazon region, this increase in VPD is more pronounced during the dry season, which is a natural phenomenon caused by seasonal variation in solar radiation and the northward migration of the Intertropical Convergence Zone over South America [53]. However, it is important to note that the increase in VPD is also related to deforestation and forest fires caused by human activities [54]. Therefore, the combination of global climate change and land-use changes in the Amazon raises concerns about the ongoing reduction in Brazil nut production as VPD increases in the region.

Regarding temperature, it was possible to observe a significant influence of temperature measurements from 1 year before seed collection. Similar results were observed by Pastana et al. [18]. These authors identified a negative relationship between Brazil nut production and temperature anomalies occurring in the third quarter before harvest in the Sul do Amapá mesoregion. Notably, these authors highlighted that the 2017 fruiting season showed a production reduction twice as large as the average for the period from 2005 to 2018.

Increasing temperature affects how plants produce organic compounds [49]. This happens because temperature influences enzymes in the leaves, leading to changes related to fruit production [55]. As the temperature rises, chemical reactions in the leaves increase, but they reach a maximum point when enzymes become deactivated, and the enzymatic structure is affected by the heat. These chemical changes affect photosynthesis, especially the action of the enzyme Rubisco, which is essential for converting CO_2 and water into glucose and oxygen using solar energy [55].

Field studies have demonstrated a reduction in gross ecosystem productivity in the Amazon forest when temperatures exceed 27°C [56]. In the study area under analysis, the average temperature ranged from 26.34°C to 27.05°C, with an average of 26.62°C, from 1989 to 1993. In the period from 2014 to 2018, the average temperature fluctuated between 27.43°C and 27.83°C, with an average of 27.59°C. These data indicate a temperature increase of 1.49°C in the mentioned intervals, considering the difference between the lowest and highest recorded average temperatures (**Figure 9**), while the average Brazil nut production decreased from 6666 tons to 4505 tons between these periods. Therefore, physiological changes associated with rising temperatures are likely reducing fruit production in the Baixo Amazonas mesoregion.

The years characterized by the lowest seed production volumes were 1992, 1993, 1996, 1997, 1998, 1999, 2003, and 2017. These years coincide with El Niño events, a recurring natural phenomenon resulting in abnormal warming of equatorial Pacific Ocean waters and surface temperatures over the Amazon. In the case of the El Niño event in November 2015, a temperature anomaly of 2.5°C was recorded in the Amazon [57]. El Niño events were observed during the study period in the years 1991/1992, 1993, 1994/1995, 1997/1998, and 2015/2016 [57, 58]. The World Meteorological Organization estimated that El Niño is likely to be positive from December 2023 to February 2024 [59]. These results suggest a relationship between past El Niño events and a reduction in Brazil nut production in the Baixo Amazonas mesoregion, which may repeat in future El Niño events.

Finally, temperature variation can interfere with the plant-animal interactions in the reproductive cycle of Brazil nut. Cavalcante et al. [44] studies showed a high inverse correlation between temperature increase and a reduction in the activity of *B. excelsa* pollinators (*Eulaema mocsaryi* and *Xylocopa frontalis*). Temperature increase also favors wildfires, which, according to observations from local producers, the smoke would be reducing the activity of Brazil nut pollinators, even in years when the number of flowers is higher, resulting in low fruit production [45]. Therefore, ecological interactions involving Brazil nut pollinators could be compromised in years when temperatures are higher, potentially reducing seed production.

4.3 Sustainability in Brazil nut production in the Amazon

The analysis of interactions affecting Brazil nut production in the Amazon region emphasizes the urgency of a sustainable approach. Achieving temperature goals of no more than 1.5°C is imperative to avoid a critical point of irreversible losses. For example, the models in this study indicate that a 2°C increase could result in decreases ranging from 5190 to 5346 tons of seeds (**Figure 11** C; D), approaching the average production volume in the analyzed period, calculated at 5192 tons (**Table 1**).

Furthermore, the implementation of industrialization processes emerges as a prominent element to add value and mitigate losses resulting from temperature increases [60]. However, industrialization in the Amazon still poses a significant challenge in the context of sustainable development. For instance, when 532 municipalities were examined, only 17 nut processing facilities were found, scattered across 16 different municipalities [41].

Industrial technology can increase the value of products derived from nuts, multiplying it from two to five times [42]. In previous years, fresh nuts, along with their shells, were purchased by factories for prices ranging from US$ 0.30 to 4.12 per kilogram. Nuts destined for oil production were traded at prices ranging from $0.3 to $1, while dehydrated nuts for consumption fluctuated between $1.5 and $4.12. The oil resulting from the pressing of the nuts reached a value of $13 per kilogram, and dehydrated nuts (**Figure 12**) were sold for $15. These examples highlight the intrinsic potential for increasing the added value of primary products through the establishment of basic technological infrastructure [42].

Figure 12.
Dehydrated seeds of Bertholletia excelsa *(Brazil nut) produced by Cooperativa Mista Agroextrativista do Rio Unini (COOMARU) in the Norte Amazonense (AM) mesoregion. Photo source: Diego Oliveira Brandão.*

Strategies to address the challenges posed by the temperature increase and its effects on Brazil nut production in the Amazon also require investments in research and the development of nut varieties more adapted to climate change. Additionally, the adoption of agroforestry systems in degraded and abandoned areas emerges as a viable solution. Proper climate change management involves the use of management systems that allow for more precise control of environmental variables such as temperature and relative humidity. Studies have highlighted the direct influence of these factors on fruit yield [31, 61], emphasizing the need for proactive approaches.

Additionally, the transition to agroforestry systems offers significant advantages. By enabling more efficient management, these systems have the potential to generate surpluses of forest products. This contrasts with the predominant extractive systems in the current Brazil nut production chain, providing a more sustainable approach to the market [62, 63]. Therefore, by investing in research, variety development, and agroforestry systems, it is possible to address the impacts of climate change on Brazil nut production.

5. Conclusions

The annual Brazil nut seed production in the Brazilian Amazon concentrated in five mesoregions between 1990 and 2021. Data analysis did not reveal a significant relationship between climatic variables and Brazil nut volume in the Baixo Amazonas mesoregion when considering data from the same year. However, significant relationships were identified between the volume of Brazil nuts in the base year and climatic variables from 1 year before seed collection, except for total precipitation. While relative humidity has a positive influence on seed volume, vapor pressure deficit and temperature had negative effects.

Maximum temperature stood out as the most influential climatic variable in the annual variation of Brazil nut production in the Baixo Amazonas. The trends of increasing temperatures and the consequent reduction in relative humidity result in an increase in vapor pressure deficit. This observation casts a new perspective on the impacts of climate change in the Amazon region on the Brazil nut market. These observations are a cause for concern, as *B. excelsa* seeds have played a fundamental role in the livelihoods of Indigenous communities for thousands of years and local communities for centuries.

To conserve Brazil nut production, it is essential to curb global temperature rise, invest in industrial processes, adopt Brazil nut varieties better adapted to climate change, and restore Brazil nut occurrence lands with agroforestry systems. These measures can not only contribute to maintaining and increasing the annual production of Brazil nut but also add value to the products, preserving the importance of this ecosystem service in providing food and income for those living in the Amazon. Without the implementation of these measures, Brazil nut production is susceptible to the negative impacts of climate change.

New studies are important to expand knowledge about annual variations in Brazil nut production, including in terms of economic value. Additional research can explore whether climate variations affect other mesoregions to determine if the results observed in this study can be generalized or specific only to the Baixo Amazonas. Finally, it is relevant to understand how the synergistic interaction between global climate change and land use changes, especially deforestation, can impact on Brazil nut production.

Acknowledgements

The authors would like to acknowledge Cristina Ribeiro, Gabriel Sperandéo, and Vinicius Leonardo Siqueira for their support in the preparation of this study.

Conflict of interest

The authors declare no conflict of interest.

Author details

Diego Oliveira Brandão[1]*, Julia Arieira[1] and Carlos Afonso Nobre[2]

1 Technical-Scientific Secretariat of the Science Panel for the Amazon (SPA), São Paulo, Brazil

2 Institute of Advanced Studies, University of São Paulo, São Paulo, Brazil

*Address all correspondence to: diegobrandao779@gmail.com

References

[1] Pires JM. The Amazon forest. In: Sioli H, editor. The Amazon: Limnology and Landscape Ecology of a Mighty Tropical River and its Basin. Dordrecht: Springer; 1984. pp. 581-601. DOI: 10.1007/978-94-009-6542-3

[2] Duchelle AE, Guariguata MR, Less G, Albornoz MA, Chavez A, Melo T. Evaluating the opportunities and limitations to multiple use of Brazil nuts and timber in Western Amazonia. Forest Ecology and Management. 2012;**268**:39-48. DOI: 10.1016/J.FORECO.2011.05.023

[3] Athayde S, Shepard G, Cardoso TM, Van Der Voort H, Zent S, Rosero-Peña M, et al. Chapter 10: Critical interconnections between cultural and biological diversity of Amazonian peoples and ecosystems. In: Nobre C et al., editors. Amazon Assessment Report 2021. New York: United Nations Sustainable Development Solutions Network; 2021. DOI: 10.55161/IOBU4861

[4] Ubiali B, Alexiades M. Forests, fields, and pastures: Unequal access to Brazil nuts and livelihood strategies in an extractive reserve, Brazilian Amazon. Land. 2022;**11**(7):1-21. DOI: 10.3390/land11070967

[5] Shepard GH, Ramirez H. "Made in Brazil": Human dispersal of the Brazil nut (*Bertholletia excelsa*, Lecythidaceae) in ancient Amazonia. Economic Botany. 2011;**65**(1):44-65. DOI: 10.1007/s12231-011-9151-6

[6] Instituto Brasileiro de Geografia e Estatística (IBGE). Produção da Extração Vegetal e da Silvicultura (PEVS) [Internet]. 2021. Available from: https://sidra.ibge.gov.br/pesquisa/pevs/quadros/brasil/2021 [Accessed: August 16, 2023]

[7] Ter Steege H et al. Hyperdominance in the Amazonian tree Flora. Science. 2013;**342**(6156). DOI: 10.1126/science.1243092

[8] Neves EG et al. Chapter 8: Peoples of the Amazon before European colonization. In: Nobre C et al., editors. Amazon Assessment Report 2021. New York: United Nations Sustainable Development Solutions Network; 2021. DOI: 10.55161/LXIT5573

[9] Ter Steege H et al. Estimating the global conservation status of more than 15,000 Amazonian tree species. Science Advances. 2015;**1-10**:e1500936. DOI: 10.1126/sciadv.1500936

[10] Fauset S et al. Hyperdominance in Amazonian forest carbon cycling. Nature Communications. 2015;**6**:6857. DOI: 10.1038/ncomms7857

[11] Pacheco J, Azevedo-Ramos C, Nakano E. The productive autonomy of public forest-dwellers in the Amazon: Two case studies of community timber management. Sustainability in Debate. 2022;**13**(1):313-351. DOI: 10.18472/SustDeb.v13n1.2022.41279

[12] Fonseca FL, Rover OJ, Wadt LHO, Cartaxo CBC. Sustainability indicators of the Brazil nut tree management. Brazilian Journal of Environmental Sciences. 2021;**56**(4):551-563. DOI: 10.5327/Z21769478889

[13] Silva TP, Pontes NA, Albuquerque AR. Cadeias de produção sustentáveis no extrativismo de castanha do Brasil na Amazônia brasileira / Sustainable production chains in Brazil brown extractivism in Brazilian Amazon. Brazilian Journal of Development. 2020;**6**(8):63460-63478. DOI: 10.34117/BJDV6N8-687

[14] Picanço CAS, Costa RC. Análise da cadeia produtiva da castanha-do-Brasil coletada na reserva biológica do Rio Trombetas, Oriximiná, Pará. Brazilian Journal of Development. 2019;**5**(10):19460-19483. DOI: 10.34117/bjdv5n10-170

[15] Waldhoff P, Souza EXF. *Bertholletia excelsa*: Key Species for Sustainable Livelihoods and Forest Conservation [Internet]. Tropical Forests – Ecology, Diversity and Conservation Status. London, UK, London, UK: IntechOpen; 2023. DOI: 10.5772/intechopen.109775

[16] Chiriboga-Arroyo F et al. Genetic threats to the Forest giants of the Amazon: Habitat degradation effects on the socio-economically important Brazil nut tree (*Bertholletia excelsa*). Plants, People, Planet. 2021;**3**(2):194-210. DOI: 10.1002/ppp3.10166

[17] Maués MM. Reproductive phenology and pollination of the Brazil nut tree (*Bertholletia excelsa* humb. & Bonpl. Lecythidaceae) in eastern Amazonia. In: Kevan P, Imperatriz Fonseca VL, editors. Pollinating Bees: The Conservation Link between Agriculture and Nature. Brasília: Ministério do Meio Ambiente do Brasil; 2002. pp. 245-254

[18] Pastana DNB et al. Strong El Niño reduces fruit production of Brazil-nut trees in the eastern Amazon. Acta Amazonica. 2021;**51**(3):270-279. DOI: 10.1590/1809-4392202003702

[19] Schöngart J et al. Age and growth patterns of Brazil nut trees (*Bertholletia excelsa* Bonpl.) in Amazonia, Brazil. Biotropica. 2015;**47**(5):550-558. DOI: 10.1111/btp.12243

[20] Esquivel-Muelbert A et al. Compositional response of Amazon forests to climate change. Global Change Biology. 2019;**25**(1):39-56. DOI: 10.1111/gcb.14413

[21] Lorenzoni-Paschoa LS et al. Climate change and the ecophysiology of *Bertholletia excelsa* seedlings. Plant Growth Regulation. 2022;**98**(1):155-165. DOI: 10.1007/s10725-022-00841-w

[22] Instituto Nacional de Pesquisas Espaciais (INPE). Terrabrasilis [Internet]. 2023. Available from: http://terrabrasilis.dpi.inpe.br/ [Accessed: August 22, 2023]

[23] Sistema de Informação Geográfica Quantum (QGIS). Version 3.32-1 Lima. QGIS Team. Chicago, United States: Open Source Geospatial Foundation; 2016

[24] Instituto Brasileiro de Geografia e Estatística (IBGE). Mapa de vegetação do Brasil. Escala 1:5.000.000 [Internet]. 2004. Available from: https://www.ibge.gov.br/geociencias/informacoes-ambientais/vegetacao/10872-vegetacao.html?=&t=acesso-ao-produto [Accessed: November 16, 2018]

[25] Instituto Brasileiro de Geografia e Estatística (IBGE). Divisão Regional do Brasil: 1990 Mesorregiões e Microrregiões Geográficas [Internet]. 2023. Available from: https://www.ibge.gov.br/geociencias/organizacao-do-territorio/divisao-regional/15778-divisoes-regionais-do-brasil.html?edicao=16163 [Accessed: June 30, 2023]

[26] Santos D. Fatos da Amazônia 2021 [Internet]. 2021. Available from: https://amazonia2030.org.br/ [Accessed: July 28, 2022]

[27] Lopes E et al. Mapping the socio-ecology of non timber forest products (NTFP) extraction in the Brazilian Amazon: The case of açaí (*Euterpe precatoria* Mart) in acre. Landscape and Urban Planning. 2019;**188**:110-117. DOI: 10.1016/j.landurbplan.2018.08.025

[28] Instituto Brasileiro de Geografia e Estatística (IBGE). Censo 2022 [Internet]. 2023. Available from: https://censo2022.ibge.gov.br/ [Accessed: September 30, 2023]

[29] Instituto Nacional de Meteorologia do Brasil (INMET). Dados Meteorológicos [Internet]. 2023. Available from: https://portal.inmet.gov.br/ [Accessed: August 28, 2023]

[30] University of Arizona. VPD Calcultor [Internet]. 2023. Available from: https://cales.arizona.edu/vpdcalc/ [Accessed: August 28, 2023]

[31] López J, Way DA, Sadok W. Systemic effects of rising atmospheric vapor pressure deficit on plant physiology and productivity. Global Change Biology. 2021;**27**(9):1704-1720. DOI: 10.1111/gcb.15548

[32] R Core Team. _R: A Language and Environment for Statistical Computing_. Vienna, Austria: R Foundation for Statistical Computing; 2023. Available from: https://www.R-project.org/

[33] Staudhammer CL et al. Comparative models disentangle drivers of fruit production variability of an economically and ecologically important long-lived Amazonian tree. Scientific Reports. 2021;**11**:2563. DOI: 10.1038/s41598-021-81948-4

[34] Tonini H, Pedrozo CA. Variações anuais na produção de frutos e sementes de Castanheira-do-Brasil (*Bertholletia excelsa* Bonpl., Lecythidaceae) em florestas nativas de Roraima. Revista Árvore. 2014;**38**(1):133-144. DOI: 10.1590/S0100-67622014000100013

[35] Corrêa V et al. The role of phosphate fertilization on physiological responses of the young *Bertholletia excelsa* plants grown in a P-deficient Amazon Ferralsol. Plants. 2022;**11**(21):2955. DOI: 10.3390/plants11212955

[36] Quesada CA et al. Variations in chemical and physical properties of Amazon forest soils in relation to their genesis. Biogeosciences. 2010;**7**:1515-1541. DOI: 10.5194/bg-7-1515-2010

[37] Darela-Filho JP et al. Reference maps of soil phosphorus for the pan-Amazon region. Earth System Science Data Discussions. 2023;**2023**:1-24. DOI: 10.5194/essd-2023-272

[38] Bentes RS, Marín RA, Emmi MF. Os cemitérios das castanheiras do Tocantins. Pará Desenvolvimento. 1988;**23**:18-23

[39] Homma AKO, Carvalho RA, Ferreira CAP, Nascimento Júnior JDBA. A destruição de recursos naturais: o caso da castanha-do-pará no Sudeste Paraense. Belém: Embrapa Amazônia Oriental; 2000. 74p

[40] Mori SA. The Brazil nut industry – past, present, and future. In: Plotkin M, Famolare L, editors. Sustainable Harvest and Marketing of Rain Forest Products. Washington, DC: Island Press; 1992. pp. 800-828

[41] Brandão DO, Barata LES, Nobre I, Nobre CA. The effects of Amazon deforestation on non-timber forest products. Regional Environmental Change. 2021;**21**(4):122. DOI: 10.1007/s10113-021-01836-5

[42] Brandão DO. Desmatamento na Amazônia e influência nos produtos florestais não-madeireiros de uso econômico local [thesis]. São José dos Campos: Instituto Nacional de Pesquisas Espaciais (INPE); 2023

[43] Cardoso GSS, Scoles R, Aragón S. O que explica a baixa produção de frutos

por árvores de *Bertholletia excelsa* em áreas de pastagem? Scientia Forestalis. 2022;**50**(e3913):1-15. DOI: 10.18671/scifor.v50.40

[44] Cavalcante MC et al. Pollination requirements and the foraging behavior of potential pollinators of cultivated Brazil nut (*Bertholletia excelsa* Bonpl.) trees in Central Amazon rainforest. Psyche. 2012:978019. DOI: 10.1155/2012/978019

[45] Kitamura PC, Müller CH. Castanhais nativas de Marabá-PA: Fatores de depredação e bases para a sua preservação. EMBRAPA, Centro de Pesquisa Agropecuária do Trópico Umido. 1984;**30**:1-32

[46] Almeida CT et al. Spatiotemporal rainfall and temperature trends throughout the Brazilian legal Amazon, 1973-2013. International Journal of Climatology. 2016;**37**(4):2013-2026. DOI: 10.1002/joc.4831

[47] Alves TCV et al. Análise da relação entre precipitação e produção de castanha-da-Amazônia em uma comunidade agroextrativista no município de Tefé-AM. Anais do Seminário Internacional em Ciências do Ambiente e Sustentabilidade na Amazônia. 2018;**5**:1-10. ISSN 2178-3500

[48] Herraiz AD, Graça PMLA, Fearnside PM. Amazonian flood impacts on managed Brazilnut stands along Brazil's Madeira River: A sustainable forest management system threatened by climate change. Forest Ecology and Management. 2017;**406**:46-52. DOI: 10.1016/j.foreco.2017.09.053

[49] Ricklefs REA. Economia da Natureza. Rio de Janeiro: Guanabara-Koogan; 2003. p. 503

[50] Mcdowell NG, Allen CD. Darcy's law predicts widespread forest mortality under climate warming. Nature. Climate Change. 2015;**5**(7):669-672. DOI: 10.1038/nclimate2641

[51] Intergovernmental Panel on Climate Change (IPCC). Climate change 2021. The Physical Science Basis. Cambridge: Cambridge University Press; 2021

[52] Yuan W. Increased atmospheric vapor pressure deficit reduces global vegetation growth. Science Advances. 2019;**5**(8): 1-12. DOI: 10.1126/sciadv.aax1396

[53] Nobre CA et al. Land-use and climate change risks in the Amazon and the need of a novel sustainable development paradigm. Proceedings of the National Academy of Sciences of the United States of America. 2016;**113**(39):10759-10768. DOI: 10.1073/pnas.1605516113

[54] Barkhordarian A et al. A recent systematic increase in vapor pressure deficit over tropical South America. Scientific Reports. 2019;**9**:15331. DOI: 10.1038/s41598-019-51857-8

[55] Moore CE et al. The effect of increasing temperature on crop photosynthesis: From enzymes to ecosystems. Journal of Experimental Botany. 2021;**72**(8):2822-2844. DOI: 10.1093/jxb/erab090

[56] Smith MN et al. Empirical evidence for resilience of tropical forest photosynthesis in a warmer world. Nature Plants. 2020;**6**:1225-1230. DOI: 10.1038/s41477-020-00780-2

[57] Jiménez-Muñoz JC et al. Record-breaking warming and extreme drought in the Amazon rainforest during the course of El Niño 2015-2016. Scientific Reports. 2016;**6**:33130. DOI: 10.1038/srep33130

[58] Sampaio GO. El Niño e você: o fenômeno climático. São José dos Campos: Transtec Editorial; 1999. p. 116

[59] World Meteorological Organization (WMO). WMO Global Annual to Decadal Climate Update (Target years: 2023-2027) [Internet]. 2023. Available from: https://library.wmo.int/index.php?lvl=notice_display&id=22272 [Accessed: May 18, 2023]

[60] Nobre I, Nobre CA. The Amazonia third way initiative: The role of technology to unveil the potential of a novel tropical biodiversity-based economy. In: Loures LC. (Editor). Land Use: Assessing the Past, Envisioning the Future. Londres: IntechOpen 2018;1:183-213. DOI: 10.5772/intechopen.80413. Available from: https://www.intechopen.com/chapters/63918 [Accessed: March 15, 2019]

[61] Alencar JC, Almeida RA, Fernandes NP. Fenologia de espécies florestais em floresta tropical úmida de terra firme na Amazônia Central. Acta Amazonica. 1979;**9**(1):163-199

[62] Gasparinetti P, Brandão DO, et al. Economic feasibility of tropical Forest restoration models based on non-timber Forest products in Brazil, Cambodia, Indonesia, and Peru. Forests. 2022;**13**(11):1878. DOI: 10.3390/f13111878

[63] Brandão DO, Barata LES, Nobre CA. The effects of environmental changes on plant species and Forest dependent communities in the Amazon region. Forests. 2022;**13**(3):466. DOI: 10.3390/f13030466

Chapter 10

Towards Overcoming the Challenges to Adopting Ecosystem-Based Management Approach for Protected Areas: The Case of Serengeti Ecosystem

Theonestina Kaiza-Boshe

Abstract

Ecosystem-based planning and management strategies concerning wildlife protected areas are a necessary development in ensuring ecological integrity of protected areas and hence the stability and survival of wildlife populations in them. Ecosystem-based planning and management strategies are however a new approach, and thus, most protected areas in Africa were established before the approach became known. Consequently, most protected areas need to adopt ecosystem-based management (EBM) to ensure ecological integrity of the areas and the survival of wildlife, as well as maintenance of other environmental services in general. Serengeti Ecosystem is one very complex system, with a large expanse of area and a multitude of stakeholders. Thus, adoption of EBM for Serengeti Ecosystem is faced by several challenges, the most daunting of which is human-wildlife conflicts (HWCs). The chapter analyzes this challenge through fairly detailed examination of the case in examples of the most outstanding HWCs and the initiatives that have been tried out to facilitate ecosystem-based management of the Serengeti, and comes to the conclusion that, with some modifications, the Greater Serengeti Conservation Society presents the best chance under the circumstances to succeed in overcoming the challenges to adoption of EBM for the Serengeti Ecosystem.

Keywords: ecosystem-based management, Tanzania wildlife protected areas, Serengeti Ecosystem, Serengeti National Park, Ngorongoro Conservation Area, Loliondo Controlled Area, Serengeti wildebeest annual migration, Maasai Mara National Game Reserve, Maasai transhumance, human-wildlife conflicts, human-elephant conflicts, wildlife management areas, Greater Serengeti Conservation Society, Serengeti Regional Conservation Strategy

1. Introduction

Ecosystem-based management (EBM) approach is one that seeks to integrate all ecosystem components, functions, interactions, processes, and all related dynamics of a given resource or area. For wildlife protected areas (WPA), the approach aims to sustainably manage natural resources, their environment, and the services they provide to humans within a defined ecosystem, as opposed to arbitrarily defined ones, which is the way most wildlife protected areas were established and are being managed.

Many protected areas in Africa had their boundaries demarcated depending on availability of land that could be set aside for respective conservation purposes or that was deemed necessary for some specific conservation purpose. This is partly because many protected areas in Africa were established before the concepts of ecology and ecosystem were very well understood, and thus, their implications on wildlife protected area management relative to human land uses were not taken into account. Moreover, wildlife management problems arising from arbitrarily demarcated protected area boundaries such as protected animals being killed outside protected areas, on the one hand, and wild animals raiding people's farms and settlements or killing and maiming humans and domestic stock, on the other, had not grown to problematic proportions.

The situation has since changed. With human population having grown tremendously and still growing, while wildlife habitats are shrinking due to human development activities encroaching upon protected areas, or destroying natural vegetation, and consequently wild animals being compelled to seek food, water, and other necessities of survival outside protected areas. This is the essence of human-wildlife conflicts (HWCs), as we have come to label it, and the number one threat to the survival of certain protected areas and wildlife species. Various measures have been taken for years to combat or mitigate HWCs, but none seems to hold a lasting solution, and this is one of the major reasons for adoption of EBM strategies.

Other major threats to the survival of natural resources in protected areas include illegal hunting or poaching, various forms of habitat destruction, and climate change.

Tanzania has taken initiative to adopting EBM strategies since the 1980s; but, to date, none of the initiatives has brought a lasting solution yet. This is because there are challenges to adopting EBM strategies that must be overcome for the strategies to provide a lasting solution to threats to ecosystem survival. An analysis of the initiatives that have been tried out to date indicate the latest one, the Greater Serengeti Conservation Society (GSCS), if improved upon, could very well provide Tanzania with an effective instrument to overcome the major challenges to EBM and hence ensure Serengeti Ecosystem of eternal survival.

This chapter presents the premises for my conclusion and the proposals of what might have to be done for Greater Serengeti Conservation Society (GSCS) or any such initiative to help overcome the challenges to EBM and hence promote the survival of Serengeti Ecosystem.

This chapter gives an overview of the general challenges to EBM strategies in planning and managing protected areas. The case of Serengeti Ecosystem is then examined, and the need and challenges to EBM are analyzed based on experience and reality on the ground. This is done by presenting fairly detailed case examples to elucidate the situations in question so as to enable the reader to see the rationale for what is concluded and ultimately proposed towards overcoming challenges to EBM adoption in the Serengeti Ecosystem.

The selection for case examples, both for challenges and solution initiatives, is based on representativeness or centrality of the case to the subject in question. What is finally proposed for action towards overcoming the challenges to EBM strategies for the Serengeti Ecosystem is based on the analysis of what has worked and what has not worked for the initiatives that have been tried to the effect, and my experience and knowledge of the workings of the legal and institutional landscape and arrangements for conservation matters in Tanzania.

2. The need for and the challenges to implementing EBM approaches in protected areas: an overview

2.1 The need for EBM approaches

A century ago, when many countries in Africa started establishing national parks and game reserves, protected areas were few and far apart, and human population was low and land uses were also few, and did not cover as much land as today. Thus, there was plenty of land for wild animals, and animals crossing protected area boundaries were not seen to be a problem if they did not raid farms or kill humans or livestock. Today, wild animals raiding farms and killing humans and domestic stock are rampant in countries like Tanzania, as is livestock grazing in protected areas and human settlements and farms neighboring protected areas. This is so much so to the extent that human-wildlife conflicts (HWCs) are probably the number one wildlife protected area management problem in the past one decade. HWCs are thus the biggest challenge to EBM, the ones threatening ecosystem management most, and hence raising the most concern and consequently receiving the most attention.

For communities living near wildlife protected areas, farm raids are a perennial problem, and wild animals maiming and killing humans and livestock is a common occurrence. Consequently, wide ranging animals such as elephants are costing the nation a lot in loss of crops and domestic stock, as well as human life and limb. On the other hand, the government is losing a tremendous amount of funds on the problem of human-elephant conflicts (HECs), for instance, in terms of money spent on research, consolation payments to victims, vermin control, and a variety of conflict mitigation measures. As I have pointed out in my article on human-elephant conflicts [1], the situation is dire and calls for institution of an integrative wildlife conservation strategy, which should also embrace a manipulative scientific wildlife management strategy [2].

For its part, the government has been fairly vigilant in addressing the HECs, largely by educating the affected communities on the problem and training them on how to live with the problem by taking mitigation measures. Government personnel are also involved in carrying out some of the mitigation measures such as conducting patrols and chasing away the problem animals from settlements. However, with a possible exception of insignificant local successes, the problem is still growing and the government has yet to find a lasting solution.

Apart from taking mitigation measures, the government has had to degazette portions of protected areas, including parts of Serengeti Ecosystem to resolve human-wildlife conflicts arising from human encroachment on protected areas, as has been the case for Maswa Game Reserve that has had parts of its area degazetted three times. In some cases, encroaching communities have had to be relocated at huge government expense to give way to wildlife conservation requirements, as has been the case for Ngorongoro Conservation Area and former Loliondo Controlled Area. At this rate, protected areas cannot be said to provide sustainable security for natural resources. This is why there have been calls for institution of ecosystem-based planning and management of protected areas in recent years.

Ecosystem-based management is indeed the widely recognized framework for promoting sustainable management of natural resources, especially for wildlife protected areas suffering from human-wildlife conflicts due to proximity of human settlements and wide-ranging nature of some animal species, as are cases of elephants and wildebeest of Serengeti Ecosystem.

2.2 The challenges of implementing EBM strategies in protected areas

Although the benefits of EBM approaches and related policies have been identified and acknowledged in natural resources conservation circles, there are also significant challenges in implementing these strategies in protected areas, Serengeti Ecosystem being the case in example. The magnitude, extent, and complexity of challenges depend on a number of factors. These include the *complexity of the ecosystem involved* in terms of the diversity of species and their interaction with each other and their environment, ecological processes, and changes over time. Consequently, an ecosystem-based approach to managing protected areas requires comprehensive understanding of all the parameters of the ecosystem, which in turn requires extensive ecological research.

Apart from the challenges deriving from the complexity of the ecological environment, there are those that derive from *the human environment*. These, too, can be quite complex, depending on expanse of protected area and what constitutes its ecosystem, the socioeconomics of surrounding communities, the economics of the country, as well as the sociopolitical setting and dynamics. These challenges and their trends need to be studied, too, and be taken into account in planning as well as in management.

Another major challenge to practicing EBM is *the diversity of stakeholders.* Although this is basically part of the human environment, it deserves special attention, as it is the one that poses the most threat to managing many wildlife protected areas (WPAs). Major among stakeholders are the management, respective boards of directors or trustees, the local communities, conservationists, donors, researchers, local politicians, tourists, tour operators, respective government authorities, and non-governmental organizations. These stakeholders have diverse and often conflicting perspectives and goals in relation to the objectives and activities of WPAs, which can lead to disagreements regarding management decisions and make it challenging to implement EBM strategies successfully.

In addition, there are unpredictable but, nonetheless, certain-to-occur *climate change challenges*. It is usually not known exactly what form climate change events might take, but as they are already occurring in terms of extreme weather events like droughts, too much rain, and flooding and have impacts on wildlife populations, it is important to make anticipative plans regarding climate change. This is because some events result in deaths, others in increased births, while others result in migration in search of food, water, and other survival necessities. Migrations may result in farm raids and cause more conflicts with farmers. In view of the damages and losses that may be caused by climate change, it is imperative that WPAs should have anticipatory mitigation plans for such occurrences.

Another challenge shared by most wildlife protected areas is that *ecosystem-based management strategies are an add-on feature* to existing management of a protected area, a consideration that came after the protected area had been established. This may entail re-demarcation of boundaries, re-settlement of surrounding communities, and any other change in surrounding land uses that may be necessitated by the requisite changes in management objectives and shift in boundaries.

Serengeti Ecosystem is faced by all of the above challenges and much more due to additional attributes. Apart from its expanse, which entail encompassing a diversity of habitats and species, as well as a large number of surrounding tribal communities, Serengeti National Park, the protected area on which the ecosystem is based, is an iconic protected area with several superlatives in its description, international statuses, and a large number of local and nonlocal stakeholders.

An overview of Serengeti National Park's historical, natural, and socioeconomic features is presented here to give the reader some idea about the complexity of Serengeti Ecosystem and its management challenges and hence the challenges to practicing EBM strategies.

2.3 Overview of Serengeti National Park

Serengeti Ecosystem encompasses several protected areas of different protection statuses, the core being Serengeti National Park, from which the ecosystem derives its name. Others (see **Figure 1**), starting with the most northerly moving clockwise, are Maasai Mara National Game Reserve (in Kenya), Pololeti Game Reserve, Malambo Game Reserve, Ngorongoro Conservation Area, Makao Wildlife Management Area, Maswa Game Reserve, Grumeti Game Reserve, Ikona Wildlife Management Area, and Ikorongo Game Reserve. The ecosystem also includes surrounding buffer zones.

Each one of the protected areas listed above has its own history, geography, and ecological features. For the purpose of this chapter, the historical and geographical notes in this section are of necessity centered around the Serengeti National Park, as it

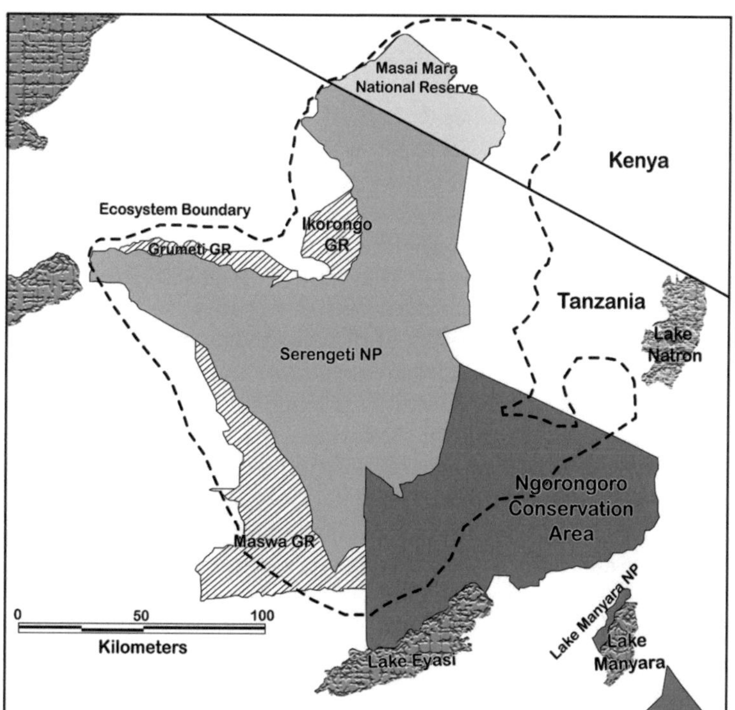

Figure 1.
A map of Serengeti Ecosystem showing the boundary and major protected areas. Source: Ref. [3]. Serengeti shall not die: Transforming an ambition into a reality.

is the core of the ecosystem by geography and ecology, as well as management activities. Other protected areas will be described as necessary in covering respective issues.

2.3.1 The history of Serengeti National Park

Widely acknowledged as the iconic national park of Tanzania and branded as the most unique area in the world by the author of two of the most used field guides to Tanzania national parks and Ngorongoro Conservation Area, Lilla N. Lyogello [4]. Serengeti National Park is the oldest protected area that was initially established as game reserve in 1921, and later upgraded and gazetted as a national park in 1951, thus becoming the first national park in Tanzania [4–6].

The idea of establishing Serengeti as a national park originated from the colonial masters in England but was strongly opposed by local colonial administrators of the then Tanganyika Territory and local communities. According to Jaffari Kideghesho [3], the most important criteria in judging the suitability of an area as a national park were interests and priorities of the Europeans. The Serengeti was rated as suitable for creation of a national park, because of its insignificant mineral deposits, presence of the tsetse fly, and scant rainfall, which made the land unattractive to European miners as well as farmers. The idea of creating national parks, however, was opposed by the colonial administrators in Tanganyika, who felt that the strategy was infringing on natives' rights and thus was posing a risk to the political stability of the colony.

The colonial masters' wish was subsequently reinforced by the 1933 London Convention on Flora and Fauna of Africa. The convention required all signatories (including Tanganyika) to investigate the possibility of creating a system of national parks. Powerful individuals in London consistently overstated the problem of what they termed "destructive behavior of Africans to wildlife" as a way of pressing the colonial government to act.

In 1940, the first game ordinance that gave the governor a mandate to declare any area a national park was enacted. Serengeti was upgraded from a game reserve into a national park in that year. However, its implementation had to be delayed largely due to the World War II (1939–1945), and although it was gazetted in 1951, it remained a national park on paper only, without effective enforcement of the laws and regulations governing national parks. The fact that there were Maasai livestock keepers within the park was contradictory to the national park idea.

According to Kideghesho's narration of the events that ensued, the gazettement of the Serengeti as a national park precipitated conflicts and opposition from the natives. This was a consequence of conservationists' placing more value on wild animals than on human beings. For example, one of the former park managers of Serengeti stated blatantly that: "The interests of fauna and flora must come first, those of man and belongings being of secondary importance."

In the eastern part of Serengeti, the Maasai resisted the proposed park boundaries through violence and sabotage/vandalism. They speared the rhinos, set fires with malicious intent, and terrorized civil servants. The Ikoma hunters in western Serengeti, on the other hand, contravened the colonial conservation laws, which barred them from hunting, while swearing to use poisoned arrows against any wildlife ranger who would interfere with their hunting activities.

To resolve these conflicts, the Colonial Government divided Serengeti National Park into two parts, the western and the eastern; the former remaining as a national park we know today and the eastern becoming Ngorongoro Conservation Area. Whereas all human activities were proscribed in remaining park, livestock keeping and a limited level of crop cultivation were allowed in the Ngorongoro Conservation Area (NCA), thus becoming a multiple land use protected area. The Serengeti Maasai were relocated to NCA through a special agreement to that effect and as provided in the Ngorongoro Conservation Ordinance of 1959. The Ordinance applied to the Maasai as well as the original residents of the area that included a small population of Tatoga (Datooga) and Barabaig in the Crater and other Mbulu tribes in the highlands, altogether making an estimated total of 8000 residents. Soon after, the Maasai chased the original residents of the area and kept the area to themselves.

For about a decade or so, the Ngorongoro's multiple land use arrangement seemed to work. But as the population of humans and livestock increased, human activities threatened the environment, and the government had to forbid crop cultivation. This was effected by enacting the 1975 Ngorongoro Conservation Area Act Cap. 284 [7]. This gave rise to a conflict. The Maasai considered the law an infringement on their human rights and a default on the 1959 agreement. Meanwhile, the population of humans and livestock continued to grow beyond what could be sustained by the area and threatened the natural resources of the area. In June 2022, Morenda [8] published an article in the Guardian quoting the Minister of Natural Resources and Tourism, Madame Pindi Chana, to have said that by 2022, there were about 110,000 Maasai and one million head of livestock in NCA.

It is worth noting that the conflicts that existed in western Serengeti when the Park was gazetted have continued to date, whereas those that existed in eastern Serengeti have changed very little. Details on these conflicts are presented by case examples in respective sections below.

2.3.2 Geography and ecology

Though with the size of 14,763 sq.km, Serengeti comes in third after Nyerere National Park (30,893 sq.km.) and Ruaha National Park (20,226 sq.km.), Serengeti is the national park with the most superlatives in terms of characteristics, history, tourism, and management. As pointed out earlier, Serengeti is the first protected area and national park, the most visited, most researched, most filmed, and most written about. Still Serengeti National Park remains arguably the wildest [4], and its wildebeest migration the world's most renowned. The name Serengeti is derived from the Maasai word *siringet*, meaning "extended area," referring to a large expanse of plain that characterizes much of Serengeti National Park landscape.

Because of its size, Serengeti National Park, and hence Serengeti Ecosystem, is surrounded by over 30 communities of different ethnicity and hence different customs, activities, and impact on the Park and Serengeti Ecosystem, at large. Serengeti's border location with Kenya and Maasai Mara National Reserve is a unique ecosystem feature in that the ecosystem transcends the national boundary, an attribute that is amply demonstrated by the annual wildebeest migration by which the animals involved spend part of the year in Serengeti, and the other part in Maasai Mara. In fact, the boundaries of Serengeti Ecosystem are defined by the Serengeti Wildebeest migration route (**Figure 2**).

Ecology is what defines the boundaries of Serengeti Ecosystem beyond those of Serengeti National Park from which it derives its name. The boundaries of the ecosystem are defined by the route of the widest ranging Serengeti National Park animal species, which is the wildebeest (*Connochaetes taurinus*) and accompanying angulates, in the form of annual migration mentioned earlier (**Figure 2**). The so defined Serengeti Ecosystem covers about 25,000–30,000 sq.km [3, 9] in the northern part of

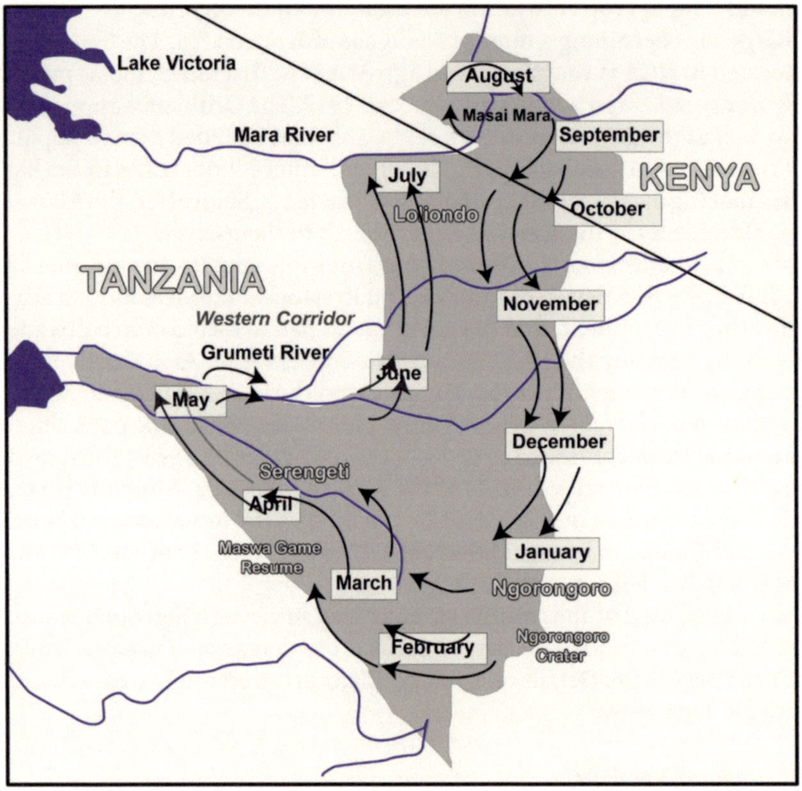

Figure 2.
Serengeti National Park wildebeest migration route. Source: Affordable AfricaSafaris.com.

Tanzania (**Figure 1**), west of the Rift Valley, in a highland savanna region with plains and woodlands ranging from 900 to 1500 m above sea level.

In addition to Serengeti National Park, the Serengeti Ecosystem encompasses several different types of protected areas, with different management regimes and falling under four different institutions (TANAPA, NCAA, TAWA, and Kenya Wildlife Services). Protected areas include the Ngorongoro Conservation Area; several game reserves including Maswa, Ikorongo, Grumeti, Kijereshi, and Pololeti; wildlife management areas including Ikona na Makao (all in Tanzania); and Maasai Mara National Reserve in Kenya (**Figure 1**).

The ecology of Serengeti Ecosystem, particularly the Serengeti National Park, has been very much studied and written about by a number of researchers, much of it of higher academic interest and not easily available to readers for practical interests, even for conservation bureaucrats and practitioners. For the purpose of this chapter, the description in a small book titled "Serengeti," by David Martin for Tanzania National Parks [6], is sufficient to give the reader some idea about the ecological setting of Serengeti Ecosystem. In this book, the Serengeti Ecosystem is described as being bounded by the Rift Valley and Ngorongoro Crater Highlands in the east, Lake Victoria to the west, and Isuria escarpment to the north. The south east of the park is flat with open grass plains interspersed with kopjes. In the south and western parts, there are undulating hill ranges, which are broken and divided by open and grassland areas. The north and north-west are more undulating with heavier rainfalls and dense tall grassland and woodland vegetation, and the north is fringed with hills bearing the densest vegetation found in Serengeti.

The Serengeti National Park is generally divided into three vegetation areas. In the south east are the open grasslands, to the north open woodlands, and in the west a mosaic of grasslands and woodlands.

It is the ungulates' ecological necessity for survival around the three major vegetation zones and water availability that gave rise to the annual migration of which Serengeti is best known. Consisting mainly of wildebeest, zebra, and gazelle, the migration begins on open grassland during the rainy season and head west and north in search of grazing during the dry season. A research by Eric Wolanski et al. [10] confirmed that wildebeest migration is determined by availability and quality of vegetation and water and hence the variation in the calendar when rainfall pattern and amount changes.

Sinclair et al. [11], a team of scientists who had studied Serengeti Ecosystem extensively, described the Serengeti Ecosystem as being of special importance because of being one of the few ecosystems with a high diversity of wildlife, one of the last protected ecosystem whose dynamics are driven by millions of migratory herbivores and at the same time containing one of the largest remaining and functioning migration of terrestrial mammals, and that though it has been subject to a wide range of disturbances, it has remained largely unaltered by human intervention. The conditions and change state of Serengeti Ecosystem have thus provided opportunities to examine naturally functioning ecosystems, to study the dynamics of a variety of major components of terrestrial food web and to explore ecological theories in order to understand the process and functioning of large ecosystems. It also provides long-term date on environmental changes in an unusually well-studied ecosystem.

3. The challenges to implementing EBM in the Serengeti Ecosystem

The complex history, geography, and ecology of Serengeti National Park are what make Serengeti Ecosystem extra complex. Thus, EBM for Serengeti Ecosystem is extra complex as is the ecosystem itself and related socioeconomic dynamics. Therefore, as pointed out in Section 2.2, Serengeti Ecosystem is faced with all the major challenges mentioned in that section and more. The challenges mentioned are the complexity of the ecosystem, human environment, diversity of stakeholders, and climate change. What is more for the Serengeti Ecosystem is the magnitude of each challenge, their impact on ecosystem management, and the consequent difficulty there is in overcoming any one of those challenges.

For such a complex ecosystem, one of the major challenges in planning and managing the ecosystem, and perhaps the number one challenge, is to mobilize, enlist support of, and forge a good working relationship with all stakeholders. Given its expanse, the number of contiguous protected areas, communities, and institutions involved make for a multitude of stakeholders. The stakeholders for Serengeti Ecosystem include protected area managers, CEOs, and Boards of Directors/Trustees of wildlife institutions concerned with the protected areas within the Serengeti Ecosystem (TANAPA, WD, TAWA, NCA, KWS), Ministry of Natural Resources and Tourism, representatives of local communities, representatives of tourist companies, representatives of hunting companies, respective local governments (regional, district, village/*mtaa*[1]), Maasai Mara Management, Narok County representative,

[1] Mtaa is the lowermost government administrative unit that can make laws in urban areas.

Tanzania Wildlife Research Institute, local and international conservation organizations, conservation NGOs, etc. Thus, any initiative aiming at overcoming challenges to EBM must be able to engage all stakeholders meaningfully and effectively.

Another challenge of concern arising from the complexity of Serengeti Ecosystem is the human-wildlife conflicts. These conflicts not only are they a big challenge to the implementation of EBM but currently they are a number one threat to the integrity and sustainability of Serengeti Ecosystem. It is for this reason that the chapter focuses on human-wildlife conflicts with view pointing to pointing out the causes and, more importantly, identifying solutions, as a way towards overcoming the major challenges to EBM.

For the purpose of this chapter, we will look at the dynamics of human-wildlife conflicts by examining one case example on either side of the Serengeti Ecosystem. Ololosokwan in Loliondo represents conflicts on the eastern side, whereas Ikona WMA neighborhood represents conflicts on the western side of the ecosystem.

4. Human-wildlife conflicts

4.1 Human-wildlife conflicts on the eastern side of the Serengeti Ecosystem

Ololosokwan: The Case of a Border Community Abutting Serengeti National Park and Maasai Mara National Reserve in Kenya.

Ololosokwan is selected as a case example that demonstrates locational effects; residents being largely from the Maasai tribe that is at the center of the conflict on the eastern side of Serengeti, plus belonging to both Tanzania and Kenya; the community being in an area affected by HWC; the community having been involved in some community natural resources management scheme that has been analyzed and documented; the document upon which much of the information has been drawn having used false statements that may have inadvertently fueled the conflict that is still raging on (August 2023) in the area.

Ololosokwan is located in northern Tanzania along the Tanzania/Kenya adjacent to the Maasai Mara National Reserve in Kenya and the Serengeti National Park in Tanzania. Its inhabitants are largely Maasai, and it is one of the most wildlife-rich areas in the world [12]. Hundreds of thousands of wildebeests, zebra, and other ungulates pass through the community's land during their annual migration between the Maasai Mara and Serengeti plains.

The authors observed that Ololosokwan's wildlife resources made it one of Tanzania's leading example of community-based ecotourism. They described two ventures that the village had developed since the late 1990s with private tourist companies that earned the village upwards of US$55,000/– annually, and which they cited as the most substantial revenues earned by any village in Tanzania from wildlife-based enterprises, and have been used for communal investments in any array of social services and infrastructure projects. They observed that the realization of these benefits from wildlife had led to increased interest in development of community land and other resource management institutions and practices. And that wildlife is seen as an important economic asset by the community, and consequently, various efforts are being made to capitalize on this natural endowment. They further observed that with this realization, however, there had been growing conflicts over use, control, and management of land and related resources.

The most outstanding of these conflicts has been one between the villagers and a hunting company that has held a hunting concession in the area since 1992. Whereas government authorities maintain that the hunting company complies with legal requirements a hunting outfit, the communities view the presence of the hunting company as an infringement on their rights to benefits, access, and control of their natural resources.

Another bone of contention over what the villagers consider to be their rights to access and use of natural resources in the area is the concept of community-based conservation (CBC) as provided by law and as practiced by the government, relative to the understanding and interests of the villagers. The government players' perspective, interests, and actions are based on the principles and procedures of managing a wildlife management area (WMA), which the villagers consider to sideline them in planning and decision-making, and as a consequence short-change them in terms of benefits. Thus, the communities are skeptical and resistant to government guidance and directives.

The conflict that has ensued following dissent, illegal activities, and complaints over what is perceived as Maasai being denied of ancestral and human rights, has attracted sympathizers and human rights activists that have for many years created an impasse due to levelling false accusations against the Government. This situation has, in the process, attracted more NGOs and researchers in the area, as the government was being seen not to pay heed to calls and advices.

Sidney Trompell's research in the area, as published in his article of 2019 titled "The Conservation Bias in Tanzania's Wildlife Management Areas," [13] is one piece of work that demonstrates some of the false accusations and notions that helped to fuel controversy and accusations over what was seen as the government denying the Maasai their rightful access to then Loliondo Controlled Area.

One of the damaging statements in Trompell's work was that, "Ololosokwan lands also fall within the boundaries of Loliondo Game Controlled Area, a purely nominal protected area category that only restricts wildlife utilization and not settlement, livestock grazing, cultivation, or any other human activity." Legally, this is a false statement. He quoted the Wildlife Conservation Act of 1974 that had long been replaced by one enacted in 2009.

According to the Wildlife Conservation Act of 2009 [14] and subsequent amendments, human settlement and livestock grazing are prohibited in Game Protected Areas (GCAs). These prohibitions are spelt out in the provisions of two sections as follows. Concerning establishing Game Protected Areas, Section 16 (5), provides that, "...The Minister shall ensure that no land falling under the village land is included in the Game Controlled Areas." Section 21 (1), on the other hand, prohibits grazing in GCAs by stating that, "Any person shall not, save with the written permission of the Director [of Wildlife] previously sought and obtained, graze any livestock in any game controlled areas."

Another damaging notion is that of referring Maasai as indigenous tribe/people when accusing the government of evacuating the Maasai from what is referred to as ancestral home. Legally, there are no indigenous tribes in Tanzania, and chronologically, the Maasai are more recent comers to Tanzania than most tribes. In fact even in Ngorongoro Conservation Area where the Maasai from Serengeti were transferred to as a compromise agreement in 1959, the Maasai were not the first to settle there. They found some Mbulu tribes, Sonjo, Barabaig, and Tatoga (Datooga) and chased them from the area [15].

The various stakeholders and actors that have ostensibly come to the aid of the villagers of Ololosokwan and other parts of Ngorongoro District have for a long time failed to move the government, as much of their premises for advocacy were based on falsehood, misinformation, lies, and what appeared to be wrong ulterior motives.

Occasionally, the conflicts between the villagers and government officials that arose from false information degenerated into violent clashes, as it happened in June 2022, which resulted in a group of villagers killing a policeman.

Meanwhile, the situation in Ngorongoro Conservation Area (NCA) was becoming intolerable. With the support of sympathizers, the Maasai in the NCA organized to confront the government to demand what they considered to be their rights to resources, social services, and livelihood, at the time when the government had plans to resettle some of them to relieve the pressure on the natural resources of the area and the environment. The people refused to be moved before they could talk to the Minister of Natural Resources and Tourism. The government realized the situation was tense and volatile. The President sent the Prime Minister to speak to the people instead of the Minister of Natural Resources and Tourism that the Maasai of NCA had asked to see.

When the Prime Minister (PM) arrived at Ngorongoro, the situation had degenerated into violent clashes. The PM managed to calm down the villagers, educate them on legal issues, and inform them about the government plan to relocate them to Msomela (Otherwise spelt as Msomera), Handeni District in Tanga Region those who were willing to. The package for moving to Msomela included free transportation of households and their properties, including livestock, a three-bedroom modern house, 3 acres of farmland per family unit, plus 5 acres grazing land; plus a common village land for grazing livestock. Moreover, the community was provided with all the basic social services. This was more than the Maasai could have legally bargained for, and it was more than what the government had ever done for any community of people in compensation for vacating conservation land.

Yet there were detractors, people who ostensibly presented themselves as Maasai human rights advocates and who cried foul and incited the Maasai to refuse to vacate NCA and Loliondo. Other Maasai were persuaded to refuse to go to Msomela where the government had already prepared the area to accommodate them, and instead asked to be relocated to other places that were not in the plan. What is really challenging is that up until August 2023, there were still foreigners persuading Maasai to refuse to relocate to the extent that some Maasai youth were being paid to engage in violent activities to make the exercise difficult, such as beating up journalists so as to hide the truth about who was resisting and why.

Unfortunately, much of the time the stories being told by the Maasai are in stark contrast to statements issued by the government. Some Maasai petitions and complaints do not even mention having been given relocation package! The government on its part has generally been tardy in responding to claims and demands, hence protracted conflicts. Thus, in some instances, it may be difficult to know the truth of the matter, and often, the public is fed with false information. In any case, it is important that the public and all concerned know the following basics about the Maasai and other community vs. government land conflicts, which are in accordance with the Village Land Law No. 5 of 1999 [16].

One, legally, all land in Tanzania is public land vested in the President as trustee on behalf of all citizens.

Two, "Where the President is minded to transfer any area of village land or reserved land *for public interest*, he may direct the Minister (responsible for lands) to proceed in accordance with the provisions of the section."

Three, for the purpose of the above provision, *public interest includes* investments of national interest.

Four, the law provides for procedures for effecting transfers and respective compensation, which if followed would prevent unnecessary conflicts.

Five, it is important to note that Maasai are semi-nomadic, practicing transhumance mode of animal husbandry such that the Maasai identifying themselves as residents of a particular area in Ngorongoro District can be found grazing their livestock in any other area within the district or even outside it during a dry season and going back to home area during the rainy season. This applies also to the Maasai from across the border in Kenya, some of whom cross into Ngorongoro District in search of better pasture. In the same vein, the Maasai from Northern Tanzania can be found as far south as Mbeya grazing their livestock anywhere they can find grass. Some may even decide to settle in new areas, outside what is generally regarded to be Maasai land. A good example is that of Maasai that have even settled in communities in the south around Ruaha National Park in Iringa Region. Thus, putting up ancestral land as the reason for refusing to move from NCA or Loliondo, or any part of Ngorongoro, for that matter is just scapegoating to justify some unreasonable motives.

4.2 Conflicts on the western side of the Serengeti Ecosystem

Human-wildlife conflicts in the Serengeti, as pointed out earlier, are a historical phenomenon. According to Kideghesho [3], there is common agreement that most of these conflicts emerge as a result of wild animals being accorded a higher priority than human beings. For example, one of the former Serengeti park managers was once quoted as saying openly: "The interests of fauna and flora must come first, those of man and belongings being of secondary importance."

The current government narrative is more positive than it was years ago, but the understanding of the communities and attitudes remain pretty much the same. This is because, though the express goal of the government is to make wildlife conservation beneficial to neighboring communities by making wildlife contribute to improved livelihoods through community-based natural resources conservation initiatives, such as WMAs, and supporting income generating activities, the results on the ground have not matched what is spoken and written by authorities.

First of all, community-based conservation initiatives are usually implemented as a way to deter communities from engaging in illegal natural resources harvesting, which is well and good for the communities if they do indeed realize the promised benefits. Unfortunately, the results have been more to the contrary. Most researchers and writers point to what has variously been seen as communities being cheated.

Bluwstein et al. [17], having worked extensively on WMAs and other community-based conservation issues in Tanzania, made an observation that encapsulate most of the researchers' observations, remarks, and conclusions about WMAs in Tanzania. He said, "Our findings suggest that WMAs foster limited ownership, participation, and collective action at community level, because WMA governance follows an austere logic of centralized control over key resources. Thus we suggest that it is difficult to argue that WMAs are community-owned conservation initiatives until genuinely devolved and more flexible conservation models are implemented to give space to popular participation rule making."

Such statements are proven correct by facts and figures of western Serengeti situation as presented by Kideghesho [3] on the benefit-based approaches, which were adopted in the Serengeti in 1990s as a strategy of promoting a positive conservation attitude and therefore motivating people to support conservation efforts that have failed to meet expectations. He mainly attributed this to the fact that the benefits granted to local communities have been too minimal to offset the costs caused by prohibitive conservation policies (opportunity costs of conservation) and damage inflicted by wildlife on property such as crops and livestock. The cost-benefit analyses conducted in the Serengeti have shown that the ratio of wildlife-induced costs to benefits received by local communities was 250:1. Furthermore, these benefits have often been realized indirectly through community development projects, although the costs are localized to individuals.

On the other hand, Kideghesho further observed that the opportunity cost of forgoing the economic activities that are ecologically damaging is often very high, thus making these activities inevitable. For example, illegal hunting in the Serengeti has been flourishing, despite stringent law enforcement, because its returns were 45 times greater compared to those provided legally through the Serengeti Regional Conservation Projects community cropping scheme. Destruction of the breeding and calving grounds for wildebeest in the Maasai Mara (Kenyan part of the Serengeti Ecosystem) between 1977 and 1997 and, consequently, reduction of the wildebeest population by 75%, were mainly caused by the high opportunity cost that landowners would incur by opting for wildlife conservation instead of pursuing mechanized agriculture. The latter was ecologically destructive but economically more attractive to farmers. Its profit was 15 times greater. Furthermore, by virtue of being too minimal, conservation benefits do not contribute adequately to poverty reduction. People's direct dependence on natural resources has therefore remained inevitable.

Currently, the problem of major concern on the western side of Serengeti is the human-elephant conflicts, which have risen to the extent that some communities have to be trained to co-exist with elephants by learning some mitigation measures and being facilitated by conservation authorities and organizations, whenever possible, to have elephant-proof food storage facilities [3, 18, 19]. HECs are said to have risen following elephant population recovery from the period of intense poaching (2009–2014) and as humans have settled in protected area buffer zone traditionally used as elephant migratory routes.

Writing about the farmers living around Ikona WMA, Lucy King of Save the Elephants, and Head of Human-Elephant Co-existence Program at the Save the Elephants and Elephant Crisis Fund observed that perennial raids on crop fields and grain stores had made the community intolerant of elephants and that they often viewed them as problem animals. She observed further that although there was enough land to grow enough food, one elephant could wipe out food that would have lasted a family several months [19].

The above observation having been made by a pro-elephant person on damage caused by elephants speaks volumes about the losses suffered by communities from elephants, considering elephants do not move about singly, and that they move about in herds, plus they may not raid a farm only once. And, apart from crops in the fields, elephants may also devour the year/season's food storage and leave the farmer without food. The situation in certain parts of western Serengeti communities is dire, and the victims thus feel compelled to turn to protected areas for bush meat for the pot and cash to survive.

5. Management and technical issues

Usually when discussing challenges or problems facing protected areas management, there is a general tendency of writing as if it were from the management view point and thus overlooking issues within the administration or management of the resources that could pose problems in advancing conservation interests. This section demonstrates the importance of having the right leadership, particularly, the chief executive officer of an institution. For you could have resources and a good board of directors, but if the chief executive officer is inept or incompetent, the institution could collapse or the conservation objectives may not be achieved.

Basically, the understanding and inclination of leadership has a tremendous bearing on what can be and what is done towards managing personnel, resources, and conservation actions, which, in turn, is reflected in the performance in advancing conservation goals. Although boards of directors are the highest leadership positions for organizations, the chief executives are central to the management of the organizations and hence the protected areas under them. Boards of directors are essentially as good as their chief executives. This is largely due to the official tradition of boards of directors meeting quarterly to deliberate on and approve what is presented to them by the CEO in a 1- or 2-day meeting. What I learnt from my experience as a member of the Board Trustees sitting in those meetings is that CEOs determine the agenda, the proceedings, and outcome of Board Meetings and hence the direction and performance of protected area management.

This was amply demonstrated by what happened to TANAPA and NCAA in the early 1980s when the two institutions almost collapsed due to management problems deriving from the personalities of the chief executives, although, on the surface, the problems of the two institutions appeared to be lack of funds. For TANAPA, the problem was that the CEO of that time was more concerned with his personal matters than the needs of the institution, personnel, and conservation activities. In addition, the CEO seemed to be lacking in requisite professional qualifications.

The CEO of NCAA, on the other hand, had the necessary professional conservation expertise and experience, plus experience in administering government entities and high offices, but by reason of attitude, he could not get along with the Maasai in the Ngorongoro Conservation Area, in spite of being a Maasai himself.

I found out about the moribund state of the two institutions through a small investigation I conducted in several northern protected areas and subsequently wrote a petition to conservation authorities imploring them to take measures to save the two institutions. The petition ended up in the National Assembly and was discussed by members of Parliament during the budget session of 1984. The National Assembly took the matter seriously and threatened to "withhold a shilling" from the budget (meaning, not to approve the budget) of the Ministry of Natural Resources and Tourism. Hon. Paul Bomani, the then Minister of MNRT, responded by appointing a Commission of members of Parliament including the petitioner to investigate the two institutions and recommend a course of action. The Commission was chaired by one of the Members of Parliament, Hon. Tabitha Siwale, hence the name Siwale Commission, and I was appointed to serve on the Commission as the technical expert member of the otherwise, all Members of Parliament. Two senior officers from the Wildlife Division in the Ministry served as the Secretariat to the Commission.

Following submission of the Siwale Commission recommendations, among other things, the two CEOs were removed from their positions, and with new management and other changes in the administration of the two institutions, the latter were revived in a very short time. Within 3 years, the institutions were back to normal level of operations and financially liquid.

The lesson I have learned from the above story and elsewhere is that, for any initiative, strategy, and management approach to succeed, it has to be led by a chief executive who is appropriately and adequately qualified for the mission, and, above all, s/he must have the passion necessary to work beyond duty.

6. Initiatives that hold lessons on overcoming ecosystem-based management challenges

There have been several initiatives in Tanzania aimed at overcoming challenges to Serengeti Ecosystem–based management approach, with different names and slightly different approaches and strategies. The one thing these initiatives have in common is that of main objective being to aim at maintaining the integrity and sustainability of Serengeti Ecosystem. However, their differences in approach have meant difference in effectiveness, success, and sustainability.

Unfortunately, to date, there seems to be no initiative that has been effective in delivering on its objectives and withstood the test of time to prove to be sustainable. In this chapter, we will look at two initiatives that seem to offer more lessons in designing effective, successful, and sustainable initiatives. One of these is the Serengeti Regional Conservation Strategy (SRCS). Although now closed, SRCS left behind considerable foundation of knowledge and institutional structures to build on or learn from.

The other initiative is current and has features that could very well make it the best initiative in overcoming ecosystem-based management challenges, if improved upon.

6.1 The Serengeti Regional Conservation Strategy

Perhaps the earliest of the Serengeti Ecosystem initiatives was a government project under the Ministry of Natural Resources and Tourism (MNRT) that was financed by the Royal Norwegian Embassy (NORAD). The project was called the Serengeti Regional Conservation Strategy (SRCS). According to the workshop report and project proposal [9, 20], the project concept was first formally declared and debated in 1986 at an IUCN and World Bank facilitated workshop at the then Seronera Research Station within Serengeti National Park. The concept was further explored with selected villages that include Robanda, Makundusi, Mbiso, and Nyiberekera in Serengeti District. The workshop to resolve the concept was attended by relevant leaders in the three Serengeti wards of Isenyi, Ikona, and Natta, and an agreement reached to start the project within identified communities. The SRCS Project was formerly initiated in 1989; the 2 years in between were used for fundraising, organizational development, and construction of the project headquarters at Fort Ikoma.

The SRCS Project worked with the following communities, Robanda, Makunwelusi, Mbiso, Singisi, and Iharara in Serengeti and Mgeta, Kyandege, Nyaliwanda, Nyamatoke, and Hinyari in Bunda District. Each village had a Natural Resources Committee of eight members, which was also a subcommittee of the Village Government. Ten individuals, at least two of whom had to be women, were elected by the Village General Assembly to be trained as Village Game Scouts at the Community Based Natural Resources Conservation Institute in Likuyu, Songea District.

Preparations also included the following activities:

- Establishment of Community Based Natural Resources Account and training of related personnel
- Establishment of hunting quotas
- Learning visits both inside and outside the country
- Establishment of tree planting nurseries

In working with other related institutions/entities, SRCS was accorded the observer status in all meetings. Such institutions included the Serengeti National Park (SENAPA), the Community Conservation Service, the Frankfurt Zoological Society (FZS), and the Wildlife Division.

Among SCRS' major achievements was its involvement in the establishment of Wildlife Management Areas (WMAs) in the area in partnership with other stakeholders. By the year 2000, SCRS had worked with over 20 communities in the establishment of Ikona WMA in Serengeti District, Eramatare in Loliondo Division, Lake Natron in Loliondo Division, and Makao WMA in Meatu District. In establishing WMAs in those area, SRCS engaged in activities and provision of services listed below:

- Wells and water points
- Water pumps
- Three seasonal boreholes
- Three dams
- Cattle dips
- Milling machines for grains
- Roads
- Health facility
- Schools
- Village offices

The project was subsequently phased out when funding stopped in 2006 [21], and there was no take over initiative to carry the initiated work forward. Although the headquarters has since been converted into WMA offices, the Project left behind a very important mark in efforts to protect the integrity of the Serengeti Ecosystem in the form of WMAs. It also left behind infrastructures that have improved the well-being of the communities living adjacent to the Serengeti Ecosystem, which is crucial in deterring illegal consumptive use of natural resources in neighboring protected areas. The Natural Resources Committees and Village Game Scouts are very important in conserving the natural resources of the area. Another important mark from the project is the conservation education it imparted to communities living adjacent to the Serengeti Ecosystem, which must have translated in some way into improved attitudes and behavior towards protected areas personnel and natural resources conservation in general.

Overall, the Serengeti Regional Conservation Strategy Project served as an important stepping stone for further work on Serengeti Ecosystem–based Management and provided lessons to aid other initiatives towards the cause. Thus, every initiative towards protecting the integrity of the Serengeti Ecosystem will do well to make reference to the Serengeti Regional Conservation Strategy Project work before concretizing its strategy, plan, and objectives.

6.2 Greater Serengeti Conservation Society (GSCS)

Another initiative aimed at facilitating ecosystem-based approach to managing Serengeti Ecosystem is what is known as the Greater Serengeti Conservation Society (GSCS, or simply, the Society). Founded by the Late Dr. Markus Borner and Hatim Karimjee as a Serengeti Ecosystem multi-stakeholder non-governmental organization seeking to maintain the integrity and resilience of the ecosystem for the benefit of present and future generation, GSCS is probably the best initiative thus far in involving all stakeholders in ensuring sustainable management of protected area resources in Tanzania.

The founders, both late now, were driven by their passion for wildlife conservation and knowledge of the dynamics involved in managing Serengeti Ecosystem as a single conservation entity against the different interests and demands of a multitude of stakeholders. Markus Borner had worked in the Serengeti as a representative of the Frankfurt Zoological Society for 40 years and served on TANAPA Board of Trustees for several years. He also sat on other wildlife conservation Boards, including that of TAWIRI, and Mweka College of Wildlife Management. He was also involved in research in the Serengeti.

Hatim Karimjee, a well-known businessman in Tanzania, coming from a family with several business lines in the country and a history of philanthropy, had also served on TANAPA Board of Trustees for several years. The impression I got of Karimjee, when we served on the TANAPA Board of Trustees together, was that, though coming from the private sector, he was very knowledgeable and had great passion for wildlife conservation. And, apart from the business acumen gained from the many years of managing the family business empire, he also had very good analytical skill, and he was good with numbers. Thus, Hatim Karimjee and Markus Borner were a very good combination of people to found a Serengeti Ecosystem management initiative, as they knew the inner workings of TANAPA, had the knowledge of Serengeti Ecosystem, and the passion and skills necessary to found an initiative with better chance of being more successful than the ones preceding it.

The founders of the initiative saw the exponential growth of human activity around the Serengeti Ecosystem as the major threat to its survival, as it was seen to have transformed the Greater Serengeti Ecosystem (Serengeti National Park and all the protected areas that surround it, as well as buffer zones and dispersal areas) and that it was encroaching on the ecosystem borders with unprecedented intensity [22]. They consequently set the initiative's vision to be, "to ensure a resilient and thriving Greater Serengeti Ecosystem to the benefit of the local and global communities." The motto of the initiative is, "Serengeti forever."

In practice, the initiative seeks to bring together Tanzania, Kenya, and international leading conservation professionals and scientists for common action in advancing the cause of saving and working to maintain the ecological integrity of the area and its natural resources, as well as its environment. To this effect, the Society was set up as an NGO with a status of a membership society based in Tanzania but with members from Tanzania, Kenya, as well as interested scientists and individuals abroad. And, in conformity with Tanzania's law, the Society is headed by a Board of Directors based in Tanzania.

Currently, the Society is also registered as a Charity Organization in London, England as well as in the USA [23]. The two charities constitute the main source of funding for the operations of the Society. The Chairman and President of the two charities, respectively, together with the Chairman of the Board of Directors for the Society in Tanzania, constitute the Board of Trustees of the Society.

The stakeholders constituting the Society's membership include managers of all protected areas within the ecosystem, major conservation entities, and individuals in Tanzania such as the Wildlife Division; Tanzania Wildlife Management Authority (TAWA); government leaders in surrounding districts; Tanzania Wildlife Research Institute (TAWIRI) and other relevant research institutions and individuals; conservation professionals and scientists both from within and outside Tanzania; conservation NGOs; relevant entities in Kenya including Kenya Wildlife Services, Maasai Mara National Reserve, Narok County, etc.

The Society meets once every year in an Annual Stakeholder Symposium, a forum to deliberate on issues pertaining to maintaining the integrity and sustainability of the Serengeti Ecosystem. The Symposium deliberates on pertinent issues, come up with resolutions, and makes recommendations that are then reported in the Society's newsletter. Implementation actions on recommendations are subsequently deliberated on at the following year's symposium, except for actions deemed urgent and for which respective stakeholders are required to take action before the following symposium.

The society's day-to-day activities are run by a management unit consisting of a Website Manager, a lawyer, and an accountant; all of them volunteers, and working on part time basis. The Unit is virtually based in Dar es Salaam, with the lawyer and accountant accommodated at the Board Chairman's Office and the website manager based overseas. The team is working under the Oversight Committee, which is composed of chief executives of the main relevant institutions in Tanzania and Kenya viz. TANAPA, NCAA, TAWA, TAWIRI, Director of Wildlife, Director of Kenya Wildlife Services, Chief Park Warden (Kenya).

On technical issues, the Society is served by a Scientific Committee and a consultant. The latter is working on part-time contractual terms; currently working 2 days per week. The consultant is the chief technical resource person of the Society, serving largely as a technical coordinator in organizing the annual symposium, serving as a rapporteur, compiling symposium reports, and coordinating the implementation of the Society's decisions, recommendations, and plans eg training. The consultant also works with the accountant to prepare the society's budget.

The Society has been in existence for a little over 6 years, and although quite lacking in institutional structure and organizational development, it has already made its mark in resolving some critical disputes deriving from the difference in stance between the Tanzanian Government policy and that of Kenya over grazing livestock in protected areas, allowing large commercial farms near protected area and cultivation in catchment areas. Initially, livestock grazing was allowed in Maasai Mara National Reserve and, this, in addition to large commercial farms adjacent to the Reserve degraded the habitat for ungulates. Cultivation in Mao Forest, on the other hand, degraded catchment area for Mara River, which had already been showing signs of drying [24]. There had also been a misunderstanding over Sasakwa dam on Tanzania side. The Kenyan side felt that by Tanzania damming Sasakwa, they were reducing water for the ungulates, which would ultimately alter the migration route. These issues could have been very complicated, if they had been approached differently and allowed political interests to filter in.

What can happen when multiple stakeholders with respect to a common natural resource have no common platform like one provided by the Society is very well demonstrated by what has been happening in Loliondo and NCA for the past two decades. Even with the government ceding 2500 km^2 out of the 4000 km^2 of the former Loliondo GCA to the communities and offering a very handsome resettlement package to those who volunteered to relocate, by providing them and their stock with relocation transport, ready-made modern homesteads, complete with modern houses, farming and livestock land, plus all necessary social services, has not completely resolved the conflict. There are those who have refused to go to government-selected area, Msomela in Handeni, Tanga Region, and demanded to be relocated to places of their choices. And, now (September 2023) a group of Maasai has taken the Government to Court contesting for the 1500 km^2 of land that was upgraded into a game reserve to protect a bit of the Serengeti Wildebeest Migration route, the breeding ground, and water catchment areas (see **Figure 3**), all of which are of critical importance in retaining some measure of protection to the function and integrity of Serengeti Ecosystem.

The strength of the Society lies in the following attributes:

a. The Society was born out of passion for conservation of wildlife and sustenance of Serengeti Ecosystem integrity, in particular.

b. The founders' knowledge of the ecosystem, the stakeholders, and failure of preceding initiatives must have helped in coming up with a strategy of involving all stakeholders in a forum that was not likely to suffer the same fate.

c. Availability of funds for holding the annual symposium and some of the initial costs of running the management unit and other initial activities.

d. Being served by a scientific committee, the factor that assures the Society of the necessary scientific information whenever it is required.

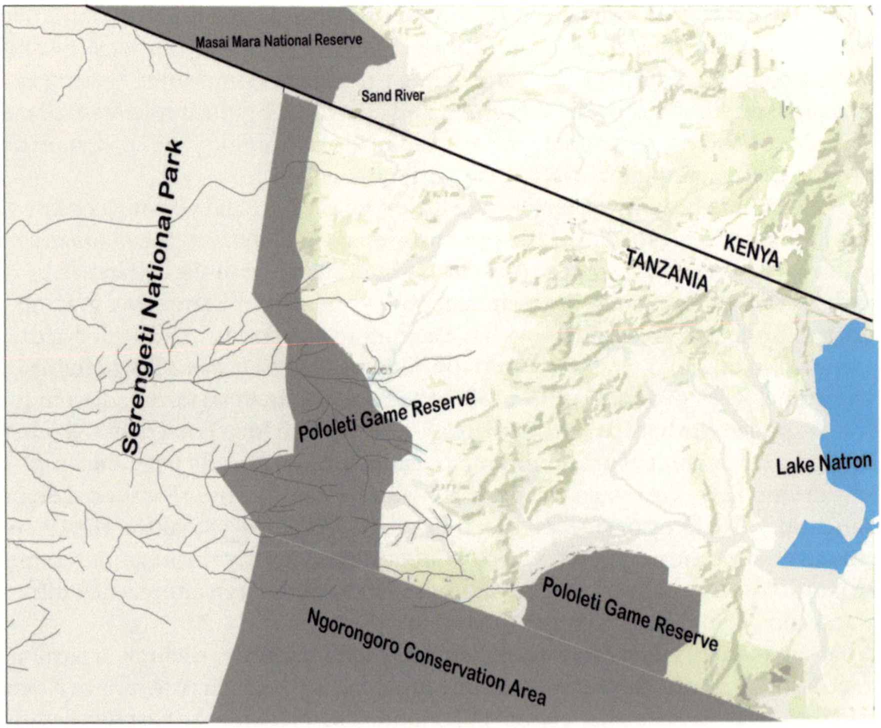

Figure 3.
Map of eastern part of Serengeti Ecosystem showing Pololet GR and Malambo GR. Source: Ministry of Natural Resources and Tourism.

e. Retaining the services of a consultant with first-hand knowledge of Serengeti Ecosystem gained from many years of working as a researcher and Managing Director of TAWIRI.

f. Being an NGO and non-partisan, and therefore not likely to be swayed due to conflicts of interest, nor be encumbered by bureaucracy in decision-making.

The Society, in its present form, appears to have the following weaknesses, which threaten its sustainability:

a. Absence of assured local source of funding. Presently the Society is funded from external sources.

b. Absence of office that is owned by the Society.

c. Absence of permanent and paid Society staff.

It is important to note, however, that, as an NGO, for national natural resources and environmental matters, the Society can only contribute to ecosystem-based management of Serengeti Ecosystem by working in partnership with or supporting the government as provided by pertinent laws and regulations. Currently, the Society has both the respective protected areas (within the ecosystem) and the WMAs to support or to work with. The Society can also support the government on any other initiative as deemed fit or necessary. The mode of engagement and operation, as well as choice of entity to work with would depend on what is legally permissible and mutually agreeable.

6.3 Wildlife management areas

Wildlife management areas (WMAs) are not one of the initiatives established to specifically overcome challenges to EBM for Serengeti Ecosystem. WMAs are a community-based wildlife conservation category of protected areas that can be established around any protected area in Tanzania, provided it fulfills the need for its establishment and satisfies the legal requirements. However, their inclusion here is necessitated by their default relevance as can be discerned from their mentions in other sections.

Indeed, in as much as HWCs are a major challenge to EBM for the Serengeti Ecosystem, WMAs, as a community-based conservation (CBC) initiative in communities around Serengeti Ecosystem, have a role to play. Besides, the shortcomings of WMAs and other forms of CBC have been variously blamed for people's negative attitudes towards protected areas and conservation, and consequent illegal utilization of natural resource in protected areas. Thus, any effort aiming to resolve HWCs, or overcome challenges to EBM, will do well to take WMAs into account. As discrete areas, with their coverage limited by the sizes of village land in question, the socio-economic impacts of WMAs are equally limited, but their influence on mindsets and attitude towards protected areas and the resources within goes much beyond the communities concerned with the WMAs in question.

Wildlife management areas within the Serengeti Ecosystem include Ikona in Serengeti District, Makao in Meatu District, Elamantare in Ngorongoro District, and Lake Natron in Ngorongoro District. Apart from increased land under community-based conservation, which means increased buffer area to respective protected areas, this year the government has published the WMA strategy that has basically changed the government narrative on WMAs and made it more positive to the livelihood needs of the surrounding communities. The stated overarching aim of the National Wildlife Management Areas Strategy (NWMAS) for the period 2023–2033 is to "align Tanzania on a path towards a rewarding community and livelihood-based approach with a high returns rate" [25].

7. Conclusion and proposals

Ecosystem-based management strategies are certainly a necessary approach to ensuring sustainable management of natural resources, and this is particularly so in wildlife protected areas. Although this is generally acknowledged by the conservation community, its adoption has been very difficult due to challenges, chiefly, by human-wildlife conflicts.

Currently, human-wildlife conflicts are Serengeti Ecosystem's major challenge to ecosystem-based planning and management, and these conflicts go back to the time Serengeti National Park was established as a national park in the 1950s. The measures that the government and conservation partners have taken over the years to resolve the various conflicts have, at best, served as temporary respite, and, at worst, they have proved futile. Today, contrary to what would be expected, conflicts have been escalating in certain areas to the extent of requiring emergency action, in addition to ongoing mitigation measures.

In addition to emergency and mitigation measures that are usually directed to specific incident or area, there have been several initiatives specifically aiming at saving Serengeti Ecosystem against HW conflicts. These initiatives have, in turn, been in addition to or in support of the WMAs. The latter, too, have not been successful, in spite of reviewing the strategy on which they are based several times since their inception in 2003. To date, none of the mitigation measures, nor Serengeti Ecosystem conservation initiatives, has been successful in resolving the HWCs. These failures, in the face of rising human-wildlife conflicts and resource degradation, have given rise to the need and calls for a solution towards overcoming challenges to EBM.

On examining the initiatives that have to date been tried out for ecosystem-based management for the Serengeti Ecosystem, both past and present, it appears the conditions listed below constitute constraints to their effectiveness in enabling EBM, largely by curtailing their sustainability.

a. Community-based natural resources conservation in the form of WMAs not delivering true on promised benefits to the targeted communities and hence the communities feeling cheated.

b. Initiatives operating as projects on limited area, and for a limited span of time, and therefore having limited impact, or no impact at all.

c. Initiatives being driven by foreign organizations, and therefore lacking genuine local ownership.

d. Initiatives operating on off-shore funding and consequently dying when funding ceases.

e. Initiatives not being mainstreamed into respective protected area management; that is, operating as stand-alone projects.

f. Initiatives lacking anchorage or linkage into TANAPA, and therefore not mainstreamed into the organization's plans and strategies.

g. Initiatives lacking anchorage into MNRT and thus missing budget link and consideration in case of funding problems.

Out of the several initiatives I read and consulted about, and the two that I have made a case example out of, the Greater Serengeti Conservation Society seemed to be better placed to provide the solution for overcoming the challenges to adopting the ecosystem-based planning and management strategies for the Serengeti Ecosystem. Below are some of its strengths.

a. Involving all stakeholders in its annual symposium, thus providing a forum for all concerned to voice their ideas and concerns.

b. The supervising committee being constituted by all concerned wildlife conservation authorities.

c. The initiative having been born out of passion and knowledge and continuing that way even after the demise of the founders.

d. Having known and established source of funding that is registered as charity.

e. Being a non-governmental organization, and therefore being less encumbered by bureaucracy, and at the same time having the potential to work in partnership with government, and in support of its work, which makes for more efficient execution of activities and effective performance.

7.1 Proposals

Based on the experience gained through the initiatives that have been implemented so far towards the management of Serengeti as an ecosystem, against the challenges inherent in managing a complex ecosystem like Serengeti, and those related to integrating the multitude of diverse stakeholder interests, as well as timely coordination of interventions, I propose the following foundation actions towards overcoming the challenges.

a. The Greater Serengeti Conservation Society, or any other stakeholder initiative with the capability to effectively carry out or facilitate the necessary activities as listed here, raises the funds necessary to carry out the foundation activities. Such an initiative is referred to here as the Foundation Initiative. This could be GSCS, its modified form, or any other choice of the GSCS majority stakeholders.

b. The Foundation Initiative should establish itself firmly by building its institutional capacity and essential infrastructure, acquiring necessary equipment, and hiring and training the necessary full-time personnel.

c. The Foundation Initiative should carry out ecosystem-wide strategic environmental assessment (SEA) to provide baseline information, establish management needs, and management strategy and plan.

d. The Foundation Initiative should, based on SEA, develop a program and schedule that will allow scaling up activities, including increasing the frequency of stakeholder meetings.

Author note

Retired Senior Instructor: Wildlife Conservation, Ecology, Climatology, and Biostatistics; for Certificate, Ordinary Diploma and Post-graduate Diploma Courses at the College of African Wildlife Management, Mweka, Tanzania.

Semi-retired Independent Natural Resources and Environmental Consultant and member of Tanzania Environmental Experts Association.

Author details

Theonestina Kaiza-Boshe
Independent Researcher, Dar es Salaam, Tanzania

*Address all correspondence to: tkaiza@gmail.com

References

[1] Kaiza-Boshe T. Tanzania in Urgent Need for an Integrative Wildlife Conservation Strategy. 2020. Available from: tkaiza.wordpress.com

[2] Kaiza-Boshe T. Human–Elephant Conflicts in Tanzania: The Need for a Manipulative Scientific Wildlife Management Strategy. 2021. Available from: tkaiza.wordpress.com

[3] Kidegesho JR. 'Serengeti shall not die': Transforming an ambition into reality. Tropical Conservation Science. 2010;**3**(3):228-248

[4] Lyogello LN. A Field Guide to Tanzania National Parks and Ngorongoro. Tanzania National Parks: Arusha, Tanzania; 2008

[5] Kaiza-Boshe T. Conservation in Tanzania: Nine decades of conservation. Kakakuona Magazine. 1989;**1**(1):1989

[6] Martin D. Serengeti. Arusha, Tanzania: Tanzania National Parks; 2002. 96 pp

[7] MNRT. Ngorongoro Conservation Area Act. Cap. 284: An Act to Control Entry into and Residence within the Ngorongoro Crater Highlands Area, to Make Provision for Conservation and Development of Natural Resources Therein and for Related Matters. Dar es Salaam, Tanzania: Government Printer; 1975

[8] Morenda J. Govt defends Loliondo demarcation, Ngorongoro relocation. In: The Citizen Online (on Internet). Tanzania; 23 June 2022

[9] MNRT. Serengeti Regional Conservation Strategy: Project Proposal. Ministry of Natural Resources and Tourism: Dar es Salaam, Tanzania; 1992

[10] Wolanski E et al. Migration and the Serengeti ecosystem. In: Gereta E, Borner M, Mduma SW, editors. American Scientist. Vol. 87, Issue 6. USA: American Scientist Journal; 1999. p. 526

[11] Sinclair ARE. Human impact on ecosystem dynamics. In: Parker C, Mduma SAR, Fryxell JM, editors. Integrative and Comparative Biology. Vol. 49, Issue 1. New York, USA: Integrative and Comparative Biology Journal (formerly, American Zoologist); 2009. 83 p

[12] Nelson F, Ole Makko S. Chapter 5. Preserving rights to gain benefits. In: Communities, Conservation, and Conflicts in the Tanzanian Serengeti. Ujamaa Community Resource Team; 2012

[13] Trompell S. 2019. The Conservation Bias in Tanzania's Wildlife Management Areas.blogs,lse.ac.uk

[14] MNRT. Wildlife Conservation Act, No. 5: 2009. Dar es Salaam, Tanzania: Government Printer; 2009

[15] Fosbrooke H. A Compilation of Pre-History of the Maasai District. National Archives; 1955

[16] MNRT. The Village Land Act No. 5 of 1999. Dar es Salaam, Tanzania: Govt. Printer; 1999

[17] Bluwstein J, Moyo F, Kicheleri RP. Austere conservation: Understanding conflicts over resource governance in Tanzanian wildlife management areas. Conservation and Society. 2016;**14**(3):218-231

[18] King L. A Sigh of Relief to Communities Living near Serengeti.

London, UK: Save the Elephants and Elephant Crisis Fund; 2022

[19] Chamba IY. Human-Elephant Conflicts: Approaches and Techniques for Managing Man-Elephant Conflicts in Western Serengeti. Morogoro, Tanzania: Sokoine University of Agriculture; 2018

[20] Malpas R, Perkins S. Towards Serengeti Regional Conservation Strategy; Up-Dating a Workshop Report of 1986. IUCN doc. Dodoma: MNRT; 1986

[21] Mfunda I. Personal Communication. Former Serengeti Regional Conservation Strategy Economist. 2023

[22] Greater Serengeti Conservation Society. Available from: https://www.serengeti-forever.org

[23] Riaz Punja's LinkedIn profile. March 2024

[24] Mduma SAR. Personal Communication. Arusha, Tanzania: Retired Director General of Tanzania Wildlife Research Institute; 2023

[25] MNRT. National Wildlife Management Areas Strategy (2023-2033). Dodoma, Tanzania: Ministry of Natural Resources and Tourism; 2023

Chapter 11

Urban Planning and Land-Use Management in Jerusalem – Chronological Analysis: Urban Perspectives in Contested Cities

Raed Najjar

Abstract

Polarized spaces and divided cities present a set of fast-changing urban policies and control powers. Of its tense history of complex spatial planning and land-use management, Jerusalem is not an exception. In less than 50 years, 1917–1967, Jerusalem was controlled by four variant regimes. The Ottoman Rule, the British Mandate, the Jordanian Control, and the Israeli Occupation respectively. In that sense, Jerusalem is considered a unique spatial entity in terms of its historical and physical development. This chapter explores the evolution of urban planning and land-use management in Jerusalem for these administrative authorities, underlining its impact on the city population and urban growth. During these subsequent administrative transformations, Jerusalem has witnessed quick and variant planning paradigms, and questionable development patterns, that produced numerous socio-spatial challenges. Principally, the altered composition of the population, as well as the paradoxical urban fabric of the city. Indeed, the successive authorities in Jerusalem, ending with the Israeli occupation of the eastern part of the city, have created a maze of wide-ranging rules and regulations, making the planning system complex, spatially unsustainable, and eventually in many ways, intensifying urban conflicts.

Keywords: conflict areas, Jerusalem, land use, master plan, urban planning

1. Introduction

The vibrant records of history date the earliest civilization in Jerusalem to the sixth millennium [1]. Along this deep time pathway, distinct multicultural groups inhabited Jerusalem. The indigenous inhabitants of Jerusalem were the Canaanites. Coexistence over the land of Canaan produced intertwined histories for its inhabitants who fought occasionally but mostly collaborated [2]. Spiritually, the city of Jerusalem has a remarkable presentation. Over three millennia ago, a tradition developed envisioned Jerusalem as a Holy City. It reflected for Jews their spiritual pole [3]. The city represented the birthplace of Christianity in the first century AD, while in the seventh century when Islam showed up, the city was perceived as a Sacred Centre [4]. The religious value of Jerusalem gave it special symbolic significance [5], no wonder it became a focus of all monotheistic religions and was regarded as the metaphoric core of the old world as shown in **Figure 1**.

The special character of Jerusalem invited forceful invaders and conquerors. This fact led to the destruction and reconstruction of the sacred city more than 18 times [7]. Under the Canaanite, the city was called Ur-Salem until King David captured it and called it the City of David in 997 BC, proclaiming it the capital of the united Israelite Kingdom which was demolished by the Egyptians who recaptured Jerusalem 40 years later. Successively, Jerusalem was seized by the Babylonians, the Persians, the Hellenistic, and the Roman-byzantine Empire [8]. Then Muslims conquered Jerusalem in 636 AD. Since then, except for nice decades extending from 1099 to 1187 AD when the city fell under Crusader control, it was under multiple Muslim rules for example, Umayyad, Ikhshidid, Fatimid, Tulunid, Abbasid, Ayyubid, Seljuk, Mameluke, and lately the Ottoman. Those various rules in Jerusalem reflect a mosaic mirror of civilizations that left marvelous imprints and monuments and created remarkable spaces of fabulous landmarks to date.

Jerusalem was kept under Muslim control until 1917 when the British ended the Ottoman Rule and imposed their Mandate in Palestine [9]. The British helped establish a Jewish state in Palestine [10], thus their mandate was dismantled after the establishment of the State of Israel in 1948. In the same year, Jerusalem was divided into East and West for the first time in its long history. The eastern part was administered by the Trans- Jordan, while the western side was declared as the capital of Israel [11]. Eighteen years later, in 1967, Israel won the Six-Day War, annexed East Jerusalem, and dismantled its Arabic municipality. In the meantime, Israeli laws were imposed by one Jewish municipality operated totally under Israeli control up to date [12]. Afterward, specifically in 1980, Israel declared United Jerusalem, East, and West, as its capital.

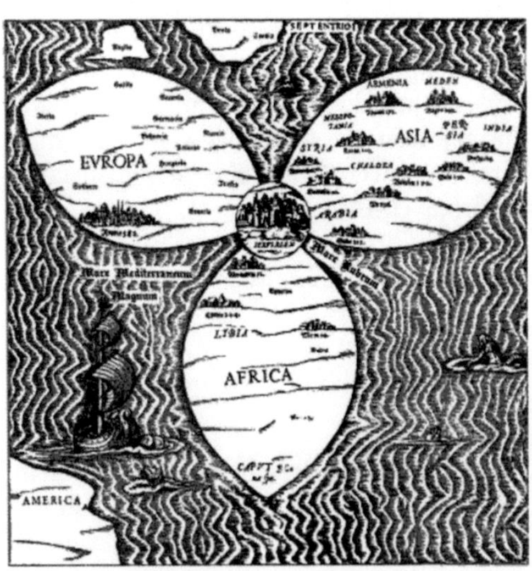

Figure 1.
Jerusalem represents the center of the Old World [6].

The geographical location of Jerusalem offered a distinguished centrality to its character, **Figure 2**. It occupies principal geopolitical status with strong connectivity to regional capitals. Jerusalem is located 55 km away from the western coast of the Mediterranean, 85 km from Amman, 290 km from Damascus, 388 km from Beirut, 528 km from Cairo, and 865 km from Baghdad. This superlative position entitles Jerusalem to exceptional geopolitical value.

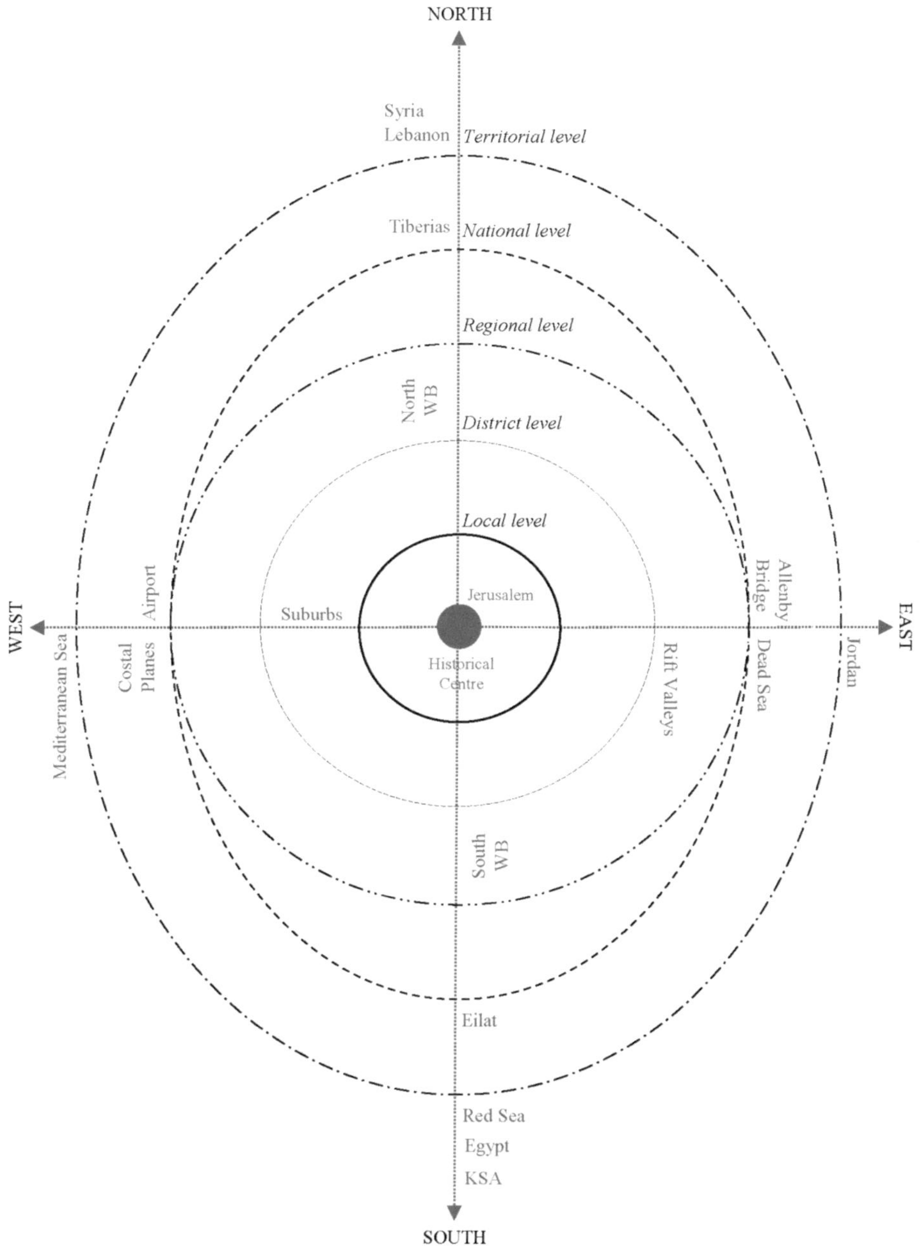

Figure 2.
Radial connectivity and geopolitical significance of Jerusalem (author).

From the past century until today, a wide range of spaces faced massive urban instabilities due to political, economic, and military conflicts worldwide. Such conflicts are more intensified in regions and cities, where ethnic separation, hypersegregation, and radical racial discrimination become phenomenal. This could be reflected in different cities like Nicosia, Mostar, Belfast, Beirut, and Jerusalem. These conflict areas or alternatively, contested cities, are perceived as detached cities, polarized cities, partitioned cities, dual cities, and divided and fragmented cities [13].

In urban and spatial contexts, conflict areas are zones where conflict is dominant. Consequently, the physical spaces and social strata are ultimately divided and thus, constitute progressively more contrasted spaces and places, opposite neighborhoods, and paradoxical blocks. Dissimilarity is remarkable in such a separated physical environment which outstandingly shows the contrasted clusters of inhabitants, i.e., the rich and the poor, the privileged and the deprived, and the dominant and the marginalized. Likewise in terms of urban fabric, conflict areas show obvious contradictions among the segregated spaces, developed or undeveloped, secured, or risky, renewal or degradation [14]. Jerusalem is an urban metropolis that represents a conflict area with a far-reaching intensity of ethnic, religious, ideological, and geopolitical struggle that exists for more than 75 years. Yet, Jerusalem is considered a contested, frontier, and deeply divided city [15].

Urban planning development in Jerusalem offers an extensive and interesting case for urban planners and scholars. The successive changes in the city definition, and the transformations of its administration during a few decades in the last century resulted in a complex set of spatial planning systems. The city population, as well as the built-up environment, have been heavily impacted.

2. Ottoman planning in Jerusalem (1516–1917)

The character and core structure of Jerusalem were formidably formed during the Ottoman rule which started in the early sixteenth century and extended for more than 400 years. Ottoman governments paid special attention to Jerusalem. Economic prosperity and social revival were the direct outcomes which, in turn, flourished the city and led to public infrastructure renovation, as well as continuous population growth. The public renovation works included rebuilding the encircling fascinating wall of the Old City. It first defined Jerusalem's spatial urban definition with a special fortress outlook. Other restoration works included the rehabilitation of internal roads, pedestrian alleys, and the installation of drinking fountains, especially in places where worshippers and pilgrims were expected. Little traces of this magnificent prosperity and urban renewal remained in the nineteenth century. This could be understood due to the economic stagnation and the arrested growth that Jerusalem underwent until the 1830s.

The growing importance of Jerusalem led the Ottomans to recognize the city as a main province in Palestine in terms of physical development and planning. This was interpreted by large-scale development plans and actions. The first monumental windmill was constructed in 1839; pedestrian sidewalks were expanded in 1863; road tiles were replaced for all streets and alleys, besides surface water drain channels were reconstructed in 1885; the first highway was constructed between Jerusalem and Jaffa coastal city in 1867, while a railway connecting both cities were opened in 1892; the city central hospital was rebuilt in 1891; as well as post offices were installed in the city. These outstanding examples show the significant Ottoman role in urban renewal in Jerusalem [16, 17].

Unlike the previous eras, under Ottoman rule, Jerusalem gained a growing "new" political value, besides its religious and administrative importance. This added a lot to Jerusalem's revival in the 19th century [18]. The intense administrative redevelopment of Jerusalem formed a dominant characteristic of Ottoman centralization in Palestine. The major universal powers approached the city by settling massive number of foreign missionaries. European and occidental consulates were established successively over a short period: Great Britain (1838), Prussia (1842), Sardinia (1843), France (1843), America (1856), and Russia (1857). In consequence, Jerusalem's political life was revitalized, and the city's urbanization gained more governmental attention which enhanced the city's population growth. These new political formations quite naturally accelerated the building boom in the city. In 1860, the Ottoman government began allowing European Christians to build outside the encircling walls of the Old City of Jerusalem. Therefore, new European building styles and architecture continued to appear influencing the urban landscape without interruption until WWI.

The unique religious perception towards Jerusalem also impacted the Ottoman planning policies and city administration. Ottomans thus established a peaceful religious environment in Jerusalem. They developed an amazing social system fed by elastic laws and regulations, including residency rights, for both: native inhabitants, and visitors. Ottomans never prohibited any Christian population from practicing their basic rights of entering the city of Jerusalem. Jews were a minority, however, they exercised religious freedom during the Ottoman period unprecedented in any country in Europe [19]. No discrimination was reported among the heterogenous population in Jerusalem, and peaceful co-existence and plurality of faiths and confessions were provident [20].

A critical announcement happened in 1869 when the founder of Political Zionism declared a desire to establish a Jewish national state in Palestine. Automatically, Ottoman Sultan, Abd-al Hamid II refused to host and settle Jewish colonists in Palestine. Within three decades later, the colonization of Palestine through the 'Basel Program' was announced in the First Zionist Congress which also founded the World Zionist Organization in 1897 in Switzerland. Accordingly, Sultan Abd-al Hamid II initiated a policy of sending members of his own palace staff to govern the province of Jerusalem. However, Jewish immigration into Jerusalem accelerated, it was even eased by diplomatic Consuls who misused a large role in the conduct of minority relations with the Ottoman Empire. Moreover, land tenure and land ownership laws could not restrict foreign immigrant Jews from buying lands in Jerusalem [21].

Ottomans did not create a comprehensive planning regime in Jerusalem, or detailed master plans and regulations. But they preserved the special character of the Old City and renovated its urban spaces and infrastructure. By this, Ottomans inherited the human community a vivid presentation of the "old fortification towns". On the other hand, Ottomans reflected their peaceful social policies upon the built-up environment, namely the Old City quarters shown in **Figure 3.** Those quarters categorize the main religious strata in Jerusalem. They form a tolerant division along well-defined geographical and demographical lines. The formation of Jerusalem's old quarters reflects the multicultural coexistence and integration of social aspects with the distinctive physical appearance of the city. Each quarter contained a small community having similar backgrounds where people preferred to live in proximity to each other, forming a "homogenous group" in a relatively wider "heterogeneous population". Honorably, Jerusalem is perceived therefore as a "Religious Open City" in the Ottoman era [22].

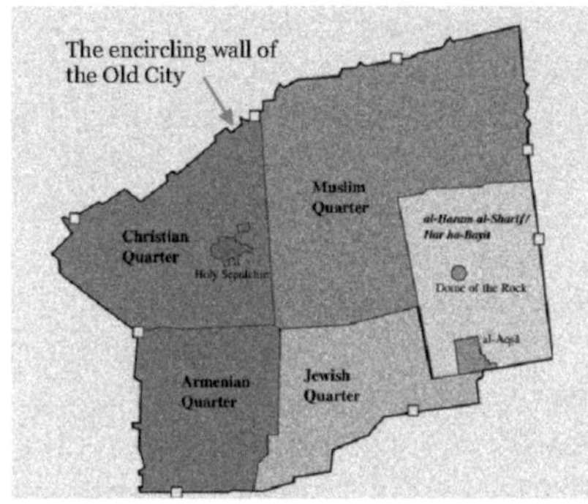

Figure 3.
Spatial affinity in Jerusalem Old City quarters [22].

Planning era	Planning perception	Spatial reflection
Jerusalem in Ottoman Rule	Fortress/Fortification City	• Reconstructing the old city walls • Place the old city as a monolithic unit serving as a regional
	Vernacular City	• Old-style city quarters with narrow alleys
	Religious Open City	• Foreign Jews and Christians could visit the city for religious activities • Enhance population diversity
	Administrative Province	• Renovate urban infrastructure, and install public services
	Diplomatic Centre	• Hub of Consulates and foreign political missionaries

Table 1.
Ottoman planning perception in Jerusalem (author).

The planning perception and the accompanying spatial reflection on Jerusalem during the Ottoman Era are shown in **Table 1**. Ottoman rule in Jerusalem ended after the dissolvement of the Ottoman Empire at the end of WWI, and Jerusalem was captured then by the British Army.

3. British planning in Jerusalem (1917–1948)

A short review of the mandate period in Palestine, especially in Jerusalem, would reveal rigorous and matchlessly more passionate political life than that during the Ottoman era. Hence, before focusing on the planning footprints British Mandate left in Jerusalem, a brief reflection on the historical background of the exceptional socio-political events during the British Mandate would be essential. As the WWI approached its end, the British Mandate (1917–1948) started and lasted for three decades in Palestine. In 1917, the British Prime Minister announced his declaration (Balfour Declaration) to reconstruct Palestine to be the Jewish homeland. As such, the British appointed a Zionist Jew as the first High Commissioner for Palestine in 1920. In 1922, the ratification of the Balfour Declaration was announced by the League of Nations, which by so, entrusted the United Kingdom to administer the "Mandate for Palestine", and to facilitate establishing a Jewish state in Palestine [10].

Unlike what was proposed by the geopolitical agreement of Sykes-Picot in1916, the internationalization of Palestine, the mandate there was only British in order to fulfill the British governmental promise of Balfour [23]. And so, the British government issued a set of "White Papers" to determine the destiny of Palestine in 1922, 1930, and 1939, besides a division plan to split Palestine in 1937. As such, the future vision of Palestine and the destiny of Jerusalem, which for many times was planned to be controlled internationally, rendered critical questions. The British mandatory administration policies aimed at changing the natural demographic composition in Palestine to minimize the number of native Palestinian Arab populations. The Jewish community at an early stage of the British Mandate in Palestine constituted less than one-tenth of the total population. The mandate facilitated a massive influx of Jewish immigration [24], more than 425,000 Jews immigrated to Palestine including illegal immigrants, **Figure 4**. In a short period, Jews composed one-third of the total population, and the accuracy of these numbers was boosted by successive studies [26].

The constant influx of Jewish settlers forced Palestinian native peasants to get displaced from their land. Then the mandatory government allotted 'illegally' thousands of hectares of Palestinian cultivable land to the Jews [27]. As such, the mandatory government tried to control the absorptive capacity of the country [28]. This sudden change in the demographic composition in Palestine created tension between the Palestinian and the foreign Jewish immigrants which led to blood-stained riots mainly in the 1920s, then the eruption of the Arab revolution of 1936–1939. Instability continued to grow and reached the top as the British Mandate drew to a close [29, 30], while Arabs organized more and more riots to liberate their lands and protect their rights [31].

The British Mandate was headquartered in Jerusalem. By so, Jerusalem acquired a new political significance and became the capital of the whole country again for the first time since the Crusader days. This had fostered urban growth which rapidly accelerated after the WWI, and most of the official British buildings were erected there. Jerusalem expanded to the north, south, and west. In consequence, new and rapid building projects marked most spaces, in different building categories including residential quarters, commercial and office centers, industrial zones, luxurious hotels, sports and recreational facilities, and religious institutions. Accordingly, Jerusalem began its transformation from the provincial town of Ottoman times to a modern administrative, political, religious, and cultural hub.

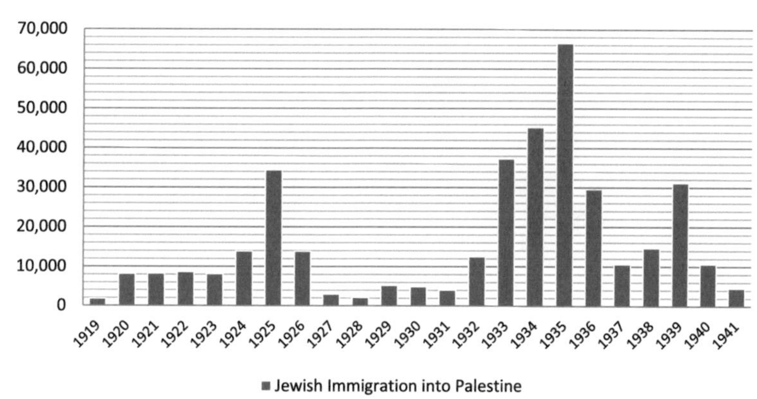

Figure 4.
Jewish immigration into Palestine during 1919–1941 [25].

Jerusalem shaped a focal point for pioneer European planners and architects. The most famous architects and planners, such as Sir William McLean, Sir Patrick Geddes, Charles Ashbee, William McLean, and Henry Kendall were invited to Jerusalem to develop master plans and design buildings. They were inspired by the "garden city" concept which influenced their planning ideas. Their role in shaping the city image of the new extension of Jerusalem was substantial. A new page of 'conventional town planning' in Jerusalem was opened during the British Mandate.

The British realized the need to preserve the old city's exclusive identity while transforming Jerusalem into a modern city. Hence, a preservative component was dominant in urban planning during the mandate period. Planners at that epoch balanced between two critical criteria, namely preservation, and urban renewal. Therefore, the British planning paradigm, specifically for the Old City of Jerusalem and its surrounding, could be classified as a "Romantic Approach" [22].

To maintain the authenticity of the Old City, the British Military Governor, in 1918, i.e., 4 months after the capture of the city, announced that no person shall destroy, improve, change, or repair the structure of any building in Jerusalem or its surroundings without first obtaining his written permit. Restrictions were also imposed for construction materials, using sheet metal and stucco for the building was forbidden, likewise, the use of beaten iron and stucco within the walls was prohibited. Those strict regulations show sensitivity towards the urban fabric, the resultant city image, and the conservation of its originality. Moreover, they shaped a conceptual foundation for the following plans that have formed Jerusalem to a large extent to date.

During the mandate period, five master plans were developed for Jerusalem: three advisory plans and two statutory outline plans. The first master plan of Jerusalem was submitted in 1918, by Sir William McLean. This plan serves as a foundation for planning Jerusalem, its strategic principles are paramount to date. It reflects the garden city concept by offering a green belt all around the Old City as shown in **Figure 5**. The plan highlighted the architectural value of the historic city center with less focus on its functional role to serve the entire city. The development of the new city, 'Modern Jerusalem', was directed mainly towards the west and north. The plan was not detailed, however, it enhanced urban uniformity throughout the city and created harmony

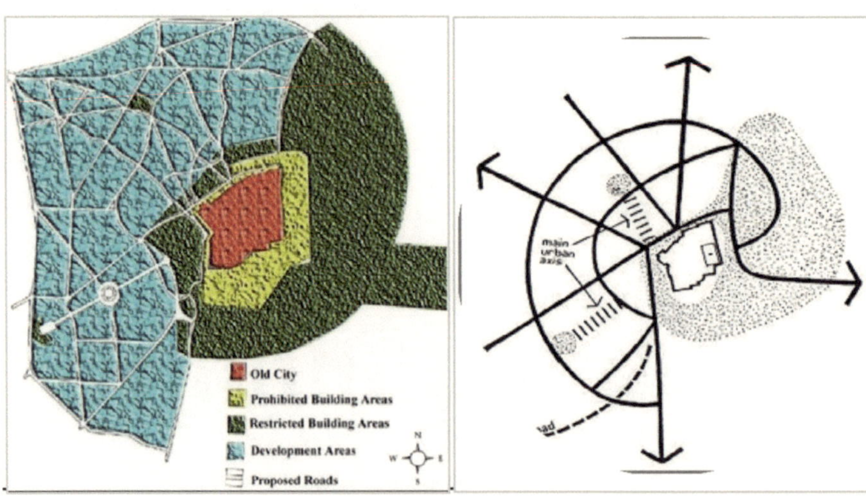

Figure 5.
McLean Master Plan 1918 with the respective schematic outline (author).

between all space components of the built environment by enforcing restrictions on types of building materials, as well as on building height to preserve the skyline. Thus, McLean offered an invaluable master plan that oriented the city development with great emphasis on preservation.

A year later, the second master plan was submitted by Patrick Geddes. This master plan paid lower attention towards preservation, it had reduced magnificently the amount of land where the building was prohibited and controlled instead the development of adjacent zones of the Old City. The development wheel followed the orientation marked by McLean plan, whereas restrictions remained on the eastern and southern sides. One year later, an interesting collaboration between Patrick Geddes and architect Chareles Ashbee produced an advisory master plan (Geddes-Ashbee) which continued to develop until 1922. It introduced greater emphasis on neighborhood planning and established building criteria according to zones. The basic urban outline of Geddes-Ashbee plan was not changed from Geddes plan, however, it indicated, for the first time, clear designations of land use "Zoning". Hence, this plan is more integral than the previous ones, it allowed for wider expansion while considering the originality of Jerusalem historic Old City.

In 1925, Clifford Holliday, the city planner of Jerusalem, proposed a new plan which was approved in 1930. It was the first legal outline plan of Jerusalem and served till 1944. Its detailed regulations defined land uses, building setbacks, building densities, heights, and building materials. In accordance with land use designations, special zones in the city were designated for commercial activities, e.g., along Jaffa Road which is considered up to date one of the most popular commercial roads in Jerusalem. Based upon Holiday's plan detailed local plans were derived and all parcellation and building plans followed it.

The city of Jerusalem demanded additional ideas and more comprehensive details about its urban context and future physical development. As a result, even during WWII, specifically in 1944, Henry Kendall as a British Town Planning Adviser developed the last plan initiated by the British Mandate Authority, **Figure 6**. Kendall Plan represents twice the area of the preceding Plan. This responds to the population growth which recorded a huge increase, almost 2.6 times the population during the previous plan [32]. Kendall plan had significantly minimized the land-use marked as

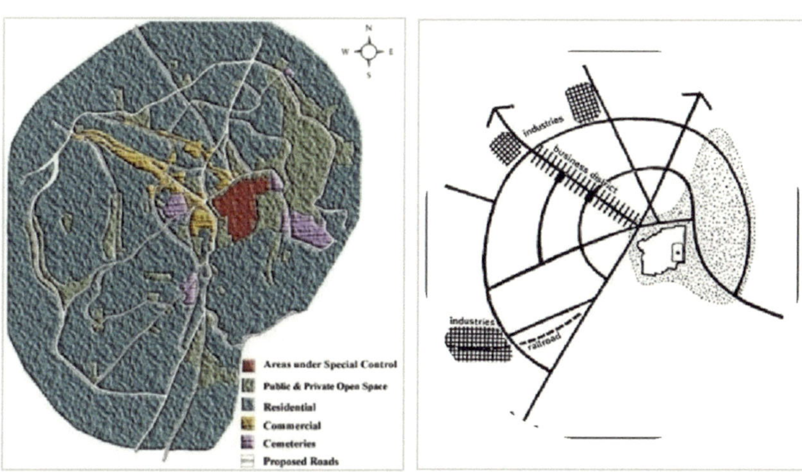

Figure 6.
Kendal Master Plan 1944 with its schematic outline (author).

Planning era	Planning perception	Spatial reflection
Jerusalem in British Mandate	Political Significance	• The administration was headquartered in Jerusalem • Jerusalem became the capital of the whole country
	Romantic Conception	• Preserve the original image of the old city while shifting Jerusalem to modernity • Sensitive regulations regarding the old city's architectural image and urban fabric
	Garden City Concept	• Prohibit building, promote and determine a green buffer zone around the old city walls • Establish building height regulations to protect the old city skyline.
	Urban Attractive City	• Jerusalem began its transformation from a provincial town to a modern administrative, political, religious, and cultural hub • Master plans were developed by eminent British planners

Table 2.
British planning perception in Jerusalem (author).

open spaces around the Old City of Jerusalem. In other words, Kendall encouraged development towards the west, north, and southern directions, and therefore allowed erecting new residential areas in the green park surrounding the Old Wall of the city. Kendal integrated multiple socio-economic planning criteria, and thus demonstrated separation of social strata by using a clever residential zoning approach. Two-thirds of those zones were designated in the western sector mainly, while the rest one-third was in the eastern part of the city.

The planning perception and the accompanying spatial reflection on Jerusalem during the British Mandate are shown in **Table 2**. The imperial administration of the British Mandate attempted to divide the city of Jerusalem into separate boroughs [23], but that failed as did the mandate. In 1947, the British government announced that the mandate in Palestine is not workable anymore. With the termination of the British Mandate in Palestine, the passionate and romantic planning fruitful days came to an end. Jerusalem, as a "Palestinian Capital" of the whole country turned into a question of hope.

4. Planning during the division of Jerusalem (1948–1967)

After the dissolvement of the mandate in Palestine, the United Nations called for the partition of Palestine and the internationalization of Jerusalem in 1947–1948 [33]. Arabs rejected this plan; war broke out between Arab and Jews and ended with the proclamation of independence of Israel in 1948. This fact reflected a practical translation of the British commitment to establish a Jewish homeland in Palestine.

Israel fostered and supported by all means the Jewish immigration to Palestine. It introduced a lot of controversial laws, among which the Law of Return of 1950, which is an ethnic-based law that gives any Jew the default right to immigrate to Israel and automatically become a citizen. Along with this immigration policy, Israel spent every effort to own lands from Palestinians [34]. During that Arab-Israeli fighting, Israel occupied the new city of the western part of Jerusalem. While Arabs kept Jerusalem Old City and its eastern new edges. Practically, the division of Jerusalem took place addressing what is known as East Jerusalem under Jordanian rule, and on other hand West Jerusalem under Israeli occupation. This separation of Jerusalem, East, and West, lasted 19 years, extending from 1948 to 1967. Each part of the city was administered and developed separately.

East Jerusalem underwent economic stagnation, a slow growth rate, and a modest development pattern. During the Jordanian administration period, Jordanians did not produce any master plan for East Jerusalem. Instead, they made some changes by issuing new planning laws (Jordanian Planning Law (79) in 1966) that replaced and amended the British planning acts [35]. In East Jerusalem, the Jordanian administration used Kendall Plan of 1944, which was the sole reference to direct urban development there. However, Kendall's Master Plan was no more appropriate to serve as a master plan, due to the fact of physical and geopolitical separation of Jerusalem. Originally, it envisioned Jerusalem as one entity that shall grow in an integrated spatial system of development, in contrast to the divisional status.

During the division period, approximately 30,000 Palestinians were driven out of their homes in the new city sectors. Local Palestinian residents in East Jerusalem suffered from severe economic and social losses. The city grew slowly, in a random, small-scale, and piecemeal pattern. Construction was initiated by families, or sometimes by limited developers. There was no harmony or consistency in the developed urban fabric, due to individual designs that were highly differentiated. The diverse forms of the single-family house were the predominant building type. In consequence, the Arabic sectors in East Jerusalem expanded fragmentary with limited speed and capacity. Likewise, infrastructure and public facilities deteriorated and lacked renovation and expansion.

On the other side, West Jerusalem was declared the capital of Israel. A new epoch of colonial administration has started. It represented for the city a period of major changes, rapid development, and speedy growth, the opposite scenario to the eastern part. The central government played a key role in accelerating the development wheel in the new city. Construction was public, and on large-scale. Housing units were a governmental priority. As such, repetitive standardized housing units characterized most neighborhoods in the western part during the 1950s and 1960s. To ensure high construction rhythm, the Israeli government overlooked the law of stone buildings, permits were issued to construct buildings in concrete or stucco.

Unlike the Jordanian administration in the eastern part, Israel produced two master plans for West Jerusalem. The first one was the Rau Plan, a conceptual plan formulated by architect Heinz Rau. It came out as a natural outcome of the new geopolitical situation which demanded establishing an urgent strategy for urban planning. Indeed, this plan took into consideration the spatial reflection of the whole city by neglecting the limits of armistice lines. Valleys besides the adjacent areas of the Old City encircling walls were designated as parks, the internal road network was much developed, and detailed zones for public and private development were carefully addressed. The Israeli government decided to prepare a legally binding plan for the city. Hence, Shaviv Plan, **Figure 7**, was introduced officially in 1955 and got approved in 1959.

Shaviv Plan shaped the major physical benchmarks of the new western city to date. It introduced different zoning criteria and multiple land use titles. Road networks and linkage to existing infrastructure and railways gained momentum in this plan. Unconventionally, the plan did not respect the preservation aspect. In consequence, it allowed the demolition of several traditional neighborhoods along commercial roads and the expansion of building rights in old neighborhoods. The focal objective of the plan was to direct the development westwards, to concentrate the Jewish population

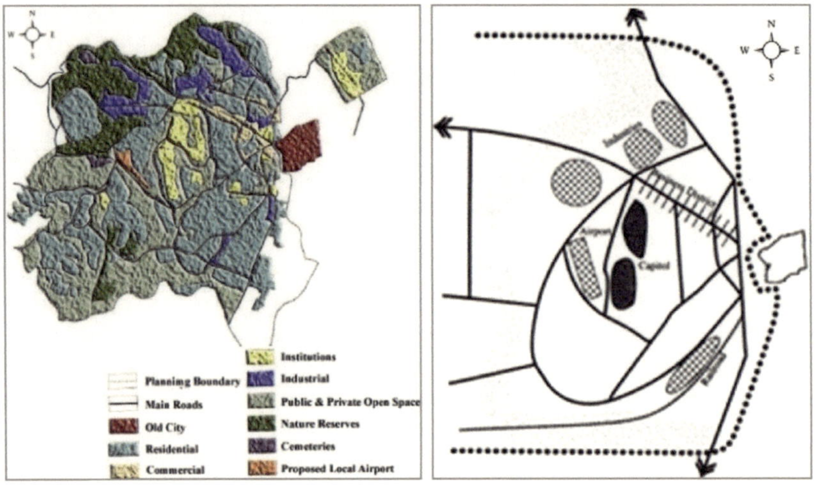

Figure 7.
Shaviv Plan 1955–1959 with its schematic outline (author).

there, and to improve the configuration of the built-up neighborhoods. This planning policy allowed population growth based on the existing infrastructure of roads and public buildings, without any large investments in new areas. Unlike the well-planned new quarters located in the western direction of the new city, the earlier existing old neighborhoods of the eastern sector got their land use titles and had been zoned in a rather general and monotonous way that did not fill the gap regarding the shortage of land for public amenities [36].

5. Planning Jerusalem during the post-1967 epoch

In mid of the 1960s, regional tensions between Israel and the surrounding Arab countries had raised. The Jewish desire of expanding the Jewish state boundaries fed numerous border clashes. Some Arab countries developed a strategic defense agreement [37], however, Jordan which controlled East Jerusalem and the West Bank at that time, complained about the weakness of strategic Arab support, and asked for Iraqi army support [38]. Egypt carefully monitored the common borders with Israel [39]. On the first of June 1967, Israel formed a National Unity Government, and on the fourth of June decision was made to originate preemptive war. The day after, Israel initiated rigorous large-scale air strikes which marked the official beginning of the Six-Day War against Egypt, Jordan, and Syria.

The war ended rapidly, and Israel got a definitive victory. Dramatic consequences faced the conquered states because of the Israeli occupation of the Sinai Peninsula in Egypt, Golan Heights in Syria, East Jerusalem, and the West Bank which were under Jordanian administration, and the Gaza Strip which was under Egyptian control [11]. Indeed, the Israeli occupation policies in Palestine present pressing issues in international law and generate far-reaching consequences in global affairs [40].

Israel annexed illegally 70.5 square kilometers of the occupied Palestinian territory (oPt) including East Jerusalem. The Israeli annexation of East Jerusalem in 1967, marked a significant event in the history of Palestine. It constituted a turning point for Jerusalem, East, and West, as both parts of the city remained under Israeli occupation to date. Israel announced the reunification of West and East Jerusalem to be one city administered by a Jewish municipality. Unifying Jerusalem earmarks a great shift in different aspects, mainly shifting from the city level to the district scale. Israel declared unified Jerusalem as its eternal capital through the Basic Law on 30 July 1980. However, this declaration is contrary to international law and thus has not been recognized by most of the international community. Accordingly, most countries maintain their embassies in Tel Aviv. In that sense, international law, resolutions of the United Nations, as well as Israeli-Palestinian signed agreements have been aggressively violated by Israel. Palestinian people underline the Resolution (No. 252) of the United Nations Security Council that condemns illegal land confiscation and refuses all actions that would change the legal status of Jerusalem. The actual status of Jerusalem is debatable and contended to date.

According to international law, namely Fourth Geneva Convention, East Jerusalem represents territory occupied by Israel because of war. As such, Israel must guarantee the rights of the native population, avoid changing the natural demographic composition of the occupied territories, and offer a suitable level of services to native inhabitants. Opposite Israeli actions constantly take place on the ground. In Jerusalem, the Israeli regressive planning has succeeded in imposing dramatic changes in the demographic compositions, physical built-up areas, urban fabric, landscape, boundaries, and legal status. By that, Israel aims at Judaizing the city. Contrary to what Israel is supposed and obliged to do according to international law and conventions, it continues to violate critical articles of the Fourth Geneva Convention such as: Article No. (47) that guarantees to offer the rights of the Convention to the occupied people; Article No. (49) (1) and (6) that prohibit residents' displacement and deportation either individually or massively; Article (53) of the Convention states "Any destruction by the Occupying Power of real or personal property belonging individually or collectively to private persons ... is prohibited."; and also Article (147) which forbids unlawful destruction and appropriation of property.

Israel has exceptional unprecedented records of violations of international law, treaties, resolutions, and conventions. Those include but are not limited to: many articles of the Universal Declaration of Human Rights such as Article (7) denial of equal protection under the law, Article (9) arbitrary arrest, detention, or exile, Article (13) denial of the right to return to one's country, Article (17) arbitrary expropriation of personal property, Article (18) interference with religious worship and observance; resolutions No. (242, 252, 338, 478, besides others) of the United Nations Security Council; the International Covenant on Civil and Political Rights (ICCPR); the Hague Convention; the Convention for the Elimination of all Forms of Racial Discrimination (CERD); the International Covenant on Economic, Social, and Cultural Rights (ICESCR); the Convention for the Rights of the Child (CRC); and the Convention for the Elimination of all forms of Discrimination Against Women (CEDA W).

The available land reserve during the 1960s was almost consumed in the western part of Jerusalem. Hence, vertical development was enhanced rather than horizontal extensions [41]. Accordingly, the lebensraum for West Jerusalem was an irresistible catalyst for the Israeli annexation of East Jerusalem and the West Bank. The urgent need for vacant spaces to serve Jewish settlers played a major factor besides the other political ones that led to the annexation, where a wide range of vacant constructible spaces was available. This facilitates understanding the speed, physical direction, and determination, with which expansion and new construction happened after 1967. All Jewish settlements are illegally constructed and represent a direct violation of international law, and contradict the spatial sustainability and its four-dimensional aspects [42], therefore, they aggravate urban conflict and complexify the geopolitical, socioeconomic, and environmental statuses on the ground. Unfortunately, the Jewish settlements degrade the Palestinian environmental profile, they consume wantonly the Palestinian scarce water resources, damage agricultural fields, and Palestinian valleys by discharging excessive quantities of wastewater which pollute surface and groundwater, besides dumping of solid wastes randomly on Palestinian lands [43].

A year later to the Israeli occupation of East Jerusalem, the plan of reunified Jerusalem was produced by Hashimshony Master Plan, **Figure 8**. The main purpose of this plan as explained before, was to add extra vacant spaces in the eastern part of Jerusalem, and so to solve the dilemma of limited urban growth in West Jerusalem. The plan achieved that objective supremely, hence it continued to serve as a regulatory plan with more than seven distributed land use categories about to mid-1980s. Jerusalem master plans, before 1967, had generally gained the characteristic of advisory and guidance plans. Whereas those prepared post-1967 period were much more regulatory and detailed plans, schematic town planning and neighborhood schemes witnessed, therefore, profound interest and precise details grounded on quantitative studies and spatial data.

Analyzing the "post-1967 epoch", would patently reveal that a lot of planning tribulations coupled with the development of Jerusalem, emerged from the geopolitical situation regarding the occupation of East Jerusalem and the adjacent parts of the West Bank. The Jewish desire to control Jerusalem with ultimate political sovereignty

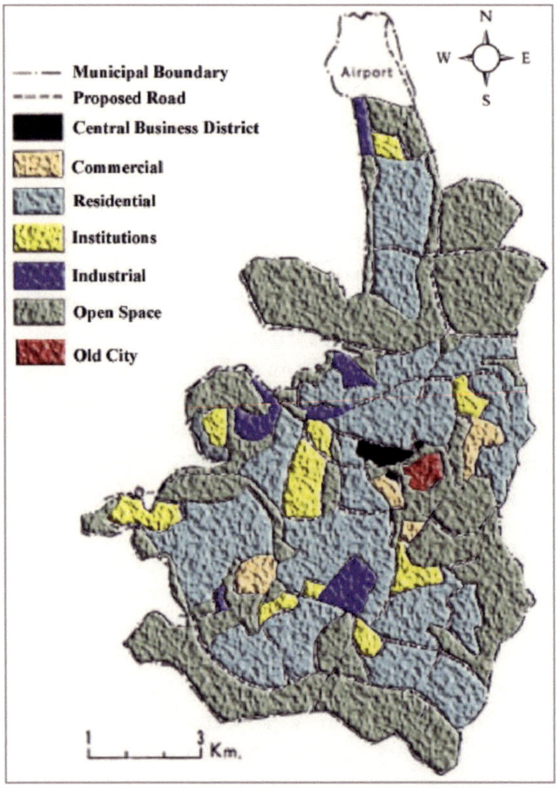

Figure 8.
Hashimshony Plan 1968 [22].

and demographic dominance, especially in the eastern part of the city, offered a chief influential impact on the normative, rational, development of Jerusalem. The Israeli perception of unified Jerusalem, as the capital of the Jewish state, inflicts planning priorities unfavorable, and inimical, towards the native Palestinian residents. In other words, the chief influential factor in the Israeli planning policies, overriding any: legal, humanitarian, historical, ethical, ecological, and topographical factors, is once more, the subject of "political sovereignty" which represents the ethnical, prejudiced, and demographic sovereignty.

Israeli planning policies in Jerusalem during the post-1967 era have been misused and widely criticized. They offer to the Israeli colonial government effective planning tools and mechanisms, for applying occupational policies and achieving objectives likely to oppose the interests of native Palestinians. Administratively, Jerusalem is unified but develops in two contradictory manners. Jerusalem municipality which has been governed by Jewish administration has set up, and adopted, two paradoxical urban planning approaches: progressive planning of West Jerusalem that responds to the actual and prospective needs of the Jewish residents; and on the other hand, regressive planning of East Jerusalem that restrains the basic needs and the future development of Palestinian residents [14, 22, 44].

Accordingly, intentional prejudiced actions against the Palestinian people continue. Israeli planning policies in Jerusalem, are therefore, inequitable, implicitly biased, and reflect not what they promise to be. Urban planning is used as a tool of control over Palestinians, rather than a tool of constructive change. Control in this context means fostering Jewish demography in Jerusalem to constitute an overwhelming majority to Israelize Jerusalem, overlooking its Arabic authenticity, and in the meantime restraining Palestinians' future development. The Israeli planning policies succeeded to impose new geopolitical, demographical, and physical facts on the ground in annexed East Jerusalem. The Israeli planning laws and regulations in Jerusalem, have been sharply articulated to simplify the process of confiscating Palestinian vacant lands to be used for constructing Jewish settlements and to restrain the growth of Palestinian neighborhoods. The available vacant lands in the Palestinian neighborhoods in East Jerusalem are majorly frozen through the current Israeli zoning and land use laws. Most of those spaces are earmarked as open landscapes, where any kind of development is blocked, and no construction is allowed. As such, Israel used land use planning as a control tool to direct the Palestinian development opportunities in an 'unsustainable' manner [45].

The Israeli discriminatory planning policies have forced Palestinians in Jerusalem to suffer in satisfying their basic needs, and also, limited them to rely on the Israeli system of services which is based on ethnonational affiliation. Jerusalem municipality allocates of the total budget only 10% to services of Palestinians who comprise, more than 30% of the total population. Regressive Israeli planning policies with inevitable adverse consequences against Palestinians continue and involve [46]:

- Palestinian land expropriation.
- Desocialization and neighborhoods shattering.
- Colonizing East Jerusalem by expanding and building Jewish settlements.
- Unfair building restrictions upon Palestinian neighborhoods.

- Destruction of Palestinian homes.
- Lack of sufficient public services and infrastructure.
- Unequal land-use laws and zoning regulations.
- Changing residency rights and permits.
- Construction of apartheid wall with massive land confiscation.

Jerusalem is planned to grow divergently, forming two comparative images. East Jerusalem represents the first portrayal, where Palestinians live in urban neighborhoods surrounded by illegal Jewish Settlements. While the other one is rendered in West Jerusalem, which is almost purely inhabited by Jewish Israelis, **Figure 9**. Since the

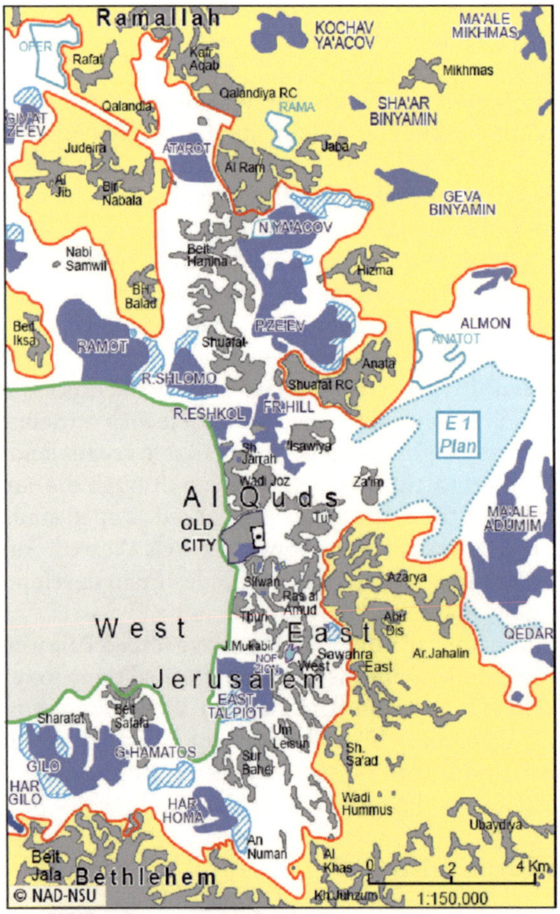

Figure 9.
Urban paradox: Walled spaces and fragmented Palestinian neighborhoods (ghettos) surrounded by Jewish settlements in Jerusalem [47].

early start of Israeli annexation to East Jerusalem, dominant Jewish politicians insisted to transform the Arabic and Islamic fabric in Jerusalem by fabricating Israeli features. This could be clearly touched in the Jewish political discourses, for instance, during the municipal council meeting held on the thirteenth of August 1967, Rabbi Cohen declared: *"And dare I say frankly that we have to do everything within our power to make Greater Jerusalem the largest Jewish city in the world, a real Jewish city, both in terms of the population numbers and in giving a permanent Jewish character to the whole city"* [48].

The Israeli-biased planning concept was the foundational cornerstone of the political architecture in Jerusalem. It reflects the Israeli determination to Judaize Jerusalem. Political architecture of the city should render in its: physical spaces a Jewish identity, while in its population, the Jewish majority. The influential political dimension demonstrates all other factors included for the future development of Jerusalem. Political architecture is, therefore, a natural output of the governmental plans determined by Israeli decision-makers who seek every single opportunity to achieve considerable political objectives. In that sense, Mordechai Ish-Shalom, former Mayor of Jerusalem, declared: *"What is required - and quickly - is Jews, many Jews in Jerusalem. No, more trickles of immigration"* [48].

Urban planning in conflict areas and contested cities, like the case of Jerusalem, form paradoxical and complex urban planning policies accompanied in most cases, by permanent physical layouts. That is, political architecture spaces, create multiple challenges in different dimensions for the local residents, remarkably when they

Dominant Axes of Israeli Planning Policies in Jerusalem		
Axis 1. Architecture of Separation and Fragmentation	**Axis 2. Architecture of Security and Surveillance**	**Axis 3. Architecture of Paradox**
The following are the chief adverse impacts on the Palestinians in Jerusalem due to these planning axes: • Palestinian neighborhoods in East Jerusalem have collectively faced a sudden rupture of their social and economic life. • Social and urban dysconnectivity in East Jerusalem, Palestinians' life is no more coherent or sustainable. • Palestinian clusters, more and more are forced to shape ghettos. • Urban instability created two groups living together under one municipal border but separately. • Demographic battle generating an overwhelming Israeli group, and another subordinate Palestinian group. • Disintegration: two ethnically separated communities classified by national affiliation: Israeli/Jewish communities and Palestinian/Arabic clusters respectively. • Ethnic separation between Palestinians and Israelis by implementing non-humanitarian and unethical segregation policies: permanent and flying checkpoints, the Separation Apartheid Wall • Social damage, urban struggle in isolated neighborhoods, and controlled transport and road systems. • Separation Wall isolates Jerusalem from oPt & severed it from its demographic, geographic, and economic support base. • Urban morphology of Jerusalem has been changing and shifting towards more Jewish identity and physical layouts. • Political unity and sovereignty but physical divergence and separated contradicted spatial development models • Growth wheel in Jerusalem is firmly correlated to political backgrounds, rather than rational planning principles.		

Table 3.
Chief regressive planning axes in Jerusalem (author).

constitute a group of minorities. Unfortunately, walled and fragmented spaces, are being produced progressively in Jerusalem due to three influential regressive planning axes identified in **Table 3**.

6. Conclusion

Jerusalem has deeply-rooted records of a long history. It has been a focal point of attraction for several universal powers. This was reflected in the city structure and the respective urban fabric. Many distinguished civilizations with variant cultural and religious backgrounds, had not only crossed the city, but also established their cornerstone and inhabited the city successively. However, in terms of the modern notion of urban planning, Jerusalem does not offer extended history in this dimension, but rather it shows very rich and intensive changes in that aspect, especially since the nineteenth century. Within 50 years, 1917–1967, Jerusalem experienced multiple administrative systems. Namely, Ottoman rule, British Mandate, Jordanian administration, and the Israeli occupation, which altogether generated different urban planning regimes. The spatial definition during each administration has changed.

Ottomans ruled Jerusalem for more than four centuries, from 1516 to 1917. At that period Jerusalem underwent an organic growth, and its limits were spatially defined by the Old Walled City. Ottomans did not produce conventional town plans but rather conducted substantial urban renewal for the Old City, public services and infrastructure, and the fascinating encircling walls. By that, Ottomans in Jerusalem adopted an interesting "conservative approach" in their planning perspective. Ottoman rule ended in 1917, after the end of WWI when Jerusalem was captured by the British Army. During the British Mandate period which extended for three decades, from 1917 to 1948, Jerusalem witnessed a new era of modernization, and the first generation of 'conventional urban planning' showed up. The spatial definition of the city expanded to involve the Old City and its adjacent environs. The British planners emphasized the authentic value of the Old City of Jerusalem, they preserved it by encircling it with a green buffer belt to reflect the garden city concept. And so, the British adopted a "romantic planning approach" in Jerusalem and the city flourished and expanded until the termination of the mandate at the end of WWII.

A substantial radical divisional period followed, from 1948 to 1967, when Jerusalem was split into three folds: the Old City, East Jerusalem, and West Jerusalem. At that time, the Old City and East Jerusalem were under Jordanian administration. Unfortunately, Jordanians did not develop any master plan for the city. They replaced some urban British regulations, and they kept Kendal Plan to guide the physical development. As such, Jordanians adopted a "primitive regulatory approach". In the meantime, West Jerusalem was occupied by Israel after the 1948 war, the Israeli government developed several master plans for the city which expanded massively westwards to cope with tremendous numbers of Jewish residents who wanted to settle in the capital of Israel. Hence, the first generation of the 'colonial planning approach' in West Jerusalem appeared.

A wider page of colonial planning in Jerusalem was opened post the 1967 War, when Israel occupied East Jerusalem. Since then, Jerusalem, East and West, were unified and subjected to paradoxical Israeli urban planning policies. Indeed, Israel worked out several master plans for Jerusalem. In areas populated by Jewish, progressive planning policies are being employed to serve the Jewish residents' needs, and to facilitate rapid and massive urban development. On the other hand, in areas populated by Palestinians, regressive planning policies are being applied to practice more control over Palestinian land and to limit Palestinian development. Although the city was reunified spatially under one Jewish municipality, it remained split and developed under contradictory planning approaches that foster urban conflict and regional tensions. The Israeli "colonial planning approach" has been used as a control tool against Palestinians. In consequence, the Palestinian presence in Jerusalem is threatened, Palestinians suffer, and pay a lot to date.

Author details

Raed Najjar
Spatial Planning, Arab American University, Ramallah, Palestine

*Address all correspondence to: raedfnajjar@gmail.com

References

[1] Fanni I. The 6000 Years Illustrated Atlas of Jerusalem. Amman: Dar Ashoruk for Publication and Distributions; 2003

[2] Walter ER. Through the Ages in Palestinian Archaeology. Philadelphia: Trinity Press International; 1992

[3] Feintuch Y. United States Policy on Jerusalem. Westport: Greenwood Publishing Group; 1987

[4] Elad A. Medieval Jerusalem and Islamic Worship: Holy Places, Ceremonies, Pilgrimage. Leiden: E. J. Brill; 1995

[5] Kanaan A. Jerusalem: Political and Religious Status of Jerusalem among Muslims. Amman: The Royal Committee for Jerusalem Affairs; 2005

[6] Rosenbilt Y. Jerusalem in Old Maps. Jerusalem: Ariel Publications; 1987

[7] Benvenisti M. Jerusalem: The Torn City. Minneapolis: The University of Minneapolis Press; 1976

[8] Prawer A, Ben-Shammai H, editors. The History of Jerusalem. New York: New York University Press; 1996

[9] Biger G. The Boundaries of Modern Palestine, 1840-1947. London: Routledge; 2005

[10] Mendelsson D. British Rule. Jerusalem: Department for Jewish Zionist Education, The Jewish Agency for Israel; 2007

[11] Pollack K. Arabs at War: Military Effectiveness 1948-1991. Nebraska: University of Nebraska Press; 2002

[12] Wasserstein B. Divided Jerusalem - the Struggle for the Holy City. London: Profile Books Ltd; 2001

[13] Caner G, Bölen F. Urban planning approaches in divided cities. A|Z ITU journal of faculty of. Architecture. 2016;**13**(1):139-156

[14] Najjar R. Planning, power, and politics (3P): Critical review of the hidden role of spatial planning in conflict areas. In: Loures LC, editor. Land Use-assessing the Past, Envisioning the Future. London, UK: IntechOpen; 2019. DOI: 10.17877/DE290R-5370

[15] Hasson S, editor. Jerusalem in the Future: The Challenge of Transition. Jerusalem: The Floersheimer Institute for Policy Studies; 2007

[16] Auld S. Ottoman Jerusalem: The Living City: 1517-1917. London: Altajir World of Islam Trust; 2000

[17] Amn C. The Guilds of Ottoman Jerusalem. Boston: Brill; 2001

[18] Scholch A. Jerusalem in the 19th century (1831-1917 AD). In: Asali KJ, editor. Jerusalem in History. New York: Olive Branch Press; 1996

[19] Cohen A. The ottoman approach to Christians and Christianity in sixteenth century Jerusalem. Islam and Christian-Muslim Relations. 1996;**7**(2):205-212

[20] Salibi K, Yusuf K. The Missionary Herald: Reports from Ottoman Syria. Royal Institute for Interfaith Studies. 1995;**1**:1819-1870

[21] Oke K. The Ottoman Empire, Zionism and the question of Palestine. International Journal of Middle East Studies. 1982;**14**:329-341

[22] Najjar R. Spatial Planning, Urban Land Management, and Political Architecture in the Conflict

Areas—Jerusalem Case Study [thesis]. Dortmund: TU Dortmund; 2013. DOI: 10.17877/DE290R-5370

[23] Pappe I. A History of Modern Palestine: One Land, Two Peoples. Cambridge: Cambridge University Press; 2004

[24] Sachar H. A History of Israel: From the Rise of Zionism to our Time. New York: Alfred A. Knopf; 1979

[25] Porath Y. Palestinian Arab National Movement: From Riots to Rebellion: 1929-1939. Historic Issues, Vol. 2. London: Frank Cass and Co., Ltd; 1977

[26] McCarthy J. The Population of Palestine: Population History and Statistics of the late Ottoman Period and the Mandate. Princeton, NJ: Darwin Press; 1995

[27] Auman M. Land Ownership in Palestine 1880-1948. Princeton, NJ: Transaction Books; 1975

[28] Cohen A. Israel and the Arab World. New York: Funk and Wagnalls; 1970

[29] O'Ballance E. The Arab-Israeli War. New York: Frederick A. Praeger; 1957

[30] Begin M. The Revolt. London: W. H. Allen; 1951

[31] Kimche J. There Could Have Been Peace: The Untold Story of Why We Failed with Palestine and Again with Israel. England: Dial Press; 1973

[32] Efrat E. Urbanization in Israel. New York: Croom Helm; 1984

[33] Rakauskas C. The Internationalization of Jerusalem. Washington: The Catholic Association for International Peace; 1957

[34] Teveth S. Ben-Gurion and the Palestinian Arabs: From Peace to War. London: Oxford University Press; 1985

[35] Khamaisi R. Israeli use of the British Mandate planning legacy as a tool for the control of Palestinians in the West Bank. Planning Perspectives. 1997;**12**(3):321-340

[36] Shapiro S. Urban Geography of Jerusalem. Jerusalem: Peli Printing Works Ltd.; 1973

[37] Gawrych GW. The Albatross of Decisive Victory: War and Policy between Egypt and Israel in the 1967 and 1973 Arab-Israeli Wars. Westport: Greenwood Press; 2000

[38] Churchill R, Churchill W. The Six Day War. Boston: Houghton Mifflin Company; 1967

[39] Mutawi S. Jordan in the 1967 War. Cambridge: Cambridge University Press; 2002

[40] Hinnebusch RA. The International Politics of the Middle East. Manchester: Manchester University Press; 2003

[41] Dumper M. The Politics of Jerusalem since 1967. Columbia: Columbia University Press; 2002

[42] Najjar R. Four dimensional spatial sustainability (4DSS): A revolutionary approach toward utopian sustainability. Discover Sustainability. 2022;**3**:21. DOI: 10.1007/s43621-022-00090-x

[43] Hosh L, Issac J. Environmental Challenges in Palestine and the Peace Process. Bethlehem: ARIJ; 1996

[44] Najjar R, Amro J. Future development of the Palestinian neighborhoods in East Jerusalem: Misuse of environmental concepts in land management. International Journal of Environmental Studies. 2011;**68**(4):531-542

[45] Abuleil W. Planning for a Sustainable Spatial Development: The Role of the

Local Level in the Palestinian Context. Birzeit: Birzeit University; 2008

[46] Najjar R, Reicher C, Amro J. Critical two-sided urbanism: The case of Jerusalem -east and west. London Art and Architecture Magazine. 2011;**1**(5):158-168

[47] 49 Jerusalem Unit. Strategic Multi Sector Development Plan for East Jerusalem. Palestine: President Office; 2010

[48] Halawani A. The Role of Israeli Planning Policies on Controlling Arabs in East Jerusalem. Birzeit: Birzeit University; 2006